IRISH AND CATHOLIC?

For
Liam S. Maher (1922-2005)

Edited by Louise Fuller, John Littleton and
Eamon Maher

Irish and Catholic?

TOWARDS AN UNDERSTANDING OF IDENTITY

the columba press

First published in 2006 by
the columba press
55A Spruce Avenue, Stillorgan Industrial Park,
Blackrock, Co Dublin

Cover by Bill Bolger
The cover illustration is a detail from an oleograph entitled 'The Death
of Ireland's Liberator', supplied by Colum Kenny (see pp 90ff).
Origination by The Columba Press
Printed in Ireland by ColourBooks Ltd, Dublin

ISBN 1 85607 538 9

Contents

Contemporary Irish Writers and Filmmakers series (Liffey Press) and of Edwin Mellen Press's Studies in Irish Literature and Irish Studies series. He is editor of *The Irish Book Review*. He is a member of the editorial board of *Nua* and reviews editor with *Minerva*. He has published more than 60 articles and reviews on Irish writing and literary and critical theory. He is also Director of the MIC Irish Studies Centre, University of Limerick, Ireland.

TIMOTHY J. WHITE is a professor in the Department of Political Science and Sociology at Xavier University in Cincinnati, Ohio, USA. He earned a PhD from the University of Michigan and taught at the University of Missouri-St Louis before moving to Xavier University. He was the Irish American Cultural Institute's Visiting Professor at the National University of Ireland, Galway in 2000-2001. He has published widely on Irish politics and sociology in journals such as *Éire-Ireland, Irish Journal of Sociology, Celtic Cultural Studies, Southeastern Political Review* and the *Journal of Social, Political, and Economic Studies*. His article on socioeconomic change in Ireland was included as a chapter in Susan Shaw Sailer's *Representing Ireland: Gender, Class, Nationality*. He recently edited a special issue of *The European Legacy* (February 2005) devoted to Irish Studies. His forthcoming works include 'Myth-Making and the Creation of Irish Nationalism in the Nineteenth Century' in *Studi Celtici* and 'Elite Construction of Identity: Comparing Nehru and de Valera as National Founders' in *India and Ireland: Colonies, Culture, and Empire* (edited by Tadhg Foley and Maureen O'Connor). He founded Xavier University's Summer Study Abroad Program in Ireland and teaches a course on Irish historical sociology there every summer. Currently, he serves as Chair of the James S. Donnelly Sr Prize for books on the History and Social Sciences Committee of the American Conference for Irish Studies and he serves as the social sciences representative of that organisation.

KEVIN WILLIAMS is Senior Lecturer in Mater Dei Institute of Education, Dublin City University and a former President of the Educational Studies Association of Ireland. He is author of *Faith and the Nation: Religion, Culture and Schooling in Ireland* (2005) and is currently writing a book on the work of Michael Oakeshott.

at Odense, Denmark, for articles on Pope John Paul II's visits to Cuba, Drumcree, and the Irish Churches' failure to practice, as opposed to preaching, reconciliation. In 2001 his books *Christianity*, a collection of essays on the subject which he edited, and *The Book of the Jesus Reports*, a rewriting of the life of Jesus based on the four gospels, which he wrote on a weekly basis in 2000 were published. The content of both books had been published in *The Irish Times* in 2000 to mark the second millennium of Christianity.

PAULA MURPHY is a lecturer in the Department of English Language and Literature in Mary Immaculate College, University of Limerick. She is associate editor of *The Irish Book Review* and advisory editor of the post-modernism journal *Kritikos*. She has published on Lacanian psycho-analytic theory, film theory, deconstruction and contemporary Irish literature and film. She is currently writing a book entitled *Ireland in the Spotlight: Contemporary Irish Dramatists* and is editing the forthcoming *New Voices in Irish Criticism* collection.

KENNETH NALLY lectures at National University of Ireland, Galway in the Department of English, where he specialises in contemporary Irish film and drama and facilitates for the online Irish Studies programme provided through the University's Centre for Irish Studies. He completed a PhD on the theatre of Frank McGuinness.

GRACE NEVILLE studied French and Irish at universities in Cork, Lille, Caen and Metz. Her research specialisations include Franco-Irish studies from the medieval to the modern period, women's studies and language legislation. She is the author of more than ninety publications, including (with Eamon Maher) *France-Ireland: Anatomy of a Relationship* (2004) and (with Joachim Fischer) *Cork Through European Eyes: A Multilingual Anthology* (2005), financed by the Cork 2005 Committee as part of the Cork European Capital of Culture programme. She has presented research papers in a wide number of international venues including Harvard, the Sorbonne and the Collège de France.

EUGENE O'BRIEN is Senior Lecturer and Head of the Department of English at Mary Immaculate College, University of Limerick and Assistant Dean (Research) in the College of Humanities, University of Limerick. He has published *The Question of Irish Identity in the Writings of William Butler Yeats and James Joyce* (1998), *Examining Irish Nationalism in the Context of Literature, Culture and Religion: A Study of the Epistemological Structure of Nationalism* (2002), *Seamus Heaney – Creating Irelands of the Mind* (2002), *Seamus Heaney and the Place of Writing* (2003) and *Seamus Heaney: Searches for Answers* (2003). He is editor of the charts cultural, social and economic changes in Ireland since the 1960s. He writes regularly for the *Sunday Independent* and is an honorary life member of the Glencree Centre for Reconciliation.

JOHN LITTLETON, a priest of the diocese of Cashel and Emly, is President of the National Conference of Priests of Ireland. He has taught theology, religious studies and religious education in several colleges and institutes in Ireland and the UK, and is a well-known preacher and retreat director. He is a regular contributor to theological and pastoral journals and is a weekly columnist in *The Catholic Times* and the *Tipperary Star*. He works at The Priory Institute, Tallaght where he is manager of the distance learning theology programme.

EAMON MAHER is the Director of the National Centre for Franco-Irish Studies at ITT Dublin. He has a particular interest in the portrayal of the supernatural and the mystical in literature, especially in the novel genre. He is an associate editor of *The Irish Book Review* and editor of *The Journal of Franco-Irish Studies*. His recent books include *John McGahern: From the Local to the Universal* (2003); with Eugene O'Brien, *La France face à la mondialisation/France and the Struggle Against Globalization* (2006); and with Grace Neville, *France-Ireland: Anatomy of a Relationship* (2004). He is currently completing a book for a French publisher on the theme of marginality in the life and works of the French priest-writer, Jean Sulivan.

JOHN McDONAGH is a lecturer in the Department of English Language and Literature at Mary Immaculate College, University of Limerick. He is the author of *Brendan Kennelly – A Host of Ghosts* (2004) and editor, with Stephen Newman, of *Michael Hartnett Remembered* (2006). He is the 2005/6 MIC Research Fellow and his biography of Brendan Kennelly will be published late in 2006. He is also an associate editor of *The Irish Book Review*.

PATSY McGARRY, from Ballaghaderreen, Co Roscommon, has been Religious Affairs Correspondent for *The Irish Times* since 1997. He was theatre critic at the *Irish Press* from 1990 until 1995. In 1989 he established the first independent radio newsroom in Ireland as Head of News at Capital Radio in Dublin, now FM 102. As a freelance journalist in the 1980/90s he worked for Sunshine Radio, the *Sunday World*, *Magill* magazine, the *Irish Press*, the *Irish Independent* and the *Sunday Independent*. In 1992 he was awarded a Journalist of the Year award for his comment and analysis in the *Sunday Independent* on the fall of Charles Haughey as Taoiseach. In 1999 he was awarded the '1998 Templeton European Religion Writer of the Year' award at a ceremony

Notes on the Contributors

BRIAN COSGROVE is Professor of English and Head of the Department of English at the National University of Ireland, Maynooth. His major areas of interest include Joyce, Wordsworth and the interface between literature and philosophy / theology. He has published *Wordsworth and the Poetry of Self-Sufficiency* (1982), edited *Literature and the Supernatural* (1995) and published articles on Newman, on Melville's attitude to Christianity and on Joyce and irony. He has also contributed reviews to the *Irish Theological Quarterly*.

PATRICK CLAFFEY is a Divine Word missionary priest. He lectures at the Milltown Institute of Theology and Philosophy, Dublin. He worked in West Africa from 1977 until 2002. He completed a PhD at the School of Oriental and African Studies, University of London, in 2005.

LOUISE FULLER is an IRCHSS Research Fellow working in the Department of Modern History at the National University of Ireland, Maynooth. Her research interests centre on political and socio-cultural changes in Ireland, the interplay between religion and society, and in particular on the role and influence of the Catholic Church. She is author of *Irish Catholicism Since 1950: The Undoing of a Culture* (2002, 2004) and several articles on Catholicism in nineteenth- and twentieth-century Ireland. She is currently researching the contribution of parish confraternities and associations to the religious and social history of modern Ireland.

SARA KEATING is completing a PhD on the Irish Catholic Family in twentieth-century drama at the School of Drama, Trinity College Dublin. Her research interests include theoretical developments in Irish Studies and twentieth-century Irish and American theatre. Her article 'Contemporary Critical Contexts in Irish Theatre Studies: or, is Martin McDonagh an Irish playwright?' will be published twice later this year – in English in a case study on Martin McDonagh, edited by Eamonn Jordan, and in French in the Canadian journal *L'Annuaire Théâtral*. Sara is also theatre and visual arts editor with *In Dublin* magazine and writes about theatre for *The Irish Times* and *Irish Theatre Magazine* among other publications.

COLUM KENNY is Associate Professor of Communications at Dublin City University. His most recent book, *Moments That Changed Us* (2005),

Introduction

There is possibly no subject that exercises Irish people's minds and arouses such heated debate as Catholicism. The majority religion has undergone a torrid time in Ireland during the past few decades. Ever since Noel Browne's ill-fated attempt to get a set of proposals known as 'The Mother and Child Scheme' through the Dáil in 1951, there have been numerous events that altered forever the attitude to Catholicism among those living in a rapidly changing Irish society. In spite of maintaining a veneer of power during the 1950s and 60s, particularly because of the special relationship it enjoyed with politicians, an increasingly well-educated Irish population was becoming more and more reluctant to allow the Church to dominate the agenda, particularly in the areas of sexual relations, education and social justice. A series of divisive referenda on divorce and abortion during the 1980s and 90s showed strong support for the Church's position in rural areas and a corresponding wave of secularism in the cities.

Contraception and divorce are now legally available in Ireland and the position in relation to abortion is somewhat ambiguous as a result of the 'X' case; homosexual practices are no longer a criminal offence; there is a crisis of vocations to the priesthood and religious life; revelations of physical and sexual abuse in industrial schools and the laundries that were administered mainly by religious orders and then, of course, clerical child abuse, have shaken the faithful to the core; the scandals involving high-powered figures like Eamonn Casey and Michael Cleary, two well-known clerics who were discovered to have fathered children, have revealed that priests are human like everyone else. The Jesuit priest, Joseph Veale, writing in 2000, pointed out that the wound inflicted by the clerical abuse scandal was nothing so superficial as the loss of influence or diminished power. It went far deeper than that, right to the core of how Irish people related to the Catholic Church. It might have been so different if evidence of genuine repentance for the hurt and damage caused had been forthcoming from the beginning:

> The Church is in shock. Many are in denial. The disclosure of sex-abuse and cruelty came when people were already disenchanted with the Church, with the whole set-up, with religion in general. That goes back a long way. It was masked by a smugness on the part of the official Church and a deference and conformism in the presence of clergy ... The sin-less priest, not fully human, was a fiction. No one really believed it, but it served a purpose to pretend. The revelations of abuse fell into a culture that for decades had seen through clerical screens.[1]

Veale rightly detected that the experience of Catholicism that many Irish people had was a negative one, especially in relation to sexuality: '... their sexual lives, the central energy of their humanity, whether they are married or not, were mucked up by Catholicism.' (Veale, p 298) Many commentators make the point that the Catholic Church in Ireland became synonymous with a distrustful attitude towards sex which seemed to be invariably linked to sin. In Kevin Myers' view, however, 'the determining factor in all this was not the priest, not the hierarchy, but the taboo.'[2] This is something that is often overlooked when dealing with the emotive issue of Irish Catholic identity: the extent to which the institutional Church was merely a reflection of the society which spawned it and allowed the Catholic clergy almost unbridled power for the best part of a century. As Myers states: 'No Taoiseach over the past three decades would have dared to

---

1. Joseph Veale, 'Meditating on abuse – and repenting', in *Doctrine and Life*, May-June 2000, pp 296-303, pp 297-8.
2. Kevin Myers, 'An Irishman's Diary', *The Irish Times*, 3 November, 2005, p 17.

instigate a wholesale investigation into clerical child abuse and survived even a day.' Society was complicit in the incarceration of young women found pregnant outside of wedlock, or in the committal to industrial schools of children engaged in 'anti-social behaviour' or from homes that could not afford to feed them. The Catholic Church and its priests and bishops acted as a sort of 'moral police force' for a long time in Ireland, because that was the role the population expected from them. They inspired much love and devotion and these in turn led to power and domination. When their authority was questioned, therefore, it is not surprising that they reacted by attempting to crush the opposition. As their power began to slip, the desire was strong to hold on to its vestiges by whatever means possible. Tom Inglis wrote in the wake of the publication of *The Ferns Report*:

> There was a time when people trusted the Church. It supposedly told us the truth about life and death. While other organisations had material interests, the Church was only interested in proclaiming the truth. Now we see that it has an almost pathological inability to tell the truth about itself.[3]

Shrewd and fair analyst that he is, however, Inglis echoes Kevin Myers's comments quoted earlier by stipulating that the Catholic hierarchy in this country merely showed itself to possess the same sort of weaknesses as those displayed by any group that enjoys a monopoly of power: 'The problem of trust is, of course, wider than the Catholic Church. We used to believe in the honesty and integrity of all those in authority – whether they were politicians, gardaí, solicitors, bank managers, journalists or many others. We were led to believe that they were above re-proach.'[4] Mary Kenny too believes that there should always be a distinction drawn between the Church as institution and the concept of faith. While the faithful can be (indeed, must be) appalled at stories of abuse perpetrated on children by priests, that does not mean that people automatically lose their faith as a

3. Tom Inglis, 'Something Rotten in the Barrel Itself', *The Irish Times*, 3 November, 2005, p 16.
4. 'Something Rotten in the Barrel Itself', p 16.

result of these revelations: 'The Church is the institution and subject to as many errors as any other institutions – the law, the media, the bureaucracies, business.'[5] But it is not possible for everyone to distinguish between the message of the gospel and the human weaknesses of those (a tiny minority) who, while involved in active ministry, perpetrated heinous crimes on innocent children.

Nevertheless, what is particularly annoying for the many people who are attracted to the positive message contained in the Catholic faith is the way in which the Irish bishops seemed prepared to do almost anything to avoid facing up to the ineptitude that characterised their management of the scandals. They needed to be more humble, more prepared to listen and repent. But the clerical mindset was not particularly adept at listening. Joseph Veale, while accepting the huge amount of damage done to the Church's reputation by the failure to deal in an adequate manner with the scandals, felt that it could have a positive side: 'The loss of power will turn out to have been a blessing. We will need to let go generously and freely because it is closer to the mind of Christ.'[6] These words find an echo in the spiritual diary of the French priest-writer, Jean Sulivan (1913-1980), who said in relation to the French Church of the 1970s: 'Like the storm clouds of the exodus, the Church's face today is more luminous than when it seemed to rule. It has found glory in its humiliation.'[7] Maybe that is what will happen to the Irish Church in the coming years as its power and influence begin to wane: it could well find 'glory in its humiliation'.

The decision to organise a conference at The Priory Institute, Tallaght on 23-24 June 2005 was prompted by a genuine desire to engage with the issue of Irish Catholic identity at what is definitely a crucial and difficult time for the Church in this country. The organisers were keen that it not be seen as simply another

5. Mary Kenny, 'Church is Damaged – but Our Faith will Endure', *The Sunday Independent*, 30 October, 2005, p 24.
6. 'Meditating on Abuse', p 302.
7. Jean Sulivan, *Morning Light*, translated by Joseph Cunneen and Patrick Gormally (New York: Paulist Press, 1988), p 149.

'clerical talk-shop' and that equally it should not just engage in a simple exercise of 'Church bashing.' Debate is very necessary between numerous stakeholders if the Catholic Church in Ireland is to have any hope of assuming an effective role in a changed society. It is natural to be fearful of change if it impacts upon you personally. Brendan Hoban makes that point forcibly:

> If you are part of a tradition, it is very difficult to become part of the dismantling of the same tradition. If you give a wedge of your life to any activity, it is extremely difficult to stand back and set that work in a realistic context. The bigger the institution, the more sacred the tradition, the more difficult it is to ask hard questions about it.[8]

Difficult, but fair, questions were posed at the conference. Participants analysed the issue of Irish Catholic identity from a number of different angles, using history, theology, literature, literary theory, sociology and personal reflection as their points of departure. What emerges is not intended to be a definitive statement in relation to what is a highly complex issue: more a starting point in a process that may well result in a more open debate going forward on the issue of Irish Catholicism and the important role it has played, continues to play and will play in forging a certain notion of Irish identity.

We are grateful to The Priory Institute and ITT Dublin for supporting the conference, to the participants for the benefit of their thoughts in the form of papers or comments, and to Seán O Boyle of The Columba Press for the vision he displayed in seeing the value of publishing this book.

---

8. Brendan Hoban, *Change or Decay: Irish Catholicism in Crisis* (Kilglass: Banley House, 2004), p 60.

CHAPTER ONE

Catholic Identity in the Irish Context

John Littleton

What does it mean to be a Catholic today? First, what it does *not* mean. It surely does *not* mean having such a rigid sense of identity that there is no room any longer for diversity and for outreach to those with different points of view, both within and outside the Church. Nor does it mean having such a soft sense of identity that there is no longer any theological, spiritual, or doctrinal core. It is one thing to say ... that there is a hierarchy of truths, such that distinctions have to be made always between the essential and the non-essential, or between the important and less important. But it is quite another matter to imply that there are no truths at all, no defining characteristics of Catholic identity, as if Catholicism is simply the sum total of its disparate parts or, worse, whatever one wishes to make of it.[1]

It is occasionally proposed that one religion is the same as another. However, that assertion is untrue because all religions – including Catholicism – make unique claims. Hence they cannot be identical and every religious tradition has a separate identity, although it may have much in common with other traditions. The American theologian Richard McBrien, in the opening quotation, acknowledges that to be Catholic means having a definite identity which, in the context of indispensable truths, incorporates diverse opinions and attitudes. Thus Catholic identity cannot be perceived as inflexible. Neither is it so vague that it lacks any precise meaning.

---

1. Richard McBrien, 'Before and After Vatican II', *Priests and People*, 10 (8,9), 1996, p 301.

A long and varied history

The Catholic Church has existed for two millennia and is un-doubtedly among the most enduring institutions in the history of human civilisation. During two thousand years it has evolved in countless ways, sometimes with beneficial results and at other times compromising its main purpose which is to pro-claim to the entire world God's unconditional love in Jesus Christ the Universal Lord and Saviour. In reality, the Catholic Church is a community of sinners and saints and, like all organ-ised religions, is *semper reformanda* (always in need of renewal). Indeed, the more regrettable episodes of history, in addition to the teaching of Christ, have challenged the Catholic Church not to understand itself anymore as *societas perfecta* (the perfect soci-ety) but as an imperfect pilgrim people slowly but surely moving towards eternity with God.

While some Catholics have described what Catholicism means for them,[2] nowadays many Catholics are unsure about their faith. Consequently, there has been a serious diminution of Catholic identity. It is often said that, until two generations ago, Catholics everywhere knew exactly what was required in their relationships and activities. Likewise they knew what to expect when going into a Catholic church, especially to attend Mass that was said in Latin. Without wishing to seem trivial, Catholicism was like McDonalds restaurants, having identical menus and tastes, regardless of the local language and cuisine; there is no substantial variation and most products are pre-packaged. That is how it was for Catholics fifty years ago. There was certainty and no desire – or encouragement – to ask probing questions about their faith or to be different. Catholics had a definite sense of their identity, although they were not always able to explain it.

But time has moved on and people have changed. Contemporary society is more materialistic and pluralistic, and

---

2. See, for example, Rowanne Pasco, *Why I Am A Catholic* (London: Hodder & Stoughton, 1995), Kevin and Marilyn Ryan (eds.), *Why I Am Still A Catholic* (New York: Riverhead Books, 1998) and Peter Stanford (ed.), *Why I Am Still A Catholic: Essays in Faith and Perseverance* (London: Continuum, 2005).

modern culture is characterised by questioning what was previously regarded as unquestionable and unchanging. The English sociologist Michael Hornsby-Smith has suggested that:

> Like everyone else, they [Catholics] have experienced the forces of reaction against the excessively mechanistic, rigid, rational world of modernity which had dominated thinking since the Enlightenment. In the so-called 'post-modern' world of recent years, the dominant values have been individualism, self-determination, expression and fulfilment, personal autonomy, and instant gratification.[3]

In contemporary Ireland, as elsewhere, many Catholics are lapsed; they do not practise the faith anymore. Others have adopted an à la carte approach; they choose what suits them from Catholic doctrines and ignore the remainder. In addition, people are generally reluctant to speak about their personal religious beliefs. This makes it difficult to describe popular Catholicism with confidence, especially when, for varied reasons, there is confusion surrounding the precise differences between the mainstream Christian denominations.

Yet in the official teaching of the Catholic Church, there is certainty about its self-understanding, with conservatives arguing that progressives have watered down Catholic beliefs and values since the 1960s to the detriment of the distinctive Catholic identity. But they also argue that this dilution has been partially counteracted by the *Catechism of the Catholic Church*.[4] Perhaps the most challenging question is: How can the traditional and liberal understandings of Catholicism be reconciled, if at all?[5]

---

3. Michael P. Hornsby-Smith, 'Catholic Identity and Evangelisation', *Priests and People*, 16 (7), 2002, p 257.
4. The *Catechism of the Catholic Church* was originally published in French in 1992 and subsequently translated into English in 1994. The Catechism is almost 700 pages long and is the most detailed and authoritative statement or compendium of Catholic faith and teachings produced since the *Catechism of the Council of Trent* (also known as the *Roman Catechism*) promulgated by Pope St Pius V in 1556.
5. The terms lapsed, à la carte, conservative, traditional, progressive and liberal are not used pejoratively; they are commonly occurring descriptive terms.

Catholicism: what is it?

There are many popular descriptions of Catholicism. Some are superficial and inaccurate, presenting a distorted image of the Catholic Church. Others are helpful because they encapsulate the essence of Catholicism. No single description of the Catholic Church, however, can ever explain adequately the mystery which the Church actually is.

Without doubt, the most negative image of the Catholic Church currently prevailing, in much of the western world, is that of the child physical and sexual abuse scandals. People have abandoned the Church in large numbers, or have lost their trust in it, because of those scandals and the secrecy and lack of transparency in how the institutional Church dealt with them. In some instances, people's faith has been destroyed by what they perceived to be a corrupt institution whose efforts at self-protection were truly shocking. While incalculable damage has been done to the credibility of the Catholic Church by the abuse scandals, they do not describe it completely. There are various dimensions to Catholicism, some more relevant and authentic than others, that cannot be neglected.

For example, when reference is made to the Catholic Church many people immediately think of the Pope who presides over one of the largest religious organisations in the world and who, through frequent pronouncements on matters of faith and morality, attempts to impose strict rules on the members' lives. Many people judge the papacy to be inconsequential, despite the fact that huge crowds of people flocked to see Pope John Paul II during his regular overseas visits. Another image of Catholicism is the Vatican, containing priceless treasures and world-famous art and sculptures, with the serving pope as a head-of-State overseeing a complex bureaucracy of civil servants.

Other well-known facts that prompt comment during discussions about Catholicism include a central belief that Jesus Christ, the Word made flesh,[6] is present in the Eucharistic species of bread and wine and that his presence there is the Real Presence.

---

6. The Second Person of the Trinity becoming human.

Many people, including those from different faith traditions, are familiar with the term 'transubstantiation' which is a technical term used to describe that Christ becomes really present under the appearances of bread and wine in the Eucharist. That term has caused difficulties in ecumenical dialogue. Aspects of Catholicism that generate heated public debate are its total opposition to abortion and euthanasia, its prohibition of divorce and remarriage, its teaching on artificial contraception (especially since Pope Paul VI's encyclical letter, *Humanae Vitae*, in 1968), the role of the laity in the Church's life and the non-admissibility of women to the ordained priesthood.

Numerous images are evoked when people mention Catholicism. Among them are Sunday Mass attendance, people making the Sign of the Cross when passing churches and cemeteries, people marking their foreheads with blessed ashes on Ash Wednesday, girls dressing in white dresses and boys wearing white rosettes when they celebrate First Holy Communion, the lighting of candles at shrines, the smoke rising from the burning incense at certain ceremonies and devotions, the fingering of beads as people pray the Rosary, the public display of holy pictures and statues representing the Blessed Virgin Mary and canonised saints, and the Christmas crib. All these rituals and practices are not confined to Catholicism. But more peculiar to Catholicism are pilgrimages to Marian shrines (for example, Fatima, Knock and Lourdes), and the practice of penitents confessing their sins to a priest and receiving sacramental absolution. In Catholic churches the red sanctuary lamp draws attention to the presence of the reserved Blessed Sacrament. Less evident images include the sprinkling of holy water, the mission collection boxes in shops, the wearing of devotional medals and scapulars and blue Children of Mary cloaks, and members of male and female religious orders wearing a distinctive habit.

Certain people, when asked about Catholicism, become conscious of the Catholic school and college system which arguably provides an excellent education – to the extent that in the UK and USA, for example, many non-Catholics seek to have their children educated in Catholic schools. Similarly the Catholic health care system is considered to be among the best in the world. Then, other people speak about famous Catholics whom they know or about whom they have heard and how those Catholics have influenced their lives. They may be internationally known Catholics such as Mother Teresa of Calcutta (1910-1997) or national public figures like Cardinal Basil Hume of Westminster (1923-1999). Alternatively, they could just as easily be Catholic neighbours or local Catholic clergy, demonstrating the witness dimension of being a Catholic. The assorted images refer either directly or indirectly to the basics of Catholicism and to its distinguishing features from different faith traditions.

What does it mean to be Catholic?
What are the central features of Catholicism that differentiate it from other Christian denominations? Or, adapting the title of one of Rosemary Haughton's books, what is the 'Catholic thing'?[7] There are several significant characteristics that distinguish Catholicism from other Christian denominations. Although not exclusive to Catholicism, they provide it with a particular identity because, realistically, it is possible to be a Christian without necessarily being a Catholic whereas it is impossible to be a Catholic unless one is also a Christian.

Catholic identity can best be defined using three terms: universality (or catholicity), tradition and sacramentality. These three principles describe the overlapping and interdependent, yet distinctive, strands of Catholicism. Ironically, those Catholics who do not reflect critically on their faith, and who may be described most accurately as nominally Catholic, are unable to identify these defining characteristics of Catholic identity. Other Catholics are unable to converse authoritatively about their faith. Furthermore, in many instances, Catholics do not know how to pass on the faith to their children. What, then, is meant by the terms universality, tradition and sacramentality?

7. See Rosemary Haughton, *The Catholic Thing* (Springfield, IL: Templegate, 1979).

Universality/Catholicity

By 'universality' (or 'catholicity') is meant the undivided, worldwide ecclesial community that gathers people of different nationalities, cultures and languages into one People of God.[8] The People of God, theoretically at least, readily embraces all people without discrimination although, regrettably, not all Catholic individuals and groups do so. Historically it is continuous with the apostolic Church. Jesus's first disciples gradually understood that the Church established by him must be all-inclusive. He had died on the Cross for the salvation of the whole human race. Therefore, all people from every culture and place should have the possibility of learning about the risen Lord Jesus and should also be offered the opportunity of making a personal faith commitment to him by being baptised into the community of his believers. The term 'catholic' was originally used to describe that community, the Church. Subsequently, the term was used to differentiate between the faithful community of disciples and heretical groups, that is, those groups whose beliefs and opinions were judged to be contrary to the revealed truths contained in orthodox (correct) doctrines of faith.

The concept of a Church that is universal implies that the Church, in and through its nature, is missionary. Thus Catholicism is convinced that the Good News about Jesus of Nazareth ought to be shared with all peoples. The Catholic Church is a universal communion of local Churches in which everyone desiring to follow Christ may find a welcome and a spiritual home. Because of its missionary nature, it continues to spread around the world in fidelity to Jesus's command and in continuity with the apostles' ministry.[9]

The Second Vatican Council (1962-1965) taught that 'the sole Church of Christ… subsists in the Catholic Church, which is governed by the successor of Peter and the bishops in commu-

---

8. The term 'universal' derives from the Greek *katholikos*, meaning general, and it refers to whatever is common to all.
9. See, for example, Matthew 28:19-20 and Acts 1:8.

nion with him'.[10] Yet it acknowledged that elements of sanctification and truth are found outside the visible confines of the Catholic Church. Accordingly, the Catholic Church recognised that other religions have a purpose. This is surely one of the major developments in official Catholic teaching that has occurred since the Council. It highlights the profound transformation from pre-conciliar to post-conciliar Catholicism. Nevertheless, Catholics believe that there is a unique Catholic identity. That identity is discovered in the specifically Catholic dogmas and doctrines, sacramental rites, moral principles, codes of behaviour and spiritual practices. In summary, Catholics belong to a worldwide Church. Hence they should have a strong sense of the universality/catholicity of their Church's mission. This notion of universality/catholicity is crucially important because there are many alternative manifestations of Christianity which are less than universal.

Tradition

'Tradition' refers to the process of passing on the lived heritage of God's self-revelation that culminated in Jesus of Nazareth and which concluded at the end of the apostolic era.[11] Tradition guarantees continuity from the Church's origins, through the present, into the future. Tradition, which forms the continuity between past, present and future, is, in the words of Hornsby-Smith, 'the chain of memory in the transmission of faith and commitment'.[12]

Faith in God is a reasonable and personal response to God's self-revelation which is God's disclosure to humankind of what was previously unknown (for example, various aspects of God's existence, nature, will or, indeed, God's desire for friendship).

10. The Second Vatican Council, *Lumen Gentium* (1964), n 8, in Austin Flannery (ed.), *Vatican Council II: The Conciliar and Post Conciliar Documents* (Dublin: Dominican Publications, 1996; revised edition), p 357.
11. The term 'tradition' derives from the Latin *traditio*, meaning transmission or handing over.
12. Hornsby-Smith, 'Catholic Identity and Evangelisation', p 258.

We are made in the 'image' and 'likeness' of God (Genesis 1:26) with the capacity to recognise the divine indwelling and we become more human if we genuinely seek God in our lives and in the world. God initiates this self-communication and invites us to respond and to share in the salvation offered to us. Salvation history describes the ongoing dialogue with God and the events occurring throughout the history of Israel ending with the birth, life, death, resurrection and ascension of Jesus the Messiah, and the outpouring of the Holy Spirit at Pentecost. Thus God's self-revelation is most perfectly expressed in the life and teachings of Christ, and these survive in sacred Scripture and in Tradition.

Scripture is the inspired word of God contained in the Bible. Tradition is the ongoing process by which the unwritten beliefs, practices and worship of believers in Jesus Christ (for example, unique customs, ethical guidelines, devotional rituals and attitudes) are transmitted to succeeding generations. The earliest Christian preaching and teaching preceded the biblical text; yet there is an intrinsic connection between Scripture and Tradition because both originate from one source, namely Christ who is the fullness of God's revelation.[13] Both are necessary for a proper understanding of revelation. In summary, Tradition is essentially about being rooted in the faith. It relates to both the old and the new, stretching back to the Church's beginning. The world is now amazingly sophisticated and fast-changing. That is why one needs to retain the old values and traditions that have been prayerfully discerned and that have borne the test of time – simply so that one knows one's identity and appreciates one's history. Tradition needs to be alive today so that there can be continuity between the past and the present, enabling us to move confidently towards the future and hand on the faith.

---

13. See The Second Vatican Council, *Dei Verbum* (1965), n 9, in Flannery (ed.), *Vatican Council II*, pp 755-756.

Sacramentality

The language of 'sacramentality' is a language of sign and symbol.[14] All life is sacramental; it is full of signs of God's presence and interaction with the world because, being part of God's creation, our existence is graced, it is blessed by God. Christians are sacramental people since, in their daily lives, they glimpse aspects of God's nature and will from the signs they discern around them in the created world order. The world is a world of grace, a world that shares God's life, where all of creation points to God's glory, from the oceans, to the mountains, to the skies, to human beings.[15]

The principle of sacramentality deals with human beings coming into God's presence. We do this through signs and symbols, words and gestures that provide us with access to the Mystery of God. We do not simply leap into God's presence; it takes much time and sustained effort and we do so using material reality (what is visible and tangible) to communicate with spiritual reality (what is invisible and intangible). Normally when people discuss sacramentality and Catholicism, they focus on the seven sacraments which are celebratory rituals that form the nucleus of Catholic worship.[16] But the seven sacraments are really seven peak moments in a life that is already sacramental.[17] They are instances of personal encounter with the risen Lord Jesus, intense moments in which those who celebrate them access God's life since the sacraments bring about what they signify. In turn, those who celebrate them are meant to become the

---

14. The term 'sacrament' translates the Latin *sacramentum*, meaning sign or pledge.

15. See Genesis 1.

16. The seven sacraments are classified in three groups: the sacraments of Christian initiation (baptism, confirmation, Eucharist), the sacraments of Christian healing (penance/reconciliation, anointing of the sick) and the sacraments of Christian mission (matrimony and holy orders).

17. See Enda Lyons, 'Sacrament of God', in Enda McDonagh (ed.), *Faith and the Hungry Grass: A Mayo Book of Theology* (Dublin: The Columba Press, 1990), pp 35-43.

sacrament of Christ to one another. This is the basis for the notion of the Church as sacrament.[18]

Thus the sacraments are visible signs of invisible reality; they
are outward signs of inner grace. Developing further the 'sign'
meaning of sacrament, Jesus is the sacrament of God and the
Church is the sacrament of Christ. This means that Jesus is the
sign of God and, correspondingly, that the Church is the visible
sign of Jesus to the world. Hence the Church is often described
as the sacrament of salvation, the sign of God's salvation to the
world.

Catholic identity and the essentials of Catholicism

The distinctive Catholic identity is succinctly presented by the
three principles of universality, tradition and sacramentality.
These principal attributes describe the Catholic Church in terms
of its breadth, depth and transparency. As already noted, they
are also evident in other expressions of Christianity. However, it
is the particular understanding and combination of them that
confers the unique Catholic identity.

The American theologian Daniel Donovan has presented a
comprehensive study of Catholic identity in which he describes
six characteristics of Christian communions which receive the
greatest emphasis in the Catholic Church.[19] The six characteristics are compatible with the three principles of universality, tradition and sacramentality. They are:

1. a stress on community, going against the modern tendency
to religious individualism;

2. taking history seriously, both the history of the Church and
its place in all of history;

3. insistence on faith (which is shared) as acceptance of revelation as well as commitment of oneself;

4. sacramentality expressed both in liturgy and in the applic-
ation of the sacramental principle to all reality;

---

18. See Avery Dulles, *Models of the Church* (Dublin: Gill and Macmillan,
1988; 2nd edition), pp 67-70.
19. Daniel Donovan, *Distinctively Catholic: An Exploration of Catholic
Identity* (New York: Paulist Press, 1997).

5. an ordering of the community through the structure of ordained ministry; and

6. tension between unity and diversity.

What, therefore, are the essentials of the Catholic faith? While accepting the centrality of Jesus Christ, the authority of the Bible (although not in the same sense as the Protestant *sola scriptura* principle which argues that Tradition has no binding authority[20]) and the additional elements shared between Catholicism and other Christian denominations, there are, nonetheless, several absolute Catholic beliefs and practices arising from the principles of universality, tradition and sacramentality.

The Eucharist (the Mass), one of the seven sacraments instituted by Christ, is at the heart of Catholic faith and lifestyle, as is the doctrine of the Real Presence. The Eucharist has been described as 'the source and summit of the Christian life'.[21] Furthermore, the Eucharist and the other six sacraments are the most personally intimate encounters possible with the risen Lord Jesus and, not surprisingly, they are considered to be essential for the spiritual life of every Catholic. The papacy, which is the office of Pope and Bishop of Rome, and papal infallibility are also crucial to Catholic identity. The Pope is Christ's Vicar on earth; he is the chief pastor and teacher of the members of the Catholic Church.[22] The universal Church, through the bishops and the people, is in union with the Pope and the Church of Rome.

Another essential trait of Catholicism is the Magisterium, the Church's official teaching authority. Catholics do not formulate doctrine and ethical principles in an impromptu manner or simply by individual choice unaided by the Church's guidance. Inspired by the Holy Spirit, the Magisterium interprets Scripture

---

20. *Sola scriptura* (literally, scripture alone) is a basic Reformation principle that acknowledges the highest religious authority in the word of God. In practice, this means that scripture alone is decisive in resolving doctrinal and ethical questions.

21. *Lumen Gentium*, n 11.

22. The Pope has traditionally been described as *Servus servorum Dei* (the Servant of the servants of God).

and Tradition and expresses authentic Church teaching so that Catholics know what is truly Catholic and what is not. The dignity of all life is fundamental to Catholicism which teaches that there is an absolute right to life for everyone, from the moment of conception to death. Respecting the dignity of life demands that justice and human rights are to the forefront of Catholic moral teaching and social action. Catholicism also teaches that marriage is valid only between a man and a woman, and is indissoluble. It condemns homosexual practices.

The role of the Blessed Virgin Mary, the Mother of Jesus, as a model of discipleship and Mother of the Church is important for Catholics. Similarly *Communio Sanctorum* (the Communion of Saints)[23] provides encouraging and challenging examples of how to live the Catholic faith. To be Catholic means to be ecumenical in spirit, faithful to the prayer of Christ 'that they may all be one' (John 17:21).

Today some people are inclined to reject one or more of Catholicism's characteristics, perceiving them as being outdated in the modern world and imposing needless restrictions on personal autonomy. Nevertheless, the characteristics describe Catholic identity because they constitute the fundamentals of the Catholic faith which are reflected in philosophy, theology, spirituality, history, sociology and anthropology, as well as providing ideas and information for literature and fiction. And yet, according to the Irish religious educators Patricia Kieran and Anne Hession:

> It would be dangerous to define one's religious identity only in terms of what distinguishes it from others. To do so would be to ignore the presence of the Holy Spirit calling us to discover new possibilities for Catholic identity in our time. Catholics seek to find ways in which the gospel is mirrored in the beliefs and lives of non-Christians thus challenging them to live their own Christian spirituality more deeply.[24]

---

23. The Communion of Saints is the spiritual union between Christ and all Christians, whether already in heaven, or in purgatory, or still living on earth.

24. Patricia Kieran and Anne Hession, *Children, Catholicism and Religious Education* (Dublin: Veritas Publications, 2005), pp.235-236.

Catholic identity and dissent

Can Catholics, including theologians, deviate from official Church teaching while retaining the Catholic identity? What if members disagree conscientiously with aspects of the Church's teaching, especially regarding morality? Can they still classify themselves as Catholics, and how flexible is Catholic identity? The answers to these questions are complex and require consideration of several significant factors.

Firstly, Catholics are obligated to adhere only to what the Catholic Church has committed itself definitively. This does not include all its teachings, although each of them deserves serious attention and the appropriate degree of obedience. In addition, Catholics use the 'hierarchy of truths' principle that interprets the truths of faith by their relative importance in the context of the central mysteries of Catholic faith, beginning with the doctrine of the Trinity. Moreover, the *sensus fidelium* (the sense of the faithful) is exercised by all members of the Church who, inspired by the Holy Spirit, collectively contribute to the resolution of faith-related questions and ethical dilemmas. Lastly, Catholics must act in accordance with an informed conscience so that they can make enlightened decisions. According to the American theologian Philip S. Kaufman:

> Everyone is obliged to follow a sincerely informed conscience. This definitely does not mean that we can do whatever we please. It does mean that once we have made an honest effort to determine what we should do or avoid doing, we have an obligation to act according to that conviction ... And the Catholic who obeys a sincerely informed conscience, even if it is opposed to official teaching ... remains a faithful Catholic.[25]

Hence he argues that conscientious Catholics can disagree with official Church teaching and still remain Catholics. This has implications for understanding Catholic identity because it is possible to be a loyal dissenter in the Catholic Church. There can be unity in diversity.

---

23. Philip S. Kaufman, *Why You Can Disagree and Remain a Faithful Catholic* (New York: Crossroad, 1995), pp 7 and 191.

Catholic identity in the Irish context

How does the understanding of Catholic identity relate to the Irish context, both historically and contemporaneously? Until the final decades of the twentieth century, nobody questioned the coupling of the terms 'Irish' and 'Catholic'. With few exceptions, being Irish meant being Catholic. In this respect, the situation in Ireland was similar to that in France, Italy, Portugal and Spain; however, in those countries many people were nominally Catholic whereas in Ireland Catholics were committed and practising.[26]

Historically, the Irish context was one of resistance to oppression and injustice. Most Irish defined themselves largely in opposition to the English, and defeating the English (not merely militarily) has long dominated the Irish psyche. Thus Catholicism was exceptionally important because it became a major symbol of Irish identity. Quite apart from the religious implications, being Catholic was one of the characteristics that made the Irish different from the English. This is still evident in Northern Ireland where Catholic identity is often equated with nationalism and republicanism.

The enactment of the Penal Laws during the seventeenth century ensured that priests were outlawed, Catholic-owned land was forfeited and Catholics were excluded from parliament.[27] Subsequently, during the Great Famine (1845-1850), there were attempts at proselytising by Protestants who offered Catholics food and assistance. Thus a strong bond was established between clergy and laity in the face of common adversities. This alliance provided the basis for the Catholic Church's dominance during the nineteenth and twentieth centuries when it exercised major influence on politicians and governments. The Church provided much needed education amenities, health-care facilities and social services for the State which had no mechanisms

---

26. See Louise Fuller, *Irish Catholicism Since 1950: The Undoing of a Culture* (Dublin: Gill and Macmillan, 2002), p xiii.
27. See Patrick J. Corish, *The Irish Catholic Experience: A Historical Survey* (Dublin: Gill and Macmillan, 1985), p 123ff.

for doing so, and article 44 of the 1937 Constitution of Ireland recognised the special position of the Catholic Church – although this article was removed from the constitution following a referendum in 1972.

However, the Irish context has changed almost completely during the past half century. In an enquiring age, all authority-figures and institutions are questioned and the majority of people, including Catholics, refuse to accept uncritically whatever is being promoted by others. Sometimes their sense of God and of religion is less obviously associated with the teachings of the Catholic Church and they believe that the Church needs to return to Gospel values, revisiting and discarding those many needless elements that accrued over the centuries without reference to the Gospel. They perceive those elements as having been foisted on the faithful in an age when obedience and absolute acceptance of both secular and religious authority was unquestioned – often with disastrous results.

Questions are being asked about what it means to be Catholic and/or Irish and the two terms can no longer be automatically paired. The Irish theologian D. Vincent Twomey has written that:

> It is a measure of the cultural sea change in Ireland that, whereas half a century ago to call oneself an 'Irish Catholic' was a badge of honour proudly worn for all the world to see and admire, today in the upwardly mobile, modern Ireland south of the border, it is more often than not an embarrassment to be reluctantly admitted.[28]

The general move towards democracy and personal freedom has resulted in antipathy towards an authoritarian Church. In addition, there is a growing secularisation in society, resulting in a loss of the sense of the sacred and a consequential loss of the sense of sin, both of which are necessary for an understanding of Catholic identity. All forms of organised religion, including Mass attendance, are in decline; and, arguably, many of those

---

28. D. Vincent Twomey, *The End of Irish Catholicism?* (Dublin: Veritas Publications, 2003), p 17.

who still go to Sunday Mass 'show little strong conviction about their Christian faith'.[29] They have no explicit consciousness of Catholic identity in terms of universality, tradition and sacramentality. Neither do they have any innate sense of them in the same way that, for example, they have an innate sense of Irishness even if they cannot explain it systematically.

The confluence of secularism and the à la carte approach to Catholicism adopted by numerous Catholics means that they have become disaffected from the Church. They engage with it when they need to or if it suits them. As already noted, the principle of sacramentality is indispensable to Catholic identity. Yet the sacrament of confirmation, normally celebrated during early adolescence, is humorously referred to as the 'sacrament of retirement' since, in many instances, its celebration marks the end of people's formal involvement with the Church, except for funerals, weddings and children's celebration of the sacraments. All the surveys verify that many of the younger generation are indifferent towards the Catholic Church, perceiving it to be 'out of touch' with the real world. In the words of the Irish journalist and broadcaster Mary Kenny, they 'no longer see Catholicity as part of their identity'.[30] Yet, in fairness, many of them admit to being spiritual – choosing to believe without belonging.

We live in an environment that is ever more critical of the Church, much of it perhaps justified. In the past the hierarchical Church was perceived as being overly preoccupied with marital and sexual morality. In recent decades, however, the official Church has frequently commented on social justice and human rights issues, for example, the rights of Travellers. There is also remarkable work being done for the homeless and for immigrants by people such as the Jesuit priest Peter McVerry and Sr Stanislaus Kennedy (affectionately known as Sr Stan). Yet still there is a noticeable anti-Catholic bias in the opinions of many

---

29. Peadar Kirby, *Is Irish Catholicism Dying?* (Cork: The Mercier Press, 1984), p 10.
30. Mary Kenny, *Goodbye to Catholic Ireland* (London: Sinclair-Stevenson, 1997), p 387.

commentators. The Catholic Church is certainly not perceived as being triumphalist and beyond reproach, as it was in the past.

Is the Catholic Church in Ireland dying?

Today Ireland is not a Catholic country as it was in the past and the majority of critics suggest that we now live in a post-Catholic Ireland. Modern Ireland is the nation of the Celtic Tiger rather than the land of saints and scholars (which, it could be argued, was a rather romantic notion anyway). Gone are the days when there were no weddings and dances during Lent. Vocations to the priesthood and religious life are nearly non-existent. Ironically, in a remarkable reversal of events, priests from Third World countries are currently ministering in Ireland. The 1979 papal visit to Ireland of Pope John Paul II is just a nostalgic memory from another age. Contraception is now freely available and divorce is permitted. The primary school system is still predominantly Catholic (culturally, if not religiously), but that is changing too. Yet despite these major changes, the Catholic Church in Ireland is not dying. While it seems to be lurching from one crisis to another, and while the credibility of the hierarchical Church has been severely damaged by scandals and secrecy, the Church will continue until the end of history. Theologically, the Church is a divine-human institution and Christ's words, 'I am with you always; yes; to the end of time' (Matthew 28:20) are unambiguous. The decisive question is: How will it continue to carry out its mission?

In the future, the Catholic Church in Ireland will be smaller – both in the number of committed members and in its influence in wider society. But it will be a more dynamic Church due to the steadfastness of those choosing to be involved. The institutional Church must become less secretive and more transparent, both to members and to outsiders. The Irish priest and writer Brendan Hoban has recognised that 'the three modern sisters – Accountability, Openness and Transparency – are discomfiting and unwelcome visitors for the Church';[31] yet they are necessary

31. Brendan Hoban, *Change or Decay: Irish Catholicism in Crisis* (Kilglass, Banley House, 2004), p 26.

if the Church's credibility is to be restored. In the spirit of the
Second Vatican Council, it needs to read the 'signs of the times'[32]
and promote its beliefs as being reasonable and transforming.
This does not imply that they should be changed; instead, it
means presenting them compassionately and relevantly. This
will be crucial in responding pastorally to those who feel alienated
from the Church and giving them a renewed sense of belonging.[33]
Undoubtedly, the Church will have to become more inclusive.

Most of all, the Church needs to offer a thorough catechesis –
in various formats – to Catholics themselves to enable them to
rediscover, or perhaps discover, at least some understanding of
the principles of universality, tradition and sacramentality.
Sunday Mass attendance alone is not sufficient for Catholic
identity and the Sunday homily does not satisfy all the requirements for adult faith development. The more that Catholics participate in the Church's life, the more they will integrate Catholic
identity in their lives and acquire a positive sense of the Catholic
ethos. In addition, the Church needs to become proactive in
dealing with the media and in communicating its message
confidently and challengingly.

If the world does not accept the Catholic Church's preaching,
it is not because one religion is the same as another. It is primarily
because the institutional Church and individual Catholics do
not witness to the faith and are not handing it on. Many people
have lost their sense of identity with the Church. This crisis is
not just a matter of declining Catholic identity; it represents a
loss of Catholic faith. There can be no Catholic identity in any
context, Irish or otherwise, without authentic Catholic faith
whose essence is best expressed in the principles of universality,
tradition and sacramentality.

---

32. The Second Vatican Council, *Gaudium et Spes* (1965), n 4, in Flannery
(ed.), *Vatican Council II*, p 905.
33. See Michael Router, 'Welcoming Back Alienated Catholics in
Ireland', in Niall Coll and Paschal Scallon (eds.), *A Church with a Future:
Challenges to Irish Catholicism Today* (Dublin: The Columba Press, 2005),
pp 74-86.

CHAPTER TWO

The Rise and Fall of
Roman Catholicism in Ireland

Patsy McGarry

As I write it is St John's Eve, also known as 'bonfire night'. I remember in the early 1960s as a child being with my grandfather, other members of the family and some elderly neighbours on St John's Eve as we sat around a bonfire at the cross roads a short distance from our house in north Roscommon. It was also midsummer. People would chat. My grandfather would play the concert flute. Some people would sing, others might dance. Further up the countryside they had bigger fires, bigger crowds, more music and lots of singing and dancing. Maybe even some comely maidens and athletic youths, but there were very few of either in rural north Roscommon in those days. They were more likely to be in England or America.

I was too young to go to those other bonfires then. While I would dearly love to have been with 'the big ones' instead of being at Mullen crossroads with old people and a few other children, I usually settled down to enjoy what we had there. At that time there was no alternative. As darkness fell, my grandfather would rise to go home. Before he left, though, he would first take a coal from the fire with a tongs, or whatever, and throw it over the ditch into our field. For luck. It was an old custom, probably a pagan fertility rite, which had endured from the millennia before Christianity arrived in Ireland.

A feature of Christianity in Ireland was how it incorporated the old gods and sacred places into tradition. So we had holy wells, most places had their own saint – probably gods or goddesses in times past – and it was still acceptable to take a coal from a fire to celebrate St John the Baptist and throw it into a field for luck. Indeed the bonfire itself – on 23 June each year – is most likely descended from old pagan celebrations of the summer solstice, Christianised in the same way as the winter solstice celebrations were incorporated into the celebration of Christmas.

Back then in the early 1960s, Catholicism was at its height in this State. Ireland was producing so many priests and nuns that between one-third and a half of them went on the missions. In 1961 it moved Pope John XXIII to say that, 'Any Christian country will produce a greater or lesser number of priests. But Ireland, that beloved country, is the most fruitful of mothers in this respect.' But all was not well in 'that beloved country'. The population of the Republic reached an historical low of 2.8 million in 1961. Average emigration figures stood at 43,000 a year between 1956 and 1961. Four out of every five children born in Ireland between 1931 and 1941 had to emigrate in the 1950s. And for those like myself who were children in 1961, opportunities were very limited, even when it came to education. Primary education was free but secondary education was open to very few. Local authorities provided scholarships, the famous 'County Council Scholarships', subsidised by the rates, for secondary school students. In 1961 only 621 scholarships of this kind were available across the entire 26 counties. Secondary schools were fee-paying and the main ones were junior seminaries run by the Church to educate boys they hoped would become priests.

Marriage rates in the State were low in the early 1960s. The bachelor had by then become as integral a part of Irish life as the husband. So too did the spinster, with her penchant for overwrought piety. The Irish mother of the day was totally dependent on her husband economically. This ensured an appalling time for many Irish women as the absolute power of the husband was frequently abused in homes. In confession she was often advised by the priest to 'offer it up'. Many an Irish mother sought solace in religion, which gave her suffering a meaning. Nothing could bring as much consolation and pride to the devout long-suffering Irish Catholic mother as seeing her son with a Roman collar. It was said of Ireland's seminaries during the middle decades of the last century that they were full of young men whose mothers had vocations to the priesthood. It helped too that becoming a priest brought with it education, power and great social status.

That said, there was something clearly unhealthy in a State where the Church prospered while society decayed. At a time when seminaries were full, the countryside was being abandoned. As Goldsmith wrote in 'The Deserted Village':

Ill fares the land,
To hastening ills a prey,
Where wealth accumulates and men decay:
Princes and lords may flourish or may fade;
A breath can make them, as a breath has made;
But a bold peasantry, their country's pride,
When once destroyed, can never be supplied.

Those that were left of our bold peasantry in 1961 were being wiped out by economic stagnation and a deeply repressive regime as far as sexuality was concerned. How had we arrived at such a sorry pass? To explain this, we must go back. Pre-Famine Ireland was a very foreign country to that of 1961. Up to the sixteenth century one of the more frequent complaints made by English commentators about the Irish was their 'licentiousness' and the lack of stigma they attached to children born outside marriage. In the sixth century, when Ireland was supposed to be the 'island of saints and scholars', every heterosexual liaison was recognised as a type of marriage under the Brehon Laws. Homosexual liaisons were seen as a problem only if they led to the men involved neglecting the sexual needs of their wives, while the concept of illegitimacy simply did not exist. Marriage in Ireland up to 150 years ago was informal, with many couples living as though they were married.

The penal laws drove Catholics in Ireland to the edges of society, depriving them of what today would be regarded as basic human rights. They were banned from practising their religion, from getting an education, joining the professions and owning any property of value. The experience wed them to their clergy and Church with a bond so deep that elements of it still survive today. However, the Church had little influence on the day-to-day life of Ireland's Catholics in pre-Famine times. There were few church buildings and weekly Mass attendance was said to be around 34%, compared to about 48% today.

Even the idea of women controlling their fertility was not the taboo subject in pre-Famine times that it was to become. By the end of the eighteenth century the Penal Laws were falling into disuse. A clear indication of this was a decision by the London government in 1795 to subsidise the building of St Patrick's College, Maynooth, as a national seminary for Catholic priests in Ireland. It was both an attempt to lessen the likelihood of dangerous ideas spreading to Ireland from seminaries on mainland Europe following the French Revolution, and an attempt by London to try to build an alliance with the Catholic bishops which was never wholly successful.

Until the Famine, beginning in 1845, the custom in Ireland among all but the larger tenant farmer class, was to divide the land between all the sons when they were getting married. Because of this, people married young and consequently there was a rapid rise in population. This was further boosted by a low infant mortality rate – said to be as a result of widespread breastfeeding and the nutritional value of the potato which was a cheap source of food in plentiful supply. The population of Ireland was around 1.5 million in 1673. It had risen to 3 million by the 1750s and to 4 million by the 1780s. By 1821 it had reached 6.8 million, 7.7 million in 1831 and was at 8.175 million in 1841.

The Famine decimated the rural poor. Almost a million died of starvation, while over a million were forced to emigrate. Their plots were taken over by the larger tenant farmers, holding 15 acres or more. For a generation before the Famine the larger tenant farmers avoided subdivision of land and early marriage. It ensured their survival. This large tenant farmer class – apart from the Anglo-Irish aristocracy – were the only elements in society to survive relatively unscathed. In 1841 only 18% of landholdings in Ireland were of more than 15 acres. Six years later in 1851, 51% of holdings were over 15 acres. By 1891, that had risen to

58%. These changes forced the rural poor to drastically change their attitude to sexuality and family. The custom of dividing land between all the sons was ended, with the holding passing to one son only. It also meant that the number of children had to be limited. The Catholic Church was crucial to these changes in family life. Most priests came from the larger tenant farmer sector. They were the Catholics who could afford to educate their children. In the early nineteenth century the cost of sending a son to Maynooth for the first year was £40 to £50. The average wage at the time was about a shilling a day. In 1808, of the 205 students in Maynooth, 78% were the sons of larger farmers.

The Church provided the ideological basis for the sexual repression which underpinned the pattern of late marriage which was to become the norm in Ireland right up to the 1960s. Changing the sexual mores of centuries would have been no easy task under normal circumstances. But the catastrophe which saw the population almost halve from 8 million in 1841 to 4.5 million in 1861, made it an imperative. It gave the Church an opportunity to become intimately involved in Irish family life. With just one son inheriting the holding, other siblings emigrated. And some, usually encouraged by a devout mother, entered the Church. This pattern persisted too into the late 1960s. Sex became taboo. Allied to a Victorian prudery rooted in an eighteenth century wave of evangelical revivalism in Britain, and a Catholic Church seemingly fixated on sex as the only sin, sensuality was suppressed in the Irish consciousness.

In time a celibate elite came to have unparalleled influence. They were educated when so many were not, and they controlled what there was of an education and healthcare system. They became a major force in politics. Parallel to these developments in post-Famine Ireland, Rome was experiencing a most dogmatic and its second longest papacy under Pius IX, now Blessed Pius the Ninth or *Pio Nono*, as he was known. He was Pope from 1846 to 1878. He began as a liberal but was forced to leave Rome in 1848, when a revolution took place. There were similar attempts at revolution throughout much of Europe at the time, including Ireland. Pius returned to Rome in 1850 a changed and deeply conservative man. He was the last pope to be a temporal ruler, losing the Papal States to Italy in 1870, something about which he was unforgiving. He was vigorously anti-liberal and anti-modern. It was he who called the First Vatican Council and who made papal infallibility a dogma of the Church. He consolidated the power of Rome throughout the Catholic world. In Ireland he worked through the doughty Cardinal Paul Cullen of Dublin, the first Irish cardinal, who received the red hat from Pius IX in 1866.

Cardinal Cullen had spent eighteen years in Rome as president of the Irish College. He was close to Pius IX who appointed him Archbishop of Armagh in 1850 and transferred him to Dublin in 1852. Cardinal Cullen 'Romanised' the Irish Church, centralised its structure, introduced pieties such as processions and devotions from the continental Church. He was also responsible for consolidating the power of institutional Irish Catholicism. Some groundwork had already been done. Led by Daniel O'Connell, and organised in part by Catholic priests, a campaign for Catholic Emancipation had been successful in 1829. And in 1831 the parish priest got his first real taste of power when he became manager of the local primary school, under an act of parliament which proposed the establishment of the national school system on multi-denominational lines, whereas in practice the schools divided very quickly along religious lines.

This was the beginning of a clerical ascendancy which saw the Church become such a powerful force in Ireland over the following one hundred and fifty years. Crucially, the mid nineteenth century Church built a solid Irish Catholic middle-class which, as well as looking after Catholic interests, was intended to act as bulwark against any possible future persecution. From the 1850s, the Church set about an extraordinary building programme which saw neo-Gothic church buildings, as well as schools and some hospitals appear throughout the country. Later, it pushed successfully for a Catholic university in Dublin. The Irish Parliamentary Party could not do without the Church in its push for Home Rule in the latter decades of the nineteenth century. Its bishops have been blamed for the downfall of Parnell, the great leader of the Irish Party, who died in 1891. This, it must be said, was unfair. Initially the Irish bishops were silent when news of the infamous O'Shea divorce case in which Parnell was cited, first broke. Deeply religious Welsh non-conformist supporters of Britain's Liberal party were the first to lead the charge. Parnell's fate was sealed before the bishops intervened. But they helped finish him off and were recognised as a force to be reckoned with in the political sphere thereafter.

Cardinal Cullen shaped the heavily centralised Irish Catholicism which answers to a heavily centralised Roman curia right up to today. As well as preaching absolute loyalty to Rome, the Vatican's celibate foot-soldiers cultivated chastity as the greatest virtue. Irish women were expected to emulate the Virgin Mary. In 1854 Pius IX promulgated the Doctrine of the Immaculate Conception and the clergy preached that celibate life was superior to married life, that 'impure thought' was evil, as was all sexual activity without a marriage licence. Sexual pleasure was taboo. It was commonly described as 'dirty', 'disgusting', powerful evidence of an inferior animal nature which constantly threatened what was divine in the human. Sex was tolerable only in marriage and then only for the procreation of children. It was, as a local wit once remarked to me at home, 'a dirty oul' job but sure someone had to do it!'

The sermons of Irish Catholic clergy for most of the 120 years between 1850 and 1970 seemed dominated by sex. This railing, allied to economic factors, had inevitable consequences. Poverty and chastity saw to it that the marriage rate plummeted. In 1926, there were 230,525 marriages in the predominantly Catholic Republic. By 1961, that rate was down to 76,669. The rate of illegitimate births during the 1950s was just 1.8% – compared to almost a fifth of all births today. By 1926 just over a quarter – 26 % – of women remained unmarried at 45, compared to about 10% before the Famine. Before the Famine about 20% of husbands were ten years older than their wives. By the early twentieth century the proportion had risen to almost 50%.

In 1930s Ireland almost three quarters of 25-34 year-old men remained single, compared to a third in England and Wales. In 1960s Ireland, half of all 25-34 year-old men remained single compared with just one in five men in England and Wales. A notable feature of emigration from Ireland compared to other countries was the high proportion of women, who made up half of all Irish emigrants – a pattern so much greater than in other countries which experienced emigration. It meant that at no time after 1881 were there enough single women to marry all the single men in Ireland. For most of the twentieth century there were over 140 men for every 100 women in the 45-54 age-group.

In 1961, in rural areas, there were 244 single men for every 100 single woman among 45-54 year-olds. In 1960, of the women aged 15-19 in 1942 more than half were then living outside Ireland. Meanwhile, the number of nuns in Ireland increased eightfold between 1841 and 1901, despite a near halving of the Catholic population. This increase had started before the Famine. At the beginning of the nineteenth century there were 11 convents in Ireland. Immediately after the Famine there were 91. By 1900 the number of convents had rocketed to 368 and the average size of each had grown. For those other women who remained on in Ireland there were just two roles outside of the convent – that of spinster dependent on male relatives or that of 'the Irish mother'.

In most countries the symbolic religious head of the household is the man. In Ireland it has generally been the woman. Women in the post-Famine period were offered the role said to be the most important in society – that of bringing up children in the Catholic faith. To a large extent they had little choice in this. In return for taking on this role, they received a level of respect, of status, even authority, which they could not otherwise have attained. The post-Famine period saw an explosion in devotion to the Virgin Mary and the practice of reciting the Rosary. All over the country, shrines of devotion to Mary sprang up. She was the model for Irish women. Told that women were an 'occasion of sin' since the time of Eve, men in Ireland were separated from them in school, at Church and social occasions. They were often frightened of them. Meanwhile the rate of psychiatric disorder in Ireland quadrupled between 1841 and 1901. Up to the 1980s men, particularly those from the rural west where the single life was most prevalent, continued to have vastly higher rates of admission to psychiatric hospitals.

By the latter part of the nineteenth century the Church had become one of the dominant forces in Ireland. Always supportive of Irish nationalism in the main, its thrust was towards Home Rule from Famine times. It supported O'Connell's repeal movement but more particularly the Home Rule efforts of Butt and Parnell. And though wary of Michael Davitt, it was also broadly supportive of the Land League. However, it always had problems with violence as a means of achieving political change. So it condemned the Fenians and later excommunicated Republicans engaged in violence. Catholicism has been linked, historically, with nationalism and 'Irishness'. Catholic priests had a common cause with Irish people against religious oppression. Priests often provided local leadership for agitation movements, although the Catholic hierarchy gained considerable religious autonomy by supporting British rule and tended to view would-be revolutionaries with distrust. In the continuum of Irish history since the Tudor conquests, to be Irish has been to be Catholic, as was almost 75% of the island's population.

At the time of independence Catholic Church influence over government decisions was enormous. The Catholic hierarchy supported the establishment of the Free State, and the social legislation of the 1920s echoed Church morality. In 1923, a film censor was appointed, with power to edit or ban films deemed to be 'subversive of public morality'. Divorce was banned in 1925 and a censorship board established. It was made an offence to circulate literature advocating birth control. The Church, which had excommunicated de Valera and his anti-Treaty supporters, was worried when he and Fianna Fáil entered the Dáil in 1927 and formed a government in 1932. The worry proved groundless. The Irish Constitution of 1937 was largely de Valera's creation, but hugely influenced by the future Archbishop of Dublin, who at that time was Fr John Charles McQuaid. Its social provisions were clearly Catholic. It proclaimed the special position of the Catholic Church as 'the guardian of the Faith professed by the great majority of the citizens' (Article 44.1.2, *Bunreacht na hÉireann*).

The Constitution's statements about family, marriage, and social responsibility reflected Church teachings. It stated, for example, that the 'State recognises the family as the natural primary and fundamental unit group of society' (Article 41.1.1). Divorce was prohibited. A woman's primary responsibility was to home and family, and the Constitution proposed that no legislation forcing women to abdicate this responsibility should be permitted (Article 41.2). A referendum removed the Catholic Church's special position in 1972, in an attempt to assuage anxiety that the Republic might be seen as sectarian.

In the political arena, politicians were free to act as they chose, as long as they did not infringe on Church teachings or prerogatives. In 1951, they were perceived to have done just that when Dr Noel Browne attempted to introduce a scheme whereby a mother and her baby's welfare would be taken care of by the State for six months after the child's birth. This was known as the 'Mother and Child Scheme'. Dr Browne proposed, the Church opposed, and the government fell, with the Taoiseach of the day, John A. Costello, telling the Dáil in April 1951, that 'I, as a Catholic, obey my Church authorities and will continue to do so, in spite of *The Irish Times* or anything else.' This statement followed an *Irish Times* editorial criticising his stance.

Successive Irish governments were very slow to depart from official Church teaching. Whether politicians actually accepted Catholic moral teaching, or simply feared electoral disapproval, Irish politics was clearly circumscribed by the acceptance, by both people and politicians, of the Catholic hierarchy's authority in social and personal matters. Unlike some European countries, there was never any significant anti-clerical movement in Ireland, and no popular political party would dare oppose the Church directly. The Church dominated community as well as political life. A study of rural community life carried out in Co Clare during the 1930s illustrated what has been described as a template for Irish communities during the early to mid decades of the twentieth century. It found a system of prestige based on economic resources and profession and isolated six social types. At the bottom was the labourer, and then the tradesman. Above both of these was the white-collar worker, the shopkeeper, and then the professional, often the sons of farmers or shopkeepers. The pre-eminent local figure was the priest. This continued even after decline set in, in the 1960s and 1970s. When the State took on more responsibility in the areas of education and social welfare, resources were found to fund existing local parish organisations rather than creating parallel State organisations. So what brought about the incredible fall from such a position of power and influence in those days to the crisis-ridden institution we have today?

Ireland changed. The Church changed. Irish television arrived in 1961, over time providing the people with another eye on the world. The Lemass era ushered in a whole new age. Under his First Programme for Economic Expansion (1958–1963), protectionism was dismantled and foreign investment encouraged. The prosperity this allowed eventually brought profound social and cultural changes to what had been one of the poorest and least technologically advanced countries in Europe. Ireland joined the European Economic Community (now the EU) in 1973. Greater prosperity allowed the State more freedom in providing services, particularly in education and health. The most obvious example of this was the introduction of free secondary education in 1967 and State-funded third level education for students who qualified. The effect of the introduction of free secondary education was immediate. Only two out of five 19 year-olds in 1960 completed secondary education. In 1975 it was three out of five. By 1997 it was four out of five. The effect was even greater for girls. Between 1971 and 1981 the number of girls at secondary school increased by over 100% and the number at third level by 180%, compared with 94% and 60% for boys. It is said that when he signed the orders introducing that scheme the then Minister for Education, Donogh O'Malley, forecast it as most likely marking the end for the Fianna Fáil party. But it was not Fianna Fáil which was to suffer most! It read the signs of the times.

Parallel to these developments on the economic front things were also changing in the Church. The Second Vatican Council, which ended in 1965, had a profound impact. Vatican II was a strange and uncomfortable experience for older people particularly. That which they had been taught throughout their lives was immutable, was changing. The Mass was in English, the priest faced the people, the three-hour fast before Communion was gone, the Friday fast was gone, Limbo was gone, and they were being told that they were just as important in the Church as the priest. And it was not necessarily a mortal sin if one did not go to Mass on a Sunday anymore. In addition, it was said that Protestants might not go to hell after all. Indeed it was unclear to many whether hell itself had survived. It was a bewildering time for them, but it did not affect their practice. They continued to go to Mass as before but more out of cultural habit than obligation.

The changes did challenge that older generation's faith, even if it hardly changed their practice. Their conviction was shaken, and this was detected by young people. And it was among the younger generation that the consequences soon became manifest. For many of the latter, Mass attendance soon became optional, but it was the 1968 *Humanae Vitae* encyclical of Pope Paul VI, banning all artificial forms of contraception, which made 'Protestants' of so many. Influenced by Vatican II thinking on the primacy of informed conscience, many ignored the encyclical and chose to use the contraceptive pill, in particular. A 1979 survey found that 75% of married couples had used a form of contraception not approved of by the Catholic Church at some time in their marriage, while the size of the Irish family halved in less than a generation. In 1979, Charles Haughey, then Minister for Health, introduced a bill to make contraception legally available to married couples for *bona fide* family planning purposes only. It permitted contraceptives to be bought legally, but only on prescription. Haughey described the law as 'an Irish solution to an Irish problem'. It was not until 1985 that the sale of condoms without prescription to over 18 year-olds was legalised.

Central to these events was the new Irish mother. Between 1971 and 1983, as emigration slowed, the total number of women at work in Ireland grew by 34%. The number of married women in the labour force grew by 425%. This latter figure was greatly influenced by the 1973 removal of the marriage bar on women in the public service. By 1996, there were 488,000 women at work, an increase of 213,000 since 1971. This compares with a growth of just 23,000 in male employment over the same period. And in 1996, half the female workforce was married. 241,400 married women were working outside the home, an increase of more than 600% since 1971. Almost half of all women with fewer than three children were working in 1997. Those with three or more children were less likely to work outside the home. In the State the birth rate went down from 22 per 1,000 women of childbearing age in 1980 to 13.5 in 1996. Women have pushed much of the social change that has taken place in the State these recent decades, despite Church opposition in the area of contraception in particular. In 1995, divorce was finally legalised.

The loss of the Irish mother as its major recruiting agent was to have a profound effect where the Church was concerned. Just one priest was ordained for the Archdiocese of Dublin in 2004 and he was a late vocation. None was ordained for Dublin in 2005. One of the largest dioceses in Europe, it has a population of approximately 1.1 million Catholics. Seminaries in Dublin, Waterford, Kilkenny, Wexford, Thurles, and Carlow have been closed in recent years and there are a total 60 seminarians in the national seminary at St Patrick's College Maynooth at the time of writing. It is the lowest number in the college in its two centuries. Just 30 years ago there were approximately 600 seminarians in Ireland, 10 times the current number. There are as I write 10,873 religious order priests, sisters, and brothers in congregations in Ireland. A 1999 survey established that at that time two thirds of their number were over 60 and 11% under 50. It means that two thirds is now over 66. In 1981, there were 23,308 religious order priests, sisters and brothers in Ireland. There has been a drop of over half their number since then. The total of diocesan priests in Ireland in 2005 is 2,949, compared to 3,944 in 1970. And the average age of the diocesan priest in Ireland is now 63. The crisis this has precipitated is clear.

But the crisis is not simply one of numbers. It also manifests itself in a deeper crisis of faith. I belonged to that great wave of young Irish people who were among the first beneficiaries of the culture created by the availability of free education and State scholarships to university introduced in 1967. Like most of that generation, I was educated at a diocesan secondary school. The girls were educated by religious sisters in convents. There were very few lay or State-run secondary schools in Ireland at the time. Yet hardly any of the friends I made at university are practising Catholics today. Most would not even consider themselves 'Catholic', although that is our common heritage. Many of them were hardly in the gates of the university before they abandoned the practice of Catholicism. Such was the depth of their faith. And I do not criticise them for that, because the quality of religious education that we received was very poor. Indeed, I remember being chastised in my fourth year at secondary school when I asked the priest who taught us Christian Doctrine how we knew God really existed. He thought I was challenging his authority. And that tended to be the response of many clergy at the time when asked even the most obvious questions about faith. Such questions were not seen as legitimate inquiry but as the expression of a doubt in or threat to Church authority. And that was not permissable

In a book published in 2003 titled *The End of Irish Catholicism?*, Father Vincent Twomey, Professor of Moral Theology at St Patrick's College, Maynooth, argued that traditional Irish Catholicism was neither 'traditional' nor 'Catholic'. Professor Twomey is a past pupil of Pope Benedict XVI, formerly prefect of the Congregation for the Doctrine of the Faith, Cardinal Joseph Ratzinger. In an article for *The Irish Times* in April 2003 Fr Twomey wrote: 'Irish writers in the early part of the twentieth century, such as Seán Ó Faoláin, sensed that something was seriously wrong with "traditional Irish Catholicism". They saw it as narrow-minded, anti-intellectual, and rigorist on moral questions.' They were right. Because of cultural and political developments in Ireland after the Great Famine, many argue persuasively that Irish Catholic culture, as it has been described here, was perhaps not authentically Irish at all. Twomey pointed out:

This was in part due to the break with its medieval past caused by centuries of persecution. More significant was the loss of the (Irish) language in the nineteenth century, when we became cultural exiles in our own country and Catholicism became the badge of our national identity. This fed into a very old temptation, namely to see the Irish nation as God's chosen people. This in fact undermines our catholicity. The imported pieties of the nineteenth century appealed to the emotions, but numbed the mind. And the new provinciality robbed us of our confidence, making us dependent on the larger Protestant, indeed largely puritanical, milieu at a time when the struggle to survive was the main priority.

This had a negative effect on Irish Catholicism, Twomey argued:

The net result was a pragmatism that tended to extinguish both the divine and the human spirit and a piety that shunned the life-affirming celebrations that are the mark of Catholic culture in other countries and indeed once marked our own feast-days and pattern days. Conformity reigned supreme and critical reflection, always a bulwark against negative influences, was discouraged. In a word, the Irish Church's catholicity was compromised by its lack of theology, in the strict sense of the term, namely faith seeking understanding. The Irish Church lacks a passion for truth. Without such a passion there is no vision. Without a vision, people are led astray.

It is that lack of passion, that lack of vision which has left the Irish Catholic Church where it is today. What we are witnessing is the death of a form of Church. We are not overseeing the obsequies of Catholicism in Ireland or of Church in Ireland. What we are witnessing is the death of the old while we await the birth of a new form of Church which, I would wager, is already taking shape. It will be predominantly lay. It will involve a greater role for women. It will be more humble, eschew political power, keep out of the bedroom, and will concentrate instead on spreading its timeless message of hope and meaning in a spirit of charity.

Books consulted in the preparation of this chapter include:

Arensberg, Conrad M., Kimball, Solon T., *Family and Community in Ireland* (Cambridge, Mass., 1968).

Louise Fuller, *Irish Catholicism Since 1950: The Undoing of a Culture*, (Dublin: Gill and Macmillan, 2002).

Goretti Hogan, 'Changing Women's Lives in Ireland' in *International Socialism Journal*, Issue 91, Autumn 2001.

Tom Inglis, *Moral Monopoly: The Catholic Church in Modern Irish Society*, (Dublin: University College Dublin Press, 1997).

Lee Komito, *Politics and Clientelism in Urban Ireland: Information, Reputation, and Brokerage*, University Microfilms International, 8603660, 1985.

J. J. Lee, *Ireland 1912-1985: Politics and Society*, (Cambridge: Cambridge University Press, 1989).

D. Vincent Twomey, *The End of Irish Catholicism?* (Dublin: Veritas Publications, 2003).

Also, statistics were sourced at the Central Statistics Office in Dublin and the Catholic Communications Office in Maynooth.

CHAPTER THREE

'Kicking Bishop Brennan up the Arse ...':
Catholicism, Deconstruction and Postmodernity in Contemporary Irish Culture

Eugene O'Brien

The title of this chapter refers to the television programme *Father Ted*, and specifically to an episode where Ted, having lost a bet to his arch-enemy, Father Dick Roche, is forced to kick his very critical boss, Bishop Len Brennan, a Limerick man, 'up the arse'. In a series of hilarious misadventures, Ted finally accomplishes this feat, being photographed in the act by his friend, Father Dougal. The popularity of this anarchic programme has been huge but what is of particular interest to me is the deconstruction of attitudes about the Church that it has exemplified. What is perhaps most interesting about the genesis of this programme is that it was offered to RTÉ who refused to take it up, before buying it to show on their station on which it became one of the most popular comedies in the TAM ratings.

This comedy could be read as being profoundly anti-Catholic – portraying the classic stereotypes of the wheeler-dealer priest (Ted himself – albeit not an especially successful wheeler-dealer); the alcoholic priest (Fr Jack – whose four-word mantra 'feck-arse-girls-drink' became the show's catchphrase); the idiot priest (Fr Dougal) and of course, that metonym of the role of women in the Church, the housekeeper Mrs Doyle (provider of another catch-phrase in terms of her urgings of cups of tea on unfortunate guests: 'ah you will, you will, you will ...!'). And yet the programme avoids any real criticism of the Church as an organisation. None of the major Church scandals of the past number of years has been directly dealt with, and all of the clerical characters are, in different ways, likeable. The eponymous Bishop Brennan who, it is discovered, has a son by another woman, is obviously an allusion to Bishop Eamonn Casey, but that aside, there is little direct attack on the Church; indeed, there is a fondness for the priests as flawed individuals who are, in their limited way, doing their best.

What is groundbreaking about this programme however, is a placing of the institutional Church in a position as target of satire, however gentle that satire may be. For so long the sacred cow of Irish media coverage, *Father Ted* levels the playing field and the Church, like the family, the law, the world of work and politics, becomes subject to a ludic glance. The Church is now seen as just another organisation, as part of the way in which society and culture are ordered, and which is subject to the same rules, regulations and expectations as the other societal structures with which it competes.

In other words, the Church is just one more way in which society structures itself: it is another example of the interaction of the system and the subject. In the same way as politics, ethnicity, ideology and community, religion as an organisation is a system which provides support, stability and a place for the subject. It provides a structure within which the individual can exist, it provides sets of rules and guidelines which structure the individual and also provides a sense of teleology, in the provision of a set of answers to the questions posed by existence.

This chapter will examine the changing role of the Catholic Church as structure in contemporary Ireland, seeing this altered role as part of a larger process of societal change across the western world. Indeed, what is remarkable is not that the Church has lost its hegemonic status, but rather that this process has been so belated. I will trace the analysis of such structural dissemination briefly through the work of Lyotard, Jacques Lacan and Jacques Derrida, before locating the iconographic image of Bishop Brennan being kicked up the arse in a polyptich with three other images which graphically illustrate this process of structural dissemination that I see as typical of the condition of postmodernity.

Jean François Lyotard, in his book, *The Postmodern Condition*, has defined postmodernism as a process whereby the grand nar-

ratives of culture have become broken down. He makes the
point that while a self does not amount to much, nevertheless
'no self is an island; each exists in a fabric of relations that is now
more complex and mobile than ever before. Young or old, man
or woman, rich or poor, a person is always located at "nodal
points" of specific communication circuits, however tiny these
may be.'[1] As he goes on to add, one is always located at a post
through which various kinds of messages pass. No one, not even
the least privileged among us, is ever entirely powerless over
the messages that traverse and position him at the post of
sender, addressee, or referent. His point is that one's mobility in
relation to these language game effects is tolerable, at least within
certain limits (and the limits are vague); it is even solicited by
regulatory mechanisms, and in particular by the self-adjust-
ments the system undertakes in order to improve its performance. He goes on:

> It may even be said that the system can and must encourage
> such movement to the extent that it combats its own entropy,
> the novelty of an unexpected 'move,' with its correlative dis-
> placement of a partner or group of partners, can supply the
> system with that increased performativity it forever de-
> mands and consumes.[2]

His point here is telling in a contemporary context: the ability of
a single overarching structure to answer all the questions, and
provide the epistemological structures wherewith to organise a
contemporary complex society has been deconstructed by the
fractured nature of selfhood, and consequently, what has
emerged is a number of smaller narratives, both complimentary
and contradictory, which compete for the attention and loyalty
of the subject.

This is in accordance with the psychoanalytic theory of
Jacques Lacan, who sees the self as split, and as motivated by a

---

1. Jean-Francois Lyotard, *The Postmodern Condition: A Report on
Knowledge*. Translated by Geoff Bennington and Brian Massumi
(Minneapolis : University of Minnesota Press, 1984), p 15.
2. *The Postmodern Condition*, p 15.

desire to in some way heal this split. Lacan, developing the work
of Freud, undercut the notion of rationality as the dominant factor in our humanity and instead began to examine language as
an index of the unconscious processes of the mind. He also
coined the phrase that the 'unconscious is structured like a language',[3] which brought the study of structures to the fore in continental thought. For Lacan, the unconscious and language could
no longer be seen as givens, or as natural; instead, they were
structures which required investigation. In this model, language, no matter what the mode of enunciation, was shot
through with metaphors, metonymies and complex codific-
ations which often masked, as opposed to revealed, the real self.
Taking the structuralist ideas of the word as divided into signifier
and signified, he stressed the lack of correlation between the
two, adding that meaning is always fraught with slippage, lack
of clarity and play.

His recasting of the Cartesian *Cogito ergo sum* (I think therefore I am) into *Desidero ergo sum* (I desire therefore I am) has led
to a revision of the primacy of reason in the human sciences. He
also suggested that selfhood was a complex construct in which
the self took on reflections and refractions from the societal context in which it was placed. His notion of the 'mirror stage'
stressed the imaginary and fictive nature of the ideal-self, which
he saw as predicated on a desire for an unattainable ideal which
could never be actualised. In a culture where repression of desire was very much part of the socio-religious mindset, this view
of language and desire would have revolutionary implications
for any analysis of culture and sexuality. By stressing the primacy
of desire, psychoanalysis conflicts directly with the tenets of the
Church.

Catholicism has generally seen desire, especially sexual desire, as a negative human quality, in need of repression. The
adequation of desire with sin has long been part of the Irish
psyche: the corollary of this ethico-moral equation – desire + sin

---

3. Jacques Lacan, *The Four Fundamental Concepts of Psychoanalysis.* Translated by Alan Sheridan. (Harmondsworth: Penguin, 1977), p 20.

= guilt – has led to serious consequences for individual development in Ireland. Indeed, it is in relation to desire that the contemporary difficulties of the Church can best be understood.
The capitalist, or post-capitalist, cultures of Western Europe and
the developed world are in many ways the enactment of desire:
capitalism is the political system which accedes to the importance of desire in the human psyche. One need only remember
the fall of the Berlin wall – there was never any great rush of
people from West Germany to East Germany – the traffic was all
one-way, another index of the primacy of desire. Despite the
radical uncertainty of moving to a capitalist system, the desire
for possessions, for a better life, for personal freedom was the
motive force in determining the direction of traffic across the
ruins of that forbidding wall. Indeed, commodity fetishism, the
engine which drives capitalist economies, is the practical em-
bodiment of desire – I need a new mobile phone, a bigger PC
with more Ram and a Pentium 4/5/6 processor. Secular western
society is really structured by this form of reified desire and the
Catholic Church, with a different attitude to the satisfaction of
desire, is very much out of step with this culture, and with the
postmodern concept of the secular self, a self which is firmly located in history.

By dividing human subjectivity into three orders, the imaginary, symbolic and real, Lacan offered an historical and social
dimension to psychoanalytic studies, the effect of which is still
being felt today, and the primacy of language is central to his
work. Until then, the individual was being examined very much
in isolation, with the psyche being the object of analysis in terms
of how the unconscious influences the self. In fact, in a Lacanian
context, all subjectivity is defined in terms of what is called the
Symbolic order, and this order is the structural matrix through
which our grasp of the word is shaped and enunciated.[4] For

---

4. See Jacques Lacan, *Écrits – A Selection*. Translated by Alan Sheridan.
(London: Tavistock, 1977) and *The Four Fundamental Concepts of Psycho-
Analysis*. Translated by Alan Sheridan. (Harmondsworth: Penguin,
1977).

Lacan, the Symbolic order is what actually constitutes our sub-jectivity: 'man speaks, then, but it is because the symbol has made him man'.[5] It is the matrix of culture and the locus through which individual desire is expressed: 'the moment in which the desire becomes human is also that in which the child is born into language.'[6] The social world of linguistic communication, inter-subjective relations, knowledge of ideological conventions, and the acceptance of the law are all connected with the acquisition of language.

Once a child enters into language and accepts the rules and dictates of society, it is able to deal with others. The symbolic, then, is made up of those laws and restrictions that control both desire and the rules of communication, which are perpetuated through societal and cultural hegemonic modes. Lacan condenses this function in the term the 'Name-of-the-Father'. Once a child enters into language and accepts the rules and dictates of soci-ety, it is able to deal with others. The symbolic is made possible because of the acceptance of the Name-of-the-Father, those laws and restrictions that control both desire and the rules of commu-nication: 'it is in the *Name of the Father* that we must recognise the support of the symbolic function which, from the dawn of history, has identified his person with the figure of the law.'[7] Through recognition of the Name-of-the-Father, you are able to enter into a community of others. The symbolic, through language, is 'the pact which links ... subjects together in one action. The human action *par excellence* is originally founded on the existence of the world of the symbol, namely on laws and contracts.'[8]

The connection with religion here is all too clear. Catholicism, as a subset of Christianity is a patristic, and patriar-chal, religion par excellence. Indeed, one of the most universal of the Catholic prayers is the blessing of the self, beginning, as we

---

5. Lacan, *Écrits*, p 72.
6. Lacan, *Écrits*, p 113.
7. Lacan, *Écrits*, p 67.
8. Jacques Lacan, *Freud's Papers on Technique 1953-1954. The Seminar of Jacques Lacan, Book 1*. Translated by John Forrester. Edited by Jacques-Alain Miller. (New York: Norton, 1991), p 230.

all know: 'In the name of the Father, and of the Son, and of the Holy Spirit ...' Lacan, writing from within a French milieu, profoundly influenced by a Catholic Symbolic order, uses this phrase as an index of the law into which an individual, as Lyotard has pointed out, is born, and which, in many ways, reconfigures that individual. This order is patriarchal, fixed and stratified, within a given temporal and spatial structure, not unlike the hierarchy of the Church itself.

What separates this order from mere notions of peer-pressure is the fact that it exerts a huge influence on the unconscious as well as the conscious self. These influences are not obvious at times, and form part of the inchoate but influential series of seemingly core values which drive our personalities. And of course, the crucial point here is that the very notion of the Name-of-the-Father, of cultural construction, law, language, societal norms is one which is constantly subject to change. The Symbolic order of 2005 is vastly different from that of 1905, to take a broad sweep, as we will see in terms of a contrast between *Ulysses* and *American Beauty* later in this chapter. As Paula Murphy has noted:

> The significance of the symbolic in Lacan's theory of subjectivity has already been highlighted: it governs both the imaginary and the real, to the extent to which the real can be articulated. For Lacanian psychoanalysis, it means that while the structure of his theory remains stable, its constituents are constantly changing, shifting and modifying. For derivative theories of Lacanian psychoanalysis, the consequences are also numerous. If one accepts that the symbolic changes and develops, then it questions the objections of feminists that are based upon a patriarchal static notion of the symbolic and it allows for a fresh analysis of whether the phallus is still a master signifier in the present symbolic order of western society.[9]

This view of the socio-symbolic order, itself hugely formative of the individual that we become, as subject to change is important

9. Paula Murphy, *Textual Practice* 19 (4), 2005, 531–549, p 544.

in terms of the politics of theory. In fact, Lacan sees the relationship between language and reality as constantly in flux, and only kept in place by specific nodal connections, what he terms *points de capiton*, quilting points (a metaphor drawn from the points in a mattress which are nailed down for stability), where signifier, signified and referent are in some form of stasis and harmony.[10] These anchoring points, which he also calls Master Signifiers, are our key to some form of certainty: in language, for example, they are to be found in punctuation, which guarantees the stability of the sentence and allows us to retroactively make sense of what we have been reading. The particular Symbolic order of a culture, a language, a temporal period, is an important aspect of any Lacanian analysis of individuality. The key question, of course, is how such structures change. If the Symbolic order is different in different times and places, how does it change? These very *points de capiton*, which keep a structure in place, must be dislodged in some way. It is here that we come to the work of Jacques Derrida.

It was with this same issue of structurality that Derrida's work was concerned, as he presented a critique of 'logocentrism' (the central set of beliefs or truth-claims around which a culture revolves) and introduces his strategy of deconstruction (the dismantling of the underlying structure of a text to expose its grounding in logocentrism). Derrida postulates that the history of any process of meaning or signification is always predicated on some 'centre', some validating point seen as a 'full presence which is beyond play.'[11] Derrida, and perhaps specifically his neologism 'deconstruction', has become a synecdoche of this process of theoretical critique. At its most basic, deconstruction consists of taking the binary oppositions which are constructive of the epistemological paradigm of western philosophy and, as Derrida himself notes: 'to deconstruct the opposition, first of all, is to overturn the hierarchy at a given moment'.[12]

10. Lacan, *Écrits*, p 303.
11. Jacques Derrida, *Writing and Difference*. Translated by Alan Bass. (London: Routledge, 1978), p 280.
12. Jacques Derrida, *Positions*. Translated by Alan Bass. (Chicago: University of Chicago Press, 1981), p 41.

Some of these centres, or to use the Lacanian term *points de capiton*, can be traced as follows:

1. Early Christian era to eighteenth century: a single God posited as the centre and cause of all things;

2. Eighteenth century/Enlightenment to late nineteenth century: God kicked out of the centre, and human thought (rationality) posited as the centre and cause of all things;

3. Late nineteenth century-1966: rationality moved out of the centre, and the unconscious, or irrationality, or desire, posited as the centre and cause of all things.

However, this reversal is only the first step in the deconstructive project. Making the point that an opposition of metaphysical concepts is never the face-to-face opposition of two terms, but a hierarchy and an order of subordination, Derrida goes on to say that deconstruction 'does not consist in passing from one concept to another, but in overturning and displacing a conceptual order, as well as the non-conceptual order with which the conceptual order is articulated.'[13] It is this sense of displacement of the static oppositional criteria that is important in the context of the present discussion. What Derrida has termed the 'structurality of structure' stresses that very little in human culture is 'natural' or 'given'; instead, all structurations are created from an ideological standpoint which, and here we would be in Foucault territory, is governed by power relationships. What we might term the 'politics of deconstruction' exerts a loosening force on these relationships by suggesting the necessity for alternative structures which are self-aware in terms of the power relationships.

For Derrida, the teleology of deconstructive critique involves the imbrication of text with context. He is unwilling to bracket any field of cultural endeavour within its own self-defined parameters. Deconstruction, he says, consists:

only of transference, and of a thinking through of transfer-

---

13. Jacques Derrida, *Margins of Philosophy*. Translated by Alan Bass. (Chicago: Chicago University Press, 1982), p 329.

ence, in all the senses that this word acquires in more than
one language, and first of all that of the transference between
languages. If I had to risk a single definition of deconstruction, one as brief, elliptical and economical as a password, I
would say simply and without overstatement: *plus d'une
langue* – both more than a language and no more of a language.[14]

The ideas of hermetically sealed-off cultures, national languages, ideologies are deconstructed to reveal a broader context
of comparison and contrast, a process which will have ramifications for any exploration of Irish social, cultural and political
mores.

While these theories referred initially to academic texts, and
were presented in language that could be described, at best as
opaque and at worst as unreadable, their political subtext was
subversive in the extreme. Derrida's oft-quoted remark that *Il
n'y a pas de hors-texte* (there is nothing outside the text),[15] meant
that such theoretical approaches could be applied to all political
and cultural paradigms, as they were all composed of linguistic
structures, and hence all capable of being deconstructed. He
would later amend this datum to the more inclusive *Il n'y a pas
de hors contexte* (there is nothing outside of context).[16] This tag
has become one of the most contested items in the discussion of
deconstruction. Derrida, basically, is stressing the constructed-
ness of almost all sociocultural and linguistic structures, and ad-
ducing the need for interpretation and contextual placement if
interpretative activities are to have any sense of closure, an issue

---

14. Jacques Derrida, *Mémoires: For Paul de Man*. Translated by Cecile
Lindsay, Jonathan Culler and Eduardo Cadava. (New York: Columbia
University Press, 1989), pp 14-15.
15. Jacques Derrida, *Of Grammatology*. Translated by Gayatri
Chakravorty Spivak. (London: Johns Hopkins Press, 1976), p 158.
16. Jacques Derrida, *Limited Inc*. Translated by Samuel Weber and
Jeffrey Mehlman. (Evanston, Illinois: Northwestern University Press,
1988), p 136.

underlined by Lacan in relation to the subject: that each individual is context specific – 'his history is unified by the law, by his
symbolic universe, which is not the same for everyone.'[17]

In other words, it is through the relationship of text and context that meaning is to be found. So, if we are to analyse the
change in role of the Catholic Church as a system or organisation,
then these theorists will prove invaluable in terms of outlining
the processes of transformation which are, in the Ireland of the
third millennium, possibly the only form of constant that exists.

The value of *Father Ted*, I would suggest, is to place the structure of the Church in the crucible of satirical commentary. Satire
is very much an interrogative discourse in its mode of operation.
As it pokes fun at objects, people and structures, it implicitly
questions the standards and codes through which these objects,
people and structures were accorded value in the first place.
Rather than seeing the Church as an organisation that in some
way transcends the norms of system, bureaucracy, hierarchy
and the normal structures of society, this programme underlines
just how much the Church is part of such structures. The visual
image of a priest kicking his bishop 'up the arse', while another
priest takes a photograph of this act, is an iconic metaphor of the
change in the attitude of people to the Church as structure, and
at this juncture, I would like to bring two other visual metaphors
to the fore in order to create an iconic image chain wherein the
change in role of the Church as structure can be traced.

These images involve two pairs of similar events – a polyptich which in their chronology, attest to the altered role of the
Church as an organisation in Ireland today. The first image is
the iconic one of Ted kicking Bishop Brennan up the arse, while
the grinning Dougal takes a photograph of this event. The second is also an image from television, involving a camera, albeit
of a different order, a bishop and a priest.

On recalling the visit of Pope John Paul II to Galway, for the
youth Mass in 1979, one of the images that stays in the mind is
that of Father Michael Cleary and Bishop Eamonn Casey warm-

---

17. Lacan, *Seminar 1*, p 197.

ing up the crowd by leading them in the hymn 'Bind us Together'. In a way, this scene was the apotheosis of Catholic power in recent Ireland – the pope was drawing huge crowds, the youth Mass was thronged with people, and two of the most popular clerics in Ireland, both men seen as being very much in touch with younger people, as well as being telegenic, were masters of ceremonies. The future for the Church in Ireland seemed bright indeed. With the wisdom of hindsight it is all too easy to unpack the personal lives of these men, and see them as synecdoches of what is wrong with the Church in Ireland, but that is not the aim of this chapter. Instead I want to juxtapose the different images of bishops and priests and then turn to a different set of signifying images.

In 1999, the film *American Beauty* appeared to widespread acclaim. The film, an intelligent probing of mid-life crises among middle class Americans, achieved both popular and critical acclaim. One of the central images of that film is the obsession of the central character, Lester Burnham, with a young friend of his daughter, Angela Hayes, a cheerleader. This obsession begins with Lester watching Angela go through her cheer-leader routine, and obsessing about one image, namely that of Angela flipping up her skirt to reveal her underwear. This is an image which will haunt Lester's daydreams, and also fuel his masturbatory fantasies. Indeed, Lester, in his voiceover, tells us that his early morning masturbation in the shower is the best part of his day: 'Look at me, jerking off in the shower ... This will be the high point of my day; it's all downhill from here.'[18] I call this to mind because nearly one hundred years earlier, another narrative has a similar scene.

In the Nausica episode of *Ulysses*, Gertie McDowell is being watched by Leopold Bloom, and as she leans back to watch fireworks, she catches her knee in her hand, revealing to Bloom's gaze her:

nainsook knickers, the fabric that caresses the skin, better

---

18. *American Beauty* (1999). Directed by Sam Mendes. Written by Alan Ball.

than those other pettiwidth, the green, four and eleven, on
account of being white and she let him and she saw that he
saw and then it went so high it went out of sight a moment
and she was trembling in every limb from being bent so far
back that he had a full view high up above her knee where
no-one ever not even on the swing or wading and she wasn't
ashamed and he wasn't either to look in that immodest way
like that because he couldn't resist the sight of the wondrous
revealment half offered like those skirtdancers behaving so
immodest before gentlemen looking and he kept on looking,
looking. She would fain have cried to him chokingly, held
out her snowy slender arms to him to come, to feel his lips
laid on her white brow, the cry of a young girl's love, a little
strangled cry, wrung from her, that cry that has rung
through the ages. And then a rocket sprang and bang shot
blind blank and O! then the Roman candle burst and it was
like a sigh of O! and everyone cried O! O! in raptures and it
gushed out of it a stream of rain gold hair threads and they
shed and ah! they were all greeny dewy stars falling with
golden, O so lovely, O, soft, sweet, soft![19]

The similarity between the two men, both engaged in advertis-
ing and in their forties, neither of whom has had sex with their
wives in years, and the two younger women who enjoy the sexual attention of the gaze is clear. The dissimilarity is also clear.
This scene in *Ulysses*, first serialised in *The Little Review*, was
deemed to transgress moral good taste, and lead to confiscation,
book burning, legal prosecution for obscenity, and banning in
1921.[20] The scene from the film translated into a number of
awards including a Golden Globe and an Academy Award for
the screenplay written by Alan Ball.[21]

---

19. James Joyce, *Ulysses*. Edited by Hans Walter Gabler, Wolfhard
Steppe and Claus Melchior. First published 1922 (London: Bodley
Head, 1989), p 274.
20. Richard Ellmann, *James Joyce*. First published 1959 (Oxford: Oxford
Oxford University Press, 1977), pp 518-519.
21. Alan Ball, The Shooting Script: *American Beauty* (New York:
Newmarket Press, 1999).

When we place these images together, two of bishops and two of sexual behaviour, what is interesting is the altered role of the Church in terms of the mindset of people exposed to those scenes. The shock and horror that followed Eamonn Casey's revelations in 1992 was exacerbated by the wave of revelations that followed in terms of child abuse in Church-run organisations. However, reaction to the image of Bishop Brennan is, I would argue, fuelled less by anger or hurt, and more by a sense that the Church is now just another organisation among many. The simple fact is that the symbolic order has changed and our views and expectations of the clergy are very much not what they were twenty or thirty years ago. Indeed, kicking Bishop Brennan up the arse could well be a metaphor for the gradual disrespect, or to put it more accurately, gradual lack of importance of the hierarchical structure of the Church in the day-to-day lives of ordinary people.

Various scandals, mainly revolving around sexual abuse, have become common knowledge in the Ireland of the Celtic Tiger – though perhaps the most disturbing fact of these is that when Brendan Smyth and Ivan Payne were complained for abuse, their superiors, bishops and cardinals did nothing to bring this to a halt, but rather sent them to different parishes, where the pattern of abuse continued. These cases of the abuse of children, together with the sexual details of Eamonn Casey (whose scandal also involved £70,000 of diocesan funds) and Michael Cleary, who had been most vociferous in his condemnation of sexual misbehaviour, and diminished support for traditional Catholic positions in the divorce and abortion referenda, further eroded the central position of the Church as a moral arbiter in Ireland. This is especially true with respect to the role of women and sexuality, as indicated in the *Ulysses* and *American Beauty* examples.

The images of the scenes of voyeurism and exhibitionism that we see from Gertie McDowell and Angela Hayes in *Ulysses* and *American Beauty* respectively, are separated in time, demonstrating the hugely different symbolic order that exists in the world of today as opposed to that of the fictive time of *Ulysses*. In both texts, there is a certain level of desire on the part of both women and men: just as the men watch, so the women are aware and participant – these are not objects of the male scopic drive: they are participants in the scopic drive. Likewise, the two wives in these two narratives, Molly Bloom and Carolyn Burnham, are active participants in the sexual aspects of the narratives. Molly, famously, is having an affair with Blazes Boylan, having arranged that he will come to her home in Eccles Street later that day, while her husband, aware of this, has obligingly left the way clear. Thus the eternal triangle, traditionally that of one man and two women, has been inverted and it is Molly who both has her cake (seed cake in her case) and eats it. Similarly Carolyn is having a torrid affair with Buddy Kane, the Real Estate king, something of which Lester is also aware. Here women are seen as free agents in terms of their sexual preferences, and no longer seen as possessions of men. The structures of the societies within which they live have radically altered, and consequently, so has their behaviours and their choices. Indeed rapid change is a characteristic of contemporary culture, and the pace of change has been rampant in Ireland over the past twenty years. This is the core problem facing the Church in this present context: it still clings to the sense of itself as an unchanging organisation, when in actual fact it has changed radically over the centuries. In almost every progressive field of social change, from the mother and child controversy, through contraception and the various social issues that have come before it, the Church has adopted an anti-progressive policy, one which it justifies by seeing itself as the guardian of immutable standards, frozen in the past. Many of the issues are involved with sexual behaviour, which reinforces the point made earlier that the culture of desire that permeates the contemporary western world is inimical to the attitudes of the Church.

Again, in terms of postmodernism, the breakdown of grand narratives means the liberation of smaller ones, and the roles of sexual minorities, like gays and lesbians, has become ever more prominent in the wake of what I term the deconstruction of the Church as we know it. Both of these texts privilege female sexuality as developing through different societies. Just as social structures change, so too does the behaviour of the subjects within those structures. Part of the problem of the Church, it seems to me, is an inability to respond to the societal changes and symbolic conditions within which it exists. The issue of structure has been a preoccupation of this paper and it is with the Church's own definition of itself as a structure that I propose to conclude.

John Paul II, in his Apostolic Letter, *Ordinatio Sacerdotalis*, of 1994, made the position of the Church clear in terms of reasons as to why women have not been, and should not be, ordained. He said:

Christ chose his apostles only from among men.

… the exclusion of women from the priesthood is in accordance with God's plan for his Church.

Christ's way of acting [only choosing men] did not proceed from sociological or cultural motives peculiar to his time. Rather it is to be seen as the faithful observance of a plan to be ascribed to the wisdom of the Lord of the universe.

[Quote from Paul VI]: The Church does not consider herself authorised to admit women into priestly ordination.

I declare … that this judgement is to be definitively held by the Church's faithful.

This tradition [of excluding women] has been faithfully maintained by the oriental Churches.[22]

The clear point here is that Christ, as Son of God, is a transcendental consciousness at work in a particular place and time: he is in it, but not of it, and as such, is not trammelled by its socio-cultural and linguistic mores and limitations. So, his reasons for not ordaining women as part of his apostolic structure had less to do with the prevailing socio-economic status of women, which was little better than livestock at the time, and more to do with a

22. http://www.vatican.va/holy_father/john_paul_ii/apost_letters/ documents/hf_jpi_apl_2205199 4_ordinatio-sacerdotalis_en.html

transcendental grand plan. The Church, by extrapolation, is above and beyond the systems and structures of particular places and times, existing as a transcendent structure.

This is fine if one is willing to accept the discourse of the Church at face value, but when deconstructive theory is brought to bear, problems arise. If this specific choice of Jesus is not to be explained by his contemporary symbolic order, why have other such choices been explained differently, and have not been subsumed into Church dogma? Jesus chose to be a carpenter, he chose his apostles from a number of trades such as fishermen, tax collectors, etc. Why are contemporary priests not asked to undergo training in carpentry or to receive certificates of mastery in different types of fishing? Jesus went to the Temple and into synagogues regularly. He argued with the learned doctors and he pruged the Temple of money changers and hucksters. How odd, then, that the Vatican could allegedly give sanctuary to Archbishop Marcinkus, who stood accused of fraud, and was liable to arrest if he left the precincts of the Vatican. All of the apostles were Jews, where does that leave a series of Italian popes, a Polish pope and German pope? Why are those decisions not seen as beyond the prevailing sociology of Christ's place and time? I would argue that the reason that those questions were not asked before was precisely because the bishops were those *points de capiton*, those master signifiers who controlled the play of meaning. Iconically, the kicking of Bishop Brennan up the arse is a ludic demonstration of the displacement of those master signifiers, and concomitantly a sign that the Church has lost its sense of being a transcendent organisation. Instead it is now just another structure in a crowded marketplace.

Indeed, further critique would reinforce this point. How can the Church claim to act outside of time, in a transcendent manner, when it avails itself of every possible safeguard of contemporary culture to defend itself against accusations? In a deal done with former minister Michael Woods, the Church has deflected payment liabilities to victims of institutional abuse onto the taxpayer. It has also taken legal action to defend itself against victims, and had Cardinal Law say one of the requiem Masses for Pope John Paul II, while he himself was under a cloud in terms of his inaction in the face of rampant child abuse in his American diocese.

Yet, despite all of this, there is a glaring need for a form of the transcendent in contemporary secular Ireland. In many instances, this desire for something in which to believe has become displaced after the fall from grace of the Church. We see it in the fetishisation of sport and spectacle, as the almost country-wide investment into the championships of the GAA in both hurling and football provides a communal outlet for people to express a sense of the beyond themselves. It has been seen in the crowds who flocked to the relics of Saint Thérèse of Lisieux, it can be seen in the popularity of alternative forms of spirituality, and in the outpouring of genuine emotion that greeted the passing away of Pope John Paul. Ironically, the grief, the communal sharing of sorrow, the widespread media coverage called to mind an event some eight years earlier, namely the death of Princess Diana. Here too there was a similar outpouring of grief, a binding of people around a departed icon – in a way the epitome of religious desire. Interestingly, however, in the aftermath of her death, things have progressed very much as normal: her name has gradually been forgotten and Prince Charles finally married the third person in his marriage to Diana, namely Camilla Parker Bowles.

I would suggest that the same is true of the religious fervour which gripped Ireland and indeed, the Catholic world, in the aftermath of the death of Pope John Paul. The emotional desire for religious experience, for that sense of communal belief, for an identity between the immanent and the transcendent, is very much part of being human, and in Ireland, the Catholic religion has for a long time filled this void. Now, however, that the two senses of the Church as structure have been deconstructed, and that it is seen as just another organisation striving to protect its own patch and its own members, people have moved on. To attempt to preach morals and ethics, while at the same time using every legal and political means to defend the organisation against legitimate charges from victims of abuse, has really just placed the Church as one more set of systems – it is the metaphorical equivalent of kicking Bishop Brennan up the arse. He is no longer seen as a religious icon, not to be touched by the venality of human failings: he is just one more abuse boss, who has instilled fear and resentment among his staff, and suffers the consequences accordingly. This, of course, is a metaphorical equivalent of the sense of disappointment felt by Catholics when two of the more charismatic figures within the Church, Eamonn Casey, the bishop who scourged governments about the third world, who reputedly drove too fast and drank too much, but who was seen as a decent man, and Michael Cleary, the original singing priest, were both found to be involved in sexual relationships. In the wake of later scandals, these were relatively minor offences among, after all, consenting adults. And indeed, the Church has had a long history of sacerdotal sexual connections: it is not for nothing that there are Irish surnames called Mac an tSagairt (McEntaggert); Mac an Easpaig (McEnespy) and Mac an Phapa (Pope).

However, what was significant here is the differentiating of the status of the Church as a transcendent system and an immanent one. To preach about the redress of poverty or about sexually correct behaviour, as both Casey and Cleary did, on the one hand, and to be found violating those very precepts themselves on the other, made it clear that the Church's warrant to be seen as a transcendental system was in no way sustainable. The position of women in this structure has also been significant, though interestingly, the Church, as already noted, as the one remaining institution which generically discriminates against women (with the exception of certain clubs) has rarely come under sustained attack from the feminist movement. Now this could be because women as a group have taken on board the pope's transcendental justification for the men-only rule on ordination. However, I think that this state of affairs is a further index of the increasing sense of irrelevance with which the Church is viewed by women – they are just not interested in this last bastion of patriarchy.

Instead, feminists have concentrated on issues of sexual liberation, stressing the freedom of women to control their own procreative processes, and with the increasing availability of contraception of all types, the control of the Church over sexual matters has waned completely. Thus the difference between those skirtdancers separated by over 100 years, Gertie McDowall and Angela, is that the latter, while still a virgin, is so by choice, and is quite happy to have sex with Lester towards the end of the film with no sense of guilt whatsoever. The pathways of desire are now open to exploration by both sexes, and any form of external control by the Church has just lost all validity. People, in this secular age, are now inclined to voice their desire, and the concomitant guilt is no longer the price that such desire must pay.

In this way, they are voicing the presence of a different structure, a new symbolic order, a dissemination of control and, in short, are joining Father Ted and Dougal in symbolically kicking bishop Brennan up the arse. Thus through two sets of visual images, one dealing with power figures and the other with sexual desire, the alteration in the grand narrative of the Catholic Church in Ireland is mapped out. The first images, one set dealing with a bishop in his pomp, accompanied by his priest, addressing the multitudes in front of the pope, the other of a bishop being kicked up the arse by one of his priests, delineates the deconstruction of the central position of the Catholic Church in Ireland. The second set, of two young women allowing themselves to be the object of the male scopic drive, but also to a degree controlling that gaze, is another index of the primacy of desire, both sexual and other, and of a form of liberation of desire from the repressive regime of traditional Irish Catholic doctrine. The change in female attitudes to sexual desire is an index of that the symbolic order of Ireland has changed and is changing, a process which has and will continue to cause reverberations within the Church.

In the wake of the revelations in October 2005 of the report on child abuse in the diocese of Ferns, with strong blame being placed on the bishops of the diocese for not taking the required action, it would seem as if the broader community is engaged in a parallel process of deconstructing the power of the Church and its pretensions to being an unchanging vehicle of moral certitude. In this context it is important to note that deconstruction, contrary to popular belief does not equate with destruction; instead it suggests a dismantling of the traditional binary oppositions and the creation of a new structure wherein the power relations are more equally defined. In our context this deconstruction has been imaged in terms of the power of the bishops being kicked up the arse, to use a colloquialism, and the desire of women being recognised as equal to that of men. If the Church is to survive within the new symbolic order of a postmodern, postcolonial, secular Ireland that has more in common with either Boston or Berlin than Rome, it will need to take these lessons seriously.

CHAPTER FOUR

New Ireland and the Undoing of the Catholic legacy: Looking Back to the Future

Louise Fuller

Any consideration of Irish identity and the profound cultural changes that have taken place in Ireland in recent years must take account of the centrality of the influence of Catholicism until the 1950s and its quite dramatic decline since that time to a point where the role of the institutional Church is now marginalised. In the first half of the twentieth century Catholicism tended to define Irish identity. From the fifties challenges to this situation began to be mounted and clearly the automatic association of Irish and Catholic no longer obtains today. This chapter takes a historic overview and some of the important milestones along the way are charted. Forces of change which were operating are examined. Policy decisions made by politicians, government reports, court judgements, the deliberations of the Second Vatican Council, individuals, organisations and the mass media all played a role in bringing about changes in Irish society, which would ultimately redefine Irish identity. The task of understanding and assessing the influence of Catholicism in the context of re-definitions of Irishness taking place today (which is the central concern addressed by this book) is posed as a question at the end, because while the importance of Catholicism cannot be disputed (given its historic role), its ongoing influence can no longer be taken for granted, but must be forged in a radically changed economic, political, socio-cultural context.

The idea of Irish and Catholic being synonymous has deep historical roots and I want to cast a backward look at the outset at how the concept came to be and how from the time of independence it was taken for granted and consolidated. By the time of independence the power of the Catholic Church in Ireland had been consolidated over the previous hundred years. In the nineteenth century the Catholic Church placed its resources and organisational ability at the disposal of Parnell and O'Connell before him and in so doing had become a powerful political force destined to wield extraordinary influence in the new State. And we can go back further to the time of the Reformation and Henry VIII's introduction of the Protestant religion into England and the passage of the Act of Supremacy which declared Henry to be Supreme Head of the Church. From then, Catholicism was destined to become, over time, the most important dimension in the English-Irish question. By the end of Elizabeth's reign in 1603, Ireland had been militarily conquered. The defeat of Kinsale delivered the final blow to the old Irish world. In the period of Elizabeth's reign, between 1558 and 1603 the Reformed religion, established by law became the Church of the nation in fact in England – but by the time of Elizabeth's death in 1603 it was evident that Ireland was going to remain Catholic.[1] Policies of cultural assimilation and religious conversion were seen as a way to secure Irish loyalty. Warfare and insurgency in Ireland stemmed primarily from opposition to the colonial policies of the State, and came to encompass a religious dimension.[2]

By the end of the seventeenth century the overwhelming majority of the Irish, in consequence of their continued adherence to the Catholic religion, had been dispossessed and excluded from the political life of the country. Yet the conflict had established a national unity among the dispossessed, in which the Catholic faith became increasingly important the more it became apparent that everything else was lost.[3] The decline in the use of

---

1. Patrick Corish, *The Irish Catholic Experience: A Historical Survey* (Dublin: Gill and Macmillan, 1985), pp 66-7.
2. Colm Lennon, 'Religious Wars in Ireland: Plantations and Martyrs of the Catholic Church' in Brendan Bradshaw and Daire Keogh (eds.), *Christianity in Ireland: Revisiting the Story* (Dublin: The Columba Press, 2002), p 86.
3. Patrick J. Corish (ed.), 'The Origins of Catholic Nationalism' in *A History of Irish Catholicism* (Dublin, Sydney: Gill and Son, 1968), pp 1-2.

the Irish language, which accelerated during the nineteenth century particularly after the Famine added a further dimension. All of these developments meant that Catholicism had become the badge of Irish identity by the close of the century. So Catholic strength in the nineteenth century came from the fact that it was an oppositional force – it was counter-cultural. The bishops became political in their efforts to gain redress for Catholic grievances. This began in the early nineteenth century when the laity, led by O'Connell, organised a massive protest against the possibility of granting the English Crown a veto over episcopal appointments, a veto which the bishops had been prepared to concede in return for emancipation at the time of the Union.[4] O'Connell mobilised a mass movement by tapping into the Catholics' sense of discontent and grievance and forging a common consciousness. He constantly appealed to the Catholic people of Ireland as a nation.[5] The success of the campaign and the granting of Catholic emancipation was a watershed for Catholics.

The bishops were never again apolitical and in the late nineteenth century they placed themselves at the very heart of the alliance between the Irish Parliamentary Party and the Land League in their long battle to secure rights for education for Catholics at third level. They were now at the very centre of a power struggle, the aims of which were to gain the right for tenants to buy back their land and the securing of Home Rule for Ireland. By virtue of the Church's own reorganisation and renewal consolidated after the arrival of Paul Cullen to Ireland in 1849, when the Catholic populace were socialised into a strong religious belief, practice and moral order and its investment in education, health and social welfare provision, the Catholic Church had become a powerful political force through the nineteenth century, destined to wield extraordinary influence in the

4. Oliver MacDonagh, 'The Politicization of the Irish Catholic Bishops, 1800-1850', *Historical Journal*, 18: 1 (1975), pp 38-41.
5. D. George Boyce, *Nineteenth Century Ireland: The Search for Stability* (Dublin: Gill and Macmillan, 1990) pp 46-7.

new State. And its position was consolidated in the period after independence. Neither Cosgrave nor de Valera needed any prompting to ensure that the Catholic moral code was upheld by legislation. The high point of the legitimisation of the Catholic ethos was de Valera's constitution in 1937, which recognised the 'special position' of the Catholic Church, which he justified in the Dáil on the basis that '93% of the people on this part of Ireland ... belong to the Catholic Church ...' He pointed out that their 'whole philosophy of life is the philosophy that comes from its teachings ...'[6] In de Valera's vision there was an almost instinctual association of Catholicism with the Irish way of life and this was extolled time and again in his speeches. His St Patrick's day broadcast to the United States in 1935 is a good indication of how he perceived Irishness:

> Since the coming of St Patrick, fifteen hundred years ago, Ireland has been a Christian and a Catholic nation. All the ruthless attempts made through the centuries to force her from this allegiance have not shaken her faith. She remains a Catholic nation.[7]

Political support for the Catholic ethos was one of the central distinctive features of Irish life since independence. Some of the other distinctive features of Irish Catholicism were the power wielded by the bishops – they adopted a very dogmatic approach, demanding and expecting conformity whether in their dealings with ordinary Catholics or political figures; the extraordinarily high level of religious practice – the first comprehensive survey of Catholic religious practice undertaken in 1974/5 by the Bishops' Research and Development Commission placed Mass attendance at 91% of the population;[8] the very high numbers of vocations to the religious life; the extent to which the media were, in present day parlance, 'Catholic friendly'. The

6. *Dáil Debates*, 67, col 1890 (4 June 1937).
7. *Irish Press*, 18 March 1935, p 2.
8. *A Survey of Religious Practice, Attitudes and Beliefs in the Republic of Ireland 1973-4*, report no 1 on Religious Practice (Dublin: Research and Development Unit, Catholic Communications Institute of Ireland, 1975, 1976), p 71.

Irish Independent, the newspaper with the largest daily circulation gave extensive coverage to news of Catholic interest well into the 1960s. As well as printing the texts of bishops' pastoral letters, often running to two or three pages of newsprint, the leader writer also on occasion made reference to them, summarising the main points and reinforcing them.[9] Radio Éireann also played a key role in legitimating the Catholic ethos. From 15 August 1950, at the instigation of Archbishop McQuaid, the ringing of the Angelus at the Pro-Cathedral was broadcast over the air at six o'clock each evening.[10] The Church's control of education and the State's acceptance and support of the Church's policy on education was crucial in the legitimisation of the Catholic ethos, as of course was the Church's involvement in the health and social welfare services, all consolidated in the nineteenth century. The Council of Education which reported on the primary school system in 1954 and on secondary education in 1962 saw the primary purpose of schooling in the former report as 'religious'[11] and in the latter report as having to do with 'the inculcation of religious ideals and values'.[12] Thus, in many different ways and by means of all manner of ritual observances, Irish life and consciousness was defined in terms of its Catholicism.

Writing in 1952 in the *Irish Rosary* Dr James Devane could, without fear of contradiction, describe Ireland as 'the most Catholic country in the world'.[13] He went on: 'Perhaps the Republic of Ireland, as it is constituted today, is the only integral Catholic State in the world; a Catholic culture as it existed in the Middle Ages.' But in the context of the religious fervour of the

---

9. See, for example, *Irish Independent*, 5 February 1951, pp 4, 6, *Irish Independent*, 1 March 1954, pp 8, 10, *Irish Independent*, 13 February 1956, pp 8-11.

10. See *Irish Catholic Directory*, 1951 (15 August 1950), p 753.

11. See *Report of the Council of Education on (1) The Function of the Primary School, (2) The Curriculum to be pursued in the Primary School* (Dublin: The Stationery Office, 1954), paras 195, 196, pp 130, 132.

12. See *Report of the Council of Education on the Curriculum of the Secondary School*, (Dublin: The Stationery Office, 1962), paras. 150, 164, pp 80, 88.

13. James Devane, *Irish Rosary*, December 1952.

time, he could perhaps be forgiven for not sensing that the days were numbered for this model of Catholicism. The 1950s and early 1960s represented the final phase of nineteenth century devotional revolution Catholicism.[14] That said, the terms Irish and Catholic were still seen as synonymous and the discourse engaged in by Church personnel played a powerful role in the formation of consciousness and identity. In 1950, Archbishop D'Alton, Archbishop of Armagh and Primate of all Ireland expressed the view:

> Where their religion is concerned, the heart of our people is essentially sound. Irish Catholics, even amidst the temptations of modern life, are deeply attached to their faith, and loyal in the practice of it.[15]

Ironically these views were expressed by Archbishop D'Alton at the launch of *The Furrow*, a journal founded in 1950 by Dr J. G. McGarry, Professor of Sacred Eloquence and Pastoral Theology at St Patrick's College Maynooth. Both *The Furrow* and *Doctrine and Life*, a Dominican publication, founded in 1951 (spawned by the *Irish Rosary*) were to adopt a more questioning and critical stance towards the prevailing ethos of Irish Catholicism. The ideas and thinking which led to the foundation of these journals were far removed from that of Fr Devane and Archbishop D'Alton. Fr Sean O'Riordan, a Redemptorist, who became co-editor with McGarry of *The Furrow*, writing on the twenty-fifth anniversary of the journal gave an insight into the mood of the group who collaborated with them in founding the journal

---

14. Emmet Larkin, 'The Devotional Revolution in Ireland' in *The Historical Dimensions of Irish Catholicism* (New York: Arno Press, 1976), p 630. The term was first coined by Larkin in 1972 to describe how Archbishop Paul Cullen championed the consolidation of a 'devotional revolution' in post-Famine Ireland. Since that time various scholars have argued that the change was a more gradual one. In a recent essay 'Before the devotional revolution' in James H. Murphy (ed.), *Evangelicals and Catholics in Nineteenth Century Ireland* (Dublin: Four Courts Press, 2005) , pp 15-37, Larkin has answered the critics of his devotional revolution theory.
15. Archbishop D'Alton, 'The Furrow and its Programme', *The Furrow*, 1:1 (1950), p 6.

when he pointed out that 'there was a general recognition of the fact that the times called for a renewal and adaptation of the pastoral life of the Irish Church at all levels'.[16] At a time when Archbishop D'Alton and the other Irish bishops and the vast majority of the clergy were quite complacent as to the health of Irish Catholicism, the clerics who provided the inspiration for these journals were of the opinion that Irish Catholicism left something to be desired.

In the first issue of *Doctrine and Life*, the Dominican provincial, Very Rev Thomas E. Garde, saw the aim of the journal as being that of initiating people into a deeper understanding of their faith and its implications. He was aware of the fact that many might question the need for such a journal 'given the obvious faith of the Irish people'.[17] But even then he was not so complacent and felt that many people were losing the faith because they had 'never really grasped it. They never fully understood its implications. It never became for them a deep personal conviction.'[18] McGarry echoed Garde's sentiments when he was reviewing the first edition of *Doctrine and Life*. He referred to the 'prevailing spiritual climate' and its 'lack of sound foundation and substance, evidenced – to name but one sign – in the popular rating of devotional publications'.[19] He went on to point out the 'general need for a spiritual life founded more securely on doctrine' drawing attention to Pope Benedict's cautionary advice against a 'soft and empty kind of piety'.[20]

Writers in *The Furrow* focused on several aspects of Catholic life in Ireland at that time that they were less than impressed with. At a time when Mass attendance was universal, engendering in the bishops and general run of clergy a certain complacency,

---

16. See Seán O'Riordan, 'Towards a Prophetic Church', *The Furrow*, 26:3 (1975).
17. See Thomas E. Garde, 'Foreword', *Doctrine and Life*, 1:1 (1951), p 2.
18. Ibid., p 3.
19. J. G. McGarry reviewing *Doctrine and Life*, 1:1, *The Furrow*, 2:3 1951), p 189.
20. Ibid.

they questioned the quality of people's liturgical experience. They did not perceive that full churches were necessarily an index of the spiritual health of the nation. To the extent that the Church authorities were concerned about the state of Irish Catholicism in the fifties and early sixties in their pastoral letters and statements, their main preoccupation was to defend and protect it from secular influences emanating from continental Europe, and repeatedly to warn Irish Catholics of the dangers to the faith. They sensed that foreign newspapers and books, the radio, cinema and in due course television would be the harbingers of change over which they would have little or no control and which they could only warn people about and this they did repeatedly. Again at the launch of *The Furrow* in 1950 Archbishop D'Alton gave voice to the kind of fears that preoccupied the bishops and their attitudes to perceived threats to the *status quo* when he wrote:

> We have to face the fact that with the rise of the new inventions such as the cinema and the radio, we no longer enjoy our former comparative isolation. Our people are constantly being brought into contact with a civilisation for the most part alien and materialistic in outlook.[21]

The first time that the Church-State consensus which had operated since independence and seemed invulnerable was threatened was in the following year during the tenure of office of the first Inter-Party government, when Noel Browne the Minister for Health in this administration sought to introduce free medical care for women and children up to the age of sixteen years. When the hierarchy and others objected to the scheme, Noel Browne was asked to tender his resignation and the Inter-Party government fell. The subsequent debate in the Dáil and statements made by the main players in the debacle, give a unique insight into the power wielded by the bishops at that time and the subservience of politicans, Browne himself in his resignation speech declaring that 'I as a Catholic accept unequivocally and

21. Archbishop D'Alton, 'The Furrow and its Programme', *Furrow*, 1:1 (February 1950), p 6.

unreservedly the views of the hierarchy on this matter.'[22] In an address to the CTSI later that year Archbishop D'Alton declared that 'we have a right to expect that our social legislation will not be in conflict with Catholic principles.'[23] And a few years later, referring back to the controversy, Bishop Lucey of Cork at a Christus Rex Congress declared that the bishops were in fact 'the final arbiters of right and wrong even in political matters'.[24] While the bishops prevailed, it was a pyrrhic victory. Anti-clericalism had not been a feature of the Irish socio-political landscape; however, this episode sowed the seeds of a culture of dissent which up to that point had been confined to the literati or intelligentsia. In my view, it was a turning point, the fall-out of which would be felt twenty to thirty years later.

The first time in the history of the State that a government went against the hierarchy's wishes was in 1959 when, on foot of the recommendations of a Commission of Inquiry set up by the Taoiseach Sean Lemass, legislation was passed relaxing the licensing laws, ignoring the warnings of the bishops which had been most peremptory in their tone and had held up change through the fifties.[25] The fact that this happened has naturally to be seen in the context of the far-reaching socio-economic changes taking place from the late fifties. De Valera retired in 1959. Whereas in his vision of Ireland and Irish identity he had prized spiritual values eschewing whatever smacked of materialism, Lemass who replaced him as Taoiseach was a more pragmatic politician interested in people's material welfare. As a result of the First Programme for Economic Expansion published in 1958[26] the economy, which had been stagnating through the fifties, was turned round and emigration was stemmed. Another important event in 1958, which would have profound implic-

---

22. *Irish Catholic Directory*, 1952 (10 October 1951), p 709.
23. *Irish Times*, 13 April 1955.
24. See Louise Fuller, *Irish Catholicism Since 1950: The Undoing of a Culture* (Dublin: Gill and Macmillan), pp 55-60.
25. Fuller, *Irish Catholicism*, pp55-60.
26. *Programme for Economic Expansion* (often referred to as the First Programme) (Dublin: The Stationery Office, 1958).

ations in Ireland and beyond, was the election of Pope John XXIII and his announcement shortly afterwards of the convocation of the Second Vatican Council. Modern developments like industrialisation and urbanisation, taking place since the turn of the century in continental Europe had led to a decline in religious practice, which raised questions for theologians and liturgical scholars and the Council essentially was a response to this.

The Second Vatican Council had a big impact on Ireland not least because the Irish Church was very authoritarian – it was very much a Church of rules, regulations and certainties. A well-coined phrase went along the following lines: everything was obligatory and what was not, was forbidden! This captures the mood of pre-Conciliar Irish Catholicism. However, the Council was a clear indication that there was much disagreement among bishops and cardinals during the debates and that there were grey areas in theology – and this was something that was very new to Irish Catholics. The fact that it happened exactly at the time when Irish television was in its infancy reinforced the impact. Book and film censorship instituted in the 1920s had kept Irish society isolated and as far as the Church authorities were concerned 'protected' from 'evil literature' and ideas and lifestyles that might corrupt. Television had the effect of liberating Irish society almost overnight. It played an iconoclastic role in challenging and deconstructing accepted notions of traditional Irish/Catholic identity. In particular the *Late Late Show*, a late night chat show, contributed to the airing of all manner of views very often not in keeping with the official Church position and clergy frequently participated. The Vatican Council of course had also liberated clergy and whereas heretofore they were seen in the context of the altar and pulpit, now they had a different kind of visibility and contributed to debate and discussion on different aspects of life, hitherto considered taboo – often to do with sexual matters, an area which had much preoccupied bishops and clergy and on which their attitudes were more and more being perceived as narrow and puritanical.

The Irish Church was characterised by simple faith, devotional piety and the idea that there were clear-cut answers to complex moral problems. Pre-Conciliar Catholicism was legalistic, authoritarian and highly defensive. This was a legacy of the Council of Trent, convened between 1545-63, so that the Catholic Church could set out very precisely and authoritatively its doctrines on faith and morals. Post-Tridentine Catholicism was very concerned to defend and consolidate its position. Any views which diverged from what was laid down at Trent were seen in an extremely fearful light. The preservation of orthodoxy was seen as crucial to the Church's very survival. Certainty was the key to this and was one of the foremost features of Catholicism until the time of the Council. Perhaps one of the biggest changes in Catholicism in the post-Conciliar era was that Catholics no longer enjoyed the security of certainty.

This situation was compounded in the late sixties in the aftermath of the promulgation by Pope Paul VI of the Encyclical *Humanae Vitae*, in which he reaffirmed the traditional Church position on artificial birth control.[27] But by this time Catholics had become more independent as regards their decision-making in the moral area. They were also more optimistic as regards their standing before God. Catholicism in the pre-Vatican II era placed a very strong emphasis on duty, self-sacrifice and mortification. God was portrayed as a stern task-master and concepts like fear of the Lord and his wrath in the event of wrong-doing predominated. Post Vatican II Catholicism developed a more human face. Catholicism had re-invented itself, or so it appeared. God was portrayed as a loving understanding God, who was not out to catch people if they made a mistake. In Ireland, changes in secular life – television, increased affluence, opportunities to travel and changes in education from the early sixties all helped to redefine Irishness at the same time that Catholicism was being revised. An American writer, Donald S. Connery, visited Ireland in 1948 and returned in 1963. His observations about the many signs of modernisation go some way to capture

---

27. See Pope Paul VI, *Humanae Vitae: on the Regulation of Births*, 21 July 1968, in *The Furrow*, 19:9 (1968), pp 542-56.

the new mood. In his book, *The Irish*, he quoted Cathal O'Shannon's assessement of what the Irish were like in the sixties – 'working harder, living on hire purchase, glued to television sets, better dressed, spending money'.[28] Another friend, Martin Sheridan made a comment that struck him forcibly: 'Now we are seeing the first free Irishmen.'[29]

Interestingly he refers to free Irishmen, because his book was published in 1968, and the Women's movement started in Ireland around 1969 and became an influential force for change in the campaign for liberation for the Irish woman from the early 1970s. Attitudes and values were being formed increasingly by more secular, liberal views of morality and pronouncements by the pope and the Irish bishops were by no means taken as the last word from that time. The late sixties was an interesting time by virtue of other developments which would be forces for change. This was the time of the Berkeley and Paris student revolts which affected the western world and had their parallel in Ireland. It was the time when at the Labour Party conference in 1967 Brendan Halligan remarked that 'it is almost respectable now to be a socialist'.[30] Speaker after speaker at the conference reiterated the fact of Labour's socialism, rhetoric that would have constituted political suicide in the fifties, considering the dire warnings about socialism and communism which emanated from bishops' pastoral letters. The Irish cultural ethos, defined in the main by Catholicism until the sixties, was gradually being redefined. The 1969 general election campaign was fought out against the background of Labour Party slogans which confidently proclaimed that 'the seventies will be socialist'.

The 1969 election was not as mould-breaking as had been anticipated by some, but it was important in that it catapulted two new arrivals on to the political stage, who would raise questions in relation to the Catholic ethos in Ireland and whether it was in

---

28. Donald S. Connery, *The Irish* (New York: Simon and Schuster, 1968) p 30.
29. Ibid., p 31.
30. Fergal Tobin, *The Best of Decades: Ireland in the 1960s* (Dublin: Gill and Macmillan, 1984), p 213.

fact discriminatory towards minority traditions. Garret FitzGerald was returned to the Dáil as a Fine Gael TD in 1969 and Conor Cruise O'Brien was returned as a Labour Deputy and both were to make their presence felt keenly in the years to come as champions of a more pluralistic Irish society. The outbreak of the 'Troubles' in Northern Ireland in 1969 lent a new urgency to this questioning. The canon of Irish political history was already being challenged and now the canon of Irish Catholic history began to be seen as problematic. In 1964 in a *Studies* article Garret FitzGerald had outlined his vision of a new Ireland which would be the product of combined Christian, liberal and socialist traditions. The new Irish society would glory 'in our mixed inheritance, despising none of it, and elevating no part to a position of prominence over the rest', he wrote.[31] The historic meeting which took place between Northern Ireland Prime Minister Terence O'Neill and Taoiseach Sean Lemass in 1965 gave rise temporarily to a new mood of co-operation between North and South and against this background the issue of whether some laws and aspects of the Irish constitution could be discriminatory to minority traditions was being raised.

In the South also, in the more liberal post-Vatican II era, in an atmosphere of friendlier ecumenical relations, questions of whether Catholic precepts should be enshrined in civil law and what should constitute a proper relationship between Church and State in Ireland were being raised. The central focus of this on-going debate tended to crystallise around issues having to do with the right or otherwise to contraception, divorce and more recently abortion. In the context of events happening in Northern Ireland and outside of Ireland, and an evolving more critical cultural climate at home, politicians, though reluctant at the outset (in the context of the prevailing Catholic ethos), were forced more and more to grapple with these issues as time went by and their resolution from the late seventies would lead to a more secularised Irish society, in which Catholicism would be

---

31. Garret FitzGerald, 'Towards a National Purpose', *Studies*, 53 (Winter, 1964), p 350.

increasingly less influential in the formation of values and attitudes.

Surveys of Catholic practice and values were becoming
available from the late sixties and what was interesting was that
they showed that a high practice rate did not necessarily presup-
pose an explicit awareness of religious values or an acceptance
of the Church's moral or doctrinal teachings. In the 1974 comprehensive survey of religious practice, attitudes and beliefs,
which was carried out by the Bishops' Council for Research and
Development, the following conclusion was drawn:

> Irish religious practice is sustained to an inadmissible extent
> by rule and law, social custom and a sense of duty, rather
> than by personal commitment of mind and heart so that such
> belief or faith is extremely vulnerable in a rapidly changing
> society.[32]

The survey showed that while 91% of those surveyed professed
themselves to be practising Catholics and as being influenced by
the value system of Catholicism, they did not always adhere to
Church rules, particularly in the area of sexual morality. While
there had been a strong historical tradition in Irish Catholicism
of the laity ignoring Church authorities when it suited them,
there is no doubt that the fundamental ground-shift that took
place in Catholicism at the time of the Second Vatican Council,
whereby it became more optimistic about human nature and the
secular world and emphasised the dignity of the person and the
role of conscience, added to people's confidence about making
up their own minds on issues and rejecting what seemed oppres-
sive. Catholicism as people knew it had been re-defined at head-
quarters, or so it appeared until the promulgation of *Humanae
Vitae*. But by then it was too late to close the stable door – the
horse had well and truly bolted. À la carte Catholicism was here
to stay.

Attempts to legalise contraception (and here Mary Robinson
was one of the first instigators of change) dominated the seven-

---

32. Quoted in Peter Connolly, 'The Church in Ireland since Vatican II',
The Furrow, 30:12 (1979) pp 755-66.

ties, starting in 1971 and culminating in 1979 with the Family
Planning Act.[33] Of course, the remark of Mr Haughey, Minister
for Health at the time, that the Bill was 'an Irish solution for an
Irish problem', which has gone down in folklore as one of those
memorable phrases which allows us to laugh at ourselves, has a
deeper resonance. The 1979 Act was a very restrictive measure.
The impression that was given was that it would not compromise our Irish Catholic ideals too much – in other words, we
could live with it. Of course it was a major turning point and
within six years, in 1985, the measure was considerably liberalised and full liberalisation of contraception came in 1992. So
1979 was very much the beginning of a process which was un-
stoppable, despite the Church's resistance.

Two months after the Family Planning legislation was
passed, Pope John Paul II visited Ireland and he too saw that
Irish society was at a crossroads. In all of his speeches he addressed the more liberal influences which began to prevail from
the late sixties. He warned that Irish society was being confronted
with values and trends formerly alien to it and that 'Irish people
[had] to choose … their way forward' whether that be the path
of materialism or 'the things of the spirit'.[34] But of course Ireland
had made that choice long before that and his message did not
halt the further progress of more liberal developments in Irish
society – Ireland was already well on course to evolve into the
kind of society warned against by the Pope. Politicians might
have been hesitant and afraid of getting their fingers burnt elec-
torally in the seventies, but all such fears were cast aside from
the early eighties – they were reading the signs of the times,
which showed that Catholicism was no longer the same dominant force. That said, they did not always get it right.

In June 1981 Garret FitzGerald came to power at the head of a
Fine Gael/Labour coalition government. Already in the 1970s
when he was Minister for Foreign Affairs, he had spoken of the

---

33. *Health (Family Planning) Act 1979*, No 20 in public statutes of the
Oireachtas, 1979.
34. See *The Pope in Ireland: Addresses and Homilies* (Dublin, 1979), p 77.

need for constitutional reform and he very quickly raised the issue again on assuming power. In a radio interview in September 1981 he pointed out that 'our laws and our constitution, our practices, our attitudes reflect those of a majority ethos and are not acceptable to Protestants in Northern Ireland'.[35] FitzGerald's 'constitutional crusade' set the political tone for the 1980s, but developments in Irish society around that time made his reform programme problematic. The electorate had moved on, but were in divided camps – the liberals who wanted Ireland to develop into a more pluralistic society and many lay-led conservative groups who came to the fore from the early eighties, who felt threatened and were fiercely opposed to FitzGerald's campaign to reform the confessional aspects of the Constitution. Each wanted to define Irish identity. In this context the next contentious issue was abortion. Against the background of the increasing availability of abortion in western societies and a growing awareness of the number of Irish women travelling to England for abortion, in 1981 an anti-abortion pressure group was formed calling itself the Pro-Life Amendment Campaign. It lobbied for the insertion into the Constitution of an amendment specifically outlawing abortion. The amendment was put to the electorate on 7 September 1983 and was carried by a percentage vote of 66% to 33% at the end of a particularly acrimonius campaign.[36] The result was seen as a victory by the more conservative lobby for the Catholicism of pre-Conciliar times. The result also pointed to a new and deep urban/rural divide in Irish society – the seamless Catholic culture of the past was well and truly gone and the battle lines were drawn.

The next round in the battle was when Barry Desmond, Minister for Health in the Fine Gael/Labour coalition government, published the Health (Family Planning) (Amendment Bill) which proposed to amend the 1979 Family Planning Act to

---

35. Garret FitzGerald, *All in a Life: An Autobiography* (Dublin: Gill and Macmillan, 1992), p 378.

36. *The Irish Times*, 9 September 1983, p 1. See also Tom Hesketh, *The Second Partitioning of Ireland: The Abortion Referendum of 1983*, (Dublin: Brandsma Books, 1990), p 364.

make non-medical contraceptives available without a medical prescription to persons of 18 years and over. Again it was contentious with three Fine Gael deputies, Alice Glenn, Tom O'Donnell and Oliver J. Flanagan and one Labour Deputy, Seán Treacy voting against the Bill. During the 1970s, in response to demands for contraception legislation, the bishops had developed a very clear position on issues having to do with Church, State, morality and the law.[37] While their position essentially had not changed, in that as far as they were concerned the espousal of Catholic values and ideals constituted what was best for the common good of Irish society, they did accept reluctantly that times had changed and that they could no longer dictate outcomes. They could argue their position along with other groups in the public forum, but after that such matters were for the people to decide. But because these matters went to the heart of Irish life and identity the atmosphere was very confrontational. Thus, when the Family Planning Act was passed in the Dáil by a narrow margin on 21 February 1985, J. H. Whyte commented that the 'Church appeared to have suffered its most clear-cut defeat since the establishment of the State'.[38]

The following year Garret FitzGerald announced details of the coalition's proposal to hold a referendum on 26 June 1986 to remove the constitutional ban on divorce. When the issue had come up in 1923, Cosgrave, on the advice of the bishops, considered the very possibility of sanctioning divorce as altogether unworthy of an Irish legislative body and the issue was well and truly closed.[39] The proposed change was presented by FitzGerald in the context of his crusade for a more pluralistic society in the republic, which would improve relations with Northern Ireland and between Unionist and Nationalists north of the border. But the results on the day reflected the resilience of traditional Catholic values – 63% of those who voted rejected the govern-

---

37. See Fuller, *Irish Catholicism Since 1950*, pp 207-12.
38. J. H. Whyte, 'Recent Developments in Church State relations', *Journal of the Department of the Public Services*, 6:3, 1985.
39. Ronan Fanning, *Independent Ireland* (Dublin, 1983), pp 54-57.

ment's proposal.[40] Again Dublin constituencies voted (narrowly) in favour of divorce, whereas the majority of rural constituencies voted overwhelmingly against it.[41]

The next milestone was in March 1992. Called the 'X' Case, it concerned a fourteen-year-old alleged rape victim who became pregnant and was prevented by court injunction from travelling to Britain for an abortion. The Supreme Court then ruled that abortion was legal in limited cases where there was a real danger that the pregnant woman was liable to commit suicide.[42] The Bishops' Conference issued a statement recording their dismay at the judgement 'which envisages legal abortion in the Republic of Ireland' and pointing out that 'no court judgement, no act of legislation can make it morally right'.[43] They went on to place the onus on legislators to 'exercise their responsibility to protect the lives of unborn children'.[44] In a referendum held on 25 November 1992, the electorate voted in favour of the right to information on abortion services, and in favour of the right to travel to avail of such services but rejected the wording of the substantive issue as to the circumstances under which abortion is permissible.[45] In July of the same year further liberalisation of the law in relation to family planning meant that contraceptive devices became freely available throughout the country.[46]

The following year 1993, legislation which legalised homosexual practices was passed as a result of a directive from the European Court of Human Rights, which called for the decriminalisation of homosexual acts between consenting adults.[47] The bill as passed defined adults as people aged 17 and over. In 1983

---

40. See *The Irish Times*, 28 June 1986, p 1.
41. Ibid.
42. *The Irish Times*, 6 March 1992.
43. 'The Sacredness of Human Life', a statement of the Irish Episcopal Conference, *The Furrow*, 43:4 (1992), p 251.
44. Ibid., pp 251-2.
45. See *The Irish Times*, 26 November 1992.
46. Health (Family Planning) (Amendment) Act 1992, No 20 in public statutes of the Oireachtas, 1992.
47. Criminal Law (Sexual Offences) Act, 1993, No 20 in public statutes of the Oireachtas, 1993.

the Supreme Court had rejected an appeal by David Norris to declare that two Acts inherited from the period of British rule were unconstitutional and cited the preamble to the 1937 Constitution, which points to the people of Ireland as 'humbly acknowledging their obligation to Our Divine Lord Jesus Christ' as the reason for their rejection of the plea.[48] In the area of social legislation, by the 1980s and 1990s not only were bishops less able to influence politicians, but politicians themselves did not have the last word as to legislation, nor did the national courts have absolute discretion as to its interpretation.

The next stage in the Church-State battle was the divorce referendum held in November 1995. As in previous referenda, much of the lobbying in favour of a no vote was done by members of the Catholic laity organised into various anti-divorce groups. The bishops issued a statement setting out their position.[49] This time the leaders of all political parties campaigned for a yes vote. The referendum proposal was carried by a narrow margin of less than 1%.[50] Again the urban rural divide was reflected in voting patterns with rural constituencies voting along traditional lines.

Just over six years later the Fianna Fáil/Progressive Democrat coalition government announced that a further referendum on abortion was to be held.[51] In the referendum voters were asked to vote Yes or No to the terms of the Protection of Human Life in Pregnancy Bill which, if appoved by referendum and subsequently enacted by the Oireachtas, would outlaw suicide as a ground for abortion, found to be constitutional by the Supreme Court in 1992.[52] The Pro-Life movement was split on the issue, the more conservative wing feeling that the proposal did not go far enough in that it protected human life from the moment of

---

48. See *The Irish Times*, 23 April 1983, pp 1, 8.
49. *The Irish Catholic*, 9 November 1995.
50. See *The Irish Times*, 27 November 1995, p 1.
51. See *The Irish Times*, 2 October 2001.
52. See *Use Your Vote, Twenty-fifth Amendment of the Constitution (Protection of Human Life in Pregnancy) Bill, 2001*, an explanatory booklet published by the Referendum Commission (Dublin, 2002).

implantation and not from the moment of conception. While the
bishops shared this concern, they nonetheless welcomed the
proposal and urged Catholics to support it.[53] However in a result which was a virtual replica of the 1995 divorce referendum,
the electorate rejected the referendum proposal by a margin of
less than 1%.[54] Many commentators saw it as the final definitive
rebuff to the influence of the Catholic Church in Ireland, *The
Irish Times* in its editorial the following day proclaiming that 'the
grand alignment of Fianna Fáil, the Catholic Church and the official Pro-Life campaign has, for the first time, failed to produce
a majority on a sensitive moral issue in middle Ireland after a
lengthy and co-ordinated campaign.[55] The Bishops' Conference
spokesperson, asked for his reaction, responded that we must
'accept with serenity the people's will'.[56] When the reaction of
the bishops in the 1960s and 1970s to issues of contraception and
divorce, to say nothing of abortion is recalled, it is a clear indication of how much their position in Irish society and their capacity to influence Irish Catholics, both lay people and politicians,
has changed over the last forty years. The result of the 2002 abortion referendum marked the final stage in the dismantling of
legislative and constitutional support for the Catholic ethos in
Ireland.

So where does this leave Catholicism in terms of its impact
on Irish identity at the current time and for the future? Against
the background of what some commentators refer to as post-
Catholic Ireland, the importance of understanding Irish Catholic
identity as inherited from the past, how it has evolved and the
implications for its future development can hardly be overstated.
At a time of European integration and increasing globalisation

---

53. See *Statement of the Irish Episcopal Conference on the Proposed Abortion
Referendum*, Press Release issued by the Catholic Communications
Office, 12 December 2001.
54. See *The Irish Times*, 8 March 2002, p 1.
55. Ibid., pp 14-15.
56. Reaction by Fr Martin Clarke, spokesperson for the bishops, when
questioned by Charlie Bird, chief news correspondent, RTÉ, on 6.01
news, RTÉ, 7 March 2002.

the quest for identity has become increasingly urgent. Clearly
the automatic identification of Irish and Catholic no longer reflects Irish society today. This is at a time when pride in identity
is at an all-time high in the Republic.[57] This could be explained
in terms of economic progress and other factors such as Irish
success on the international stage in the arts and in sport. That
said, in a country in which, despite the decline in religious practice,[58] 88% of the population still profess themselves as
Catholic,[59] there can be no denying the importance of the
Catholic legacy, but the cultural context has altered to such an
extent that if Catholicism purports to be more than just a legacy
from the past, it must cast itself anew. The Church's concern for
the education and social mobility of Catholics in the nineteenth
century in part explains the vibrancy of Catholicism in the first
half of the twentieth century. Given that these central aspirations have long since been secured, there are different kinds of
battles to be fought and challenges to be faced.

Sociologists of religion have pointed to the emergence of the
'new' Catholic in Ireland. These new Catholics, they found, had
'a liberal attitude to sexual matters' and an optimistic interpretation of religion, one's standing before God and the world and
an outlook which questioned the Church's right to speak with
absolute authority on matters of personal morality.[60] What dis-
tinguishes 'new' Catholics is that they do not feel bound by the
tenets of Catholicism as laid down by official Church teaching.
They have re-defined Catholicism to meet their needs and accommodate their life situation. The Church's response over the

---

57. See Tony Fahey, Bernadette C. Hayes, Richard Sinnott (eds.) *Conflict
and Consensus: A Study of Values and Attitudes in the Republic of Ireland and
Northern Ireland* (Dublin: Institute of Public Administration, 2005), p 65.
58. In the 1974 survey *Religious Practice* (above mentioned) weekly Mass
attendance was recorded at 91%. A 2002 Millward Brown IMS poll
recorded weekly Mass attendance at 48%.
59. Census 2002, Central Statistics Office, Dublin.
60. See Michael P. Hornsby-Smith and Christopher T. Whelan,
'Religious and Moral Values' in Christopher T. Whelan (ed.), *Values and
Social Change in Ireland* (Dublin: Gill and Macmillan, 1994), p 44

past thirty years has been to resist and then only reluctantly accept changes, when there was no alternative. In the twenty-first century a more positive pro-active response to evolving cultural change is called for. It is high time for the Catholic Church to reinterpret its role in modern Ireland. But engaging with the modern has been highly problematical for the universal Church over centuries. At the local level, it represents the central challenge for the Irish Catholic Church, if Catholicism is to reclaim its historic place in Irish identity.

CHAPTER FIVE

'God Help Us!': The Media and Irish Catholicism

Colum Kenny

I have at home an old press-cutting that was first framed in 1849, within two years of Daniel O'Connell's death. The cutting must have been important to my ancestors, because it was the oldest item that I found in a box of papers belonging to one of them.

The image depicts O'Connell on his death-bed in Genoa, where his attempt to reach Rome ended. He is shown surrounded by five people. Underneath the image, a description is given as follows: 'The Vicar-General with the clergy were round his bed as the prayers were recited. His hands were fervently clasped upon his noble breast, his countenance perfectly serene. When at last his mighty voice was hushed, his countenance, [and] his hands responded to the prayer.'[1]

The whole scene is entitled, 'The Death of Ireland's Liberator', and my ancestor who framed it in 1849 was no doubt as familiar as most of his countrymen with the tragic circumstances in which O'Connell died. O'Connell had gone to London, reduced to begging in parliament for help for those Irish people being ravaged by the Great Famine. He fell ill, and was prevented by bad weather from returning to Ireland. His doctor and others prevailed upon him to try moving to a warmer region for the sake of his declining health and, in consultation with his personal chaplain, he formed the intent to go to Rome and secure a blessing from the new Pope.

O'Connell travelled painfully down through France, and into

---

1. This is actually a quotation from a letter that O'Connell's chaplain, Fr John Miley, wrote to O'Connell's second son, Morgan, from Genoa, on the morning after Daniel O'Connell died. It was published in the *Evening Freeman*, 25 May 1847 (W. B. MacCabe, *The Last Days of O'Connell* (Dublin, 1847), p 90).

Italy, where he finally succumbed to the effects of what seems to have been an abscess on his brain. Many of O'Connell's last days were spent in terrible despair and delirium. However, some hours before his death his mind cleared, a common occurrence in the case of such illness, and he died peacefully. His heart was later taken to Rome, encased in a silver urn. This was done in accordance with a dying wish, it is said, and the choice of faith over motherland as the ultimate resting-place of his heart has considerable emotional resonance even today. For he was, as it would transpire, the founding father of modern Irish politics.

O'Connell's recent biographer, the distinguished Oliver MacDonagh, has written that, 'At 2 am on 15 May 1847 he received the last sacrament in a scene worthy of the brush of Goya though it received nothing better than an ill-drawn oleograph [a print made to resemble an oil-painting].'[2] It is, I presume, a copy of that very oleograph that my ancestor framed two years after O'Connell's death. The return of his remains to Dublin, without its heart, was the occasion for remarkable scenes. A contemporary notes that, 'when he departed from this world, the Church militant assumed the garb of mourning, and on every altar there was a Holy Sacrifice for the repose of his soul.' No less than 1,600 people per hour are said to have passed through the warehouse where he was laid out for four days.[3]

My ancestor may have framed the cutting as much from pity as from admiration, for it was still not long since Catholic Emancipation had been granted in 1828 and its first impact was severely blunted by the Great Famine. In the late 1840s, O'Connell cut a somewhat tragic figure and possibly feared that his life's work was wasted.

However, by 1898, things had changed. That year, according to an old note found with my cutting, a more recent Kenny took the image out of its frame, cleaned it up and reframed it. It was indeed a respected Irish Catholic icon, and by 1898 the true con-

---

2. Oliver MacDonagh, *The Emancipist: Daniel O'Connell, 1830-1847* (London: Weidenfeld and Nicolson, 1989), p 317.
3. MacCabe, *Last Days*, iv, 211.

sequences of O'Connell's achievement were manifest. The Catholic classes were rising in both power and relative wealth and some measure of political independence or repeal of the Union was clearly possible.

Catholic Emancipation, won under the leadership of 'The Liberator' (as O'Connell was widely known), led inevitably to a growth in the power of the Catholic middle classes and, later, to the creation of an Irish State dominated by a very conservative Catholic Church.

Yet Daniel O'Connell himself was regarded in Europe at the end of his life as 'the avatar [incarnation] of Liberal Catholicism on the Continent'.[4] He believed in the separation of Church from politics. Pius IX, the new pope by whom he wanted so much to be blessed, was initially liberal.[5] O'Connell himself had once even been an active Freemason, but such inconvenient ambiguities were to be swept aside as a version of Irish identity was later forged which was quite narrow. This development may have been partly a response to the shock of the Great Famine and to the defeat of O'Connell's campaign to repeal the political union of Ireland with Britain.

During the nineteenth century, the Irish Catholic Church became focused on a morality moulded by the pressures of agricultural survival and bourgeois respectability. Later, after the Free State was founded, if you were not an orthodox Catholic then you were somehow less than truly Irish. If you spoke Irish, played GAA and voted Fianna Fáil or Fine Gael, then so much the better. It got so that it became difficult, and remains difficult, to distinguish between being Irish and Catholic, and being 'an Irish Catholic'.

The item framed in 1849, as I have said, happens to be the oldest heirloom in my family's possession. That alone speaks of the power of the particular item, but also of the power of images in general.

Today, we expect to see pictures in our newspapers, not least

---

4. MacDonagh, *The Emancipist*. p 315.
5. *Dictionary of National Biography* (2004), xli, 448 (O'Connell).

pictures of politicians, but I have recently been reading the Dublin papers for 1792 and one finds no pictures in them. However, by the second quarter of the nineteenth century, periodicals such as the *Dublin Penny Journal* and the *Illustrated London News* were delighting the public with their black and white visual sketches. It was still sometime before photographs appeared in the papers.

This particular image of O'Connell was reassuring for Catholics in Dublin in the 1840s, for it testified that one could reconcile ambition, enterprise, political activity and religious conviction. Our heroes could be saints, no matter their wheeling-dealing, implicit threats of violence and perhaps even their sexual prowess (as folk rumours of O'Connell had it[6]).

If pictures like this legitimated the acquisition of power by the Catholic middle classes, such power itself eventually came to compromise the Irish Catholic Church. That this may still be a contentious thing to say strikes me as quite remarkable.

However, as I see it, there has yet to be on the part of the Irish hierarchy a clear acknowledgement of persistent institutional failure in respect of its role in the Irish State in the twentieth century. Facing criticism, few bishops have appeared willing or able to cope with the crisis of their and their predecessors' making. Instead, they have maintained a fundamentally adversarial posture which is unenlightening and defensive and closed to dialogue with Irish society at large. Forced admissions by bishops that they could have done more about child abuse do not even begin to address the underlying problem of unequal power relationships and secretive manipulation within the Irish Catholic Church.

It is probably unrealistic to expect an organisation that is hierarchical and dogmatic to adopt an open model of communication when it comes to dealing with the broader world. Why should the media expect to encounter a welcoming response to

6. Diarmaid Ó Muirithe, 'O'Connell in Irish Folk Tradition', in K. B. Nowlan and M. R. O'Connell, *Daniel O'Connell: Portrait of a Radical* (New York, 1985), pp 59-60.

its efforts at dialogue or to its queries when there is such an inadequate system of communications for ordinary Catholics, lay
or clerical, within the Catholic Church? A clear recent example
of this problem is the way in which difficulties at Cura over
abortion information were handled .

The media provide an alternative locus for debates about
religion and the Churches. I believe that some bishops in Ireland
in the late twentieth and early twenty-first centuries have
deeply resented the media. The episcopal press conference has
been too rare an event. Not even journalists who work for mainstream media such as RTÉ, *The Irish Times* or Independent
Newspapers are always regarded by senior Church figures as
worthy participants in public dialogue about religious issues.

Some attempts to communicate with the laity have been particularly unfortunate. During the 1970s and 1980s, blundering efforts to encourage certain priests to patronise the lower orders
with the sort of song-and-dance routines of the likes of Michael
Cleary and Seán Fortune were an excruciating exercise in superficial faith and false communications. They met their match in
Dermot Morgan and ended in obscene scandals. I am not convinced that the hierarchy as a whole yet understands why such
sleights of hand and tricks of entertainment should never have
been envisaged as part of an appropriate communications strategy for a religious organisation.

Yet, how much better than singing priests are corporate
mouthpieces whose training has been in the managerial and
public relations practices of private business? Not a great deal
better, necessarily, if one is seeking dialogue rather than simply
wishing to ascertain the position of Church authorities on a particular matter. In my opinion, when the media deals with the
Church, the experience ought to feel qualitatively different from
that of dealing with more worldly organisations.

For years, I have been writing for various publications and
reporting for broadcasting organisations about the Irish
Catholic Church. It has frequently been a depressing and unin-
spiring experience, and I have come to the conclusion that the

Catholic Church in Ireland is stuck in a time-warp, where modes of authority stifle initiative and aggressively resist open discussion within the walls of the Catholic Church itself – never mind discussion with those outside. From conversations with other journalists, I do not think that my depressing experience of that organisation is unique.

The hierarchy of the Irish Catholic Church has clung to a power structure that became a cause of scandal, appropriating to itself the concept 'Catholic Church' when that term belongs as much to the laity as it does to clergy. In the gospels, Jesus asks who would give their son a stone when that child asks for bread. Public relations on its own is a stone.

Another aspect of the communications deficit in respect to religion in Ireland, as I see it, is that sometimes bishops and editors share a limited view of what constitutes an Irish Catholic. Both groups may be most comfortable with a mental image that is far from the complex or confused realities of contemporary everyday life. When I write as a journalist I try to understand what it actually means for people to regard themselves still as Catholics in Ireland. And I think that it means very many things and I cannot say which of those things is best or superior. Indeed, what on earth does it even mean to be 'an Irish Catholic' in that generic sense? Is calling oneself 'Irish Catholic' simply a mild sectarian allegiance? If so, that is surely not a matter of identity as much as it is a matter of loss of identity in the national crowd. And does one have to be very familiar with the Bible to be an Irish Catholic? My parents' generation was sometimes actively advised by priests not to read that most basic Christian text. Today, it seems, most Irish Catholics are only exposed to the Bible at Mass (if they go to Mass). However, many do not go frequently to Mass, yet still consider themselves Catholic.

I was struck recently by a press release from the Catholic Dublin archdiocese in respect of the launch of a wrist-band to raise money for charity (31 May 2005). The phrase 'Be not afraid' on that wrist-band was attributed to the late Pope John Paul II, rather than to Jesus or to one of the scribes of the Hebrew scriptures where it is also found. While John Paul II liked to use the phrase, it seemed to me almost as if there is a desperate need to 'relate' and appeal to young people by reference to recent media spectacles such as the latest papal funeral rather than dare to anchor their identity in a more fundamental form of conversion to spiritual roots. This incident of the wrist-band reminded me of a little research that I carried out recently with a class of third-year undergraduates at Dublin City University. On 8 February 2005, 35 third-year BA in Communication Studies students were handed a photocopied list of the books of the Bible and asked to tick those books that they had read 'in whole or nearly whole'. Each was also asked to identify her or his particular family's religious background and to say (a) whether or not they had opened the Bible and read some verses during the past two years and (b) if so, to state how many times. The forms were anonymous. This was, of course, far from being a satisfactory or scientific survey. It is just a straw poll. But when another 49 students were polled in 2006, the results were similar.

I need hardly point out that the Bible is the, or one of the, most important books in western culture and civilisation. Its direct and indirect influence has been without parallel. Moreover, apart from its spiritual relevance, it is of great literary interest. Among its books, the Hebrew tale of Job is a Jewish masterpiece. The Bible also has a particular relevance in Ireland, where differences between communities and traditions that style themselves Christian have been of great importance to society. Most of our secondary schools are ostensibly Christian in ethos. While the Bible is not a work to be read straight through from start to finish, one supposes that students at school are given some instruction in how to approach and appreciate it.

Of the 35 students, 34 ticked the 'Christian' box in respect of family background. One ticked 'Other' and specified 'Atheist'. (A distinction between 'Catholic' and 'Other Christian' was not requested.) Of the 35 students, 28 had never read a book of the Bible either 'in whole or nearly whole'. Of the 7 who had, the most widely read book was the first of those in the Old

Testament, Genesis (6 students), suggesting that people will try to read the Bible as an ordinary book only to be quickly deterred by its style and format.

One (the atheist background) had read Genesis only. Two had read Genesis and Exodus only. One had read Genesis and Revelation. One had read Genesis, Exodus, Psalms, Proverbs and the four gospels. One student had read Ecclesiastes, and the gospels of Mark and John. Just one had read all of the New Testament (and he had also read Genesis, Exodus, Leviticus, Numbers and Deuteronomy). Of the 35 students, only six had opened a Bible and read some verses during the past two years. One had actually done it once a week but the other five had done it less than a handful of times. One opened it four times during the two years, one three, one two, and two students did it once.

This leads me to ask some specific questions. What does it mean to say that Ireland is a Christian country, never mind 'Catholic'? What does a Christian education mean? What are the implications for European culture of our bright young students being so ignorant of one of the chief reference points in western civilisation? In such circumstances, what possible meaning has the term 'Irish Catholic identity', other than perhaps as something equivalent to the wearing of a Glasgow Celtic football jersey that marks one as not a Protestant and not British? And should I as a journalist take into account such nuances when reporting 'Irish Catholic' thinking? For people like my ancestor who reframed the newspaper illustration of Daniel O'Connell on his death-bed, being an 'Irish Catholic' was very much a political statement as well as a religious one. It was about the return of the dispossessed, the rebuffing of the British, the reversal of misfortune, the riposte to arrogant Anglicans who had long humiliated people of genuine Christian faith who happened to be Catholics. Such 'Irish Catholic identity' was fundamentally political and it served people well as a negative force, as a source of energy in the face of oppression. To some extent, it still serves that purpose in Northern Ireland. But it began to cease to serve a clear and certain purpose once most Irish Catholics lived in a State independent of Britain. By then, the Catholic authorities had hitched their spiritual cart to the horse of political energy. They did not reckon with the price that they would one day pay for going along for the ride. What they gained in influence they eventually lost in respect. Then, they lost influence again.

In my opinion, it has not been the media that has mainly damaged the Catholic Church in Ireland. The Irish hierarchy first narrowed Irish Catholic identity. Then, it destroyed its own power through scandals that were too lightly checked, and some of the hierarchy may be still in denial about just how far the rot has gone. The whole edifice may be on the point of collapse and there is still no obvious sense of responsibility for the crisis.

It is my belief that there is little evidence that the media in general was ever hostile to the Catholic Church in Ireland, although it probably grew increasingly frustrated by the ambivalence and evasion of Church authorities. In fact, one might fault the media not for being too negative but for having been not critical enough of Catholic authorities for most of the twentieth century. Most journalists who write frequently about the Irish Catholic Church have their own tales to tell. In my opinion, many of these journalists are actually sympathetic to the message of religion, even if they are regarded poorly by some of the Church hierarchy. At times, basic communications from journalists have gone unanswered, questions have been evaded or even responded to deviously, the very idea of open-ended discussion seemingly scoffed at.

And still some Catholic authorities cling to events such as the recent burial of Pope John Paul II as though a media event will bring the public on side and reduce the faithful to their traditional posture of subdued deference. No fusion of twenty-first century satellite TV stunt and medieval pageantry will resonate significantly with the desperate inner needs of people in these doleful times, or help them significantly to understand the relevance of the teachings of Christ to their lives. The funeral of John Paul II was a seven-day wonder, on a par with any other leading

TV spectacle. The sacred space that it appeared to constitute was similar to that generated by the coverage of the funeral of Princess Diana. The late pope's funeral was not entirely devoid of inspirational value, and was at points quite beautiful, but it is scarcely a basis on which to build realistic expectations that Irish 'young people' have suddenly re-awoken to the value of Irish Catholicism, as has been suggested by some bishops and priests from the altar.

The media generally treats something like the late pope's funeral as a public spectacle of passing interest. The media does not see itself as a supporter of any particular set of beliefs, which is not to say that those who work for the media are themselves devoid of personal beliefs. For myself, I am conscious that when I write for a mass circulation family newspaper like the *Sunday Independent*, which reaches out across all classes and ages and segments of the population, my words (insofar as they have any effect) may shake people's faith or be read in a way that increases cynicism. But I chose to believe that spiritual identity transcends the fixed identity of concepts such as 'Irish Catholic' and that a Catholic who is genuinely in search of a spiritual identity would prefer me to write as honestly as I can rather than to be 'responsible' (in the sense of conservative) and suppress or play down the truth as I see it in favour of some national or religious ideal.

There is, admittedly, much rubbish that appears in the media about religion, as there is about many other aspects of Irish life, and I am sure that I have written some of it. Some of the rubbish is sentimental nonsense spouted by religious commentators. Much of it is not written by those reporters who frequently cover religious stories. But by comparison with the rubbish written in the Irish media about religion, the sheer poverty of dialogue emanating from the hierarchy of the Irish Catholic Church in respect of the future of the Church in this society is also disturbing to me as a communicator. Where are the prophets? Where are the idealists? Where are the true believers who rely confidently on persuasion?

There is so much of interest that might be said about the

media and religion, but it is far removed from where we are at in Ireland at present in relation to public religious discourse. During the past two years, I have been slowly nudging the School of Communications at DCU towards a greater exploration of the relationship between belief and communication. This year, DCU is offering students a new module on Belief and Communications, designed by myself and taught jointly by staff from DCU, St Patrick's College, Drumcondra and Mater Dei Institute of Education. Maybe this will be a platform for interesting dialogue. I also set up a closed on-line discussion forum for journalists who frequently cover religious stories and for those spokespeople for religious organisations who deal with the press. It was disappointing to find that only a few participants seemed interested in getting debates going or sustaining them.

I have also explored what is happening internationally in this field, delivering papers at international conferences on religion and media in the United States and France and making study visits elsewhere, including the University of Colorado at Boulder where there is considerable understanding of the persistent need for forms of religious expression even when so many people feel that the established Churches have lost their way and no longer speak directly to the human heart. At another level, I have been fortunate to participate in a series of dialogues involving a small group of Buddhists, led by the Dalai Lama, and a small group of Christian meditators, led by Fr Laurence Freeman. These meetings took place in India, Italy and Belfast, and I also travelled to Los Angeles in July 2005 to renew my acquaintanceship with the Christian group involved.

There is so much that can be exciting, that can engage, when it comes to religious dialogue. But there is little sign that such dialogue is widely welcome or wanted in Ireland, except in certain quiet corners such as Tallaght. The one organisation that is best-placed to spearhead or embrace new and vital forms of multi-cultural and spiritual dialogue in Ireland, the Catholic Church, seems to me to have become mired at the highest level in self-righteous despondency or false self-satisfaction. It seems full of fear, not full of faith. Talk of Irish Catholic identity! What does that mean? If there ever was such a monolith, it is well gone. Much of what remains of the old form is an empty shell that constitutes a barrier between those who cling to it and the broader world that exists around them.

Most Irish Catholics now constitute their identity in a way that refracts all sorts of international cultural and political influences, and one Irish Catholic may be as different from another as an Irish Muslim is from an Irish Methodist. Many people who describe themselves on a census form as Catholics go to Mass infrequently and feel forgotten by an organisation that has resisted change. If being born in Ireland and being baptised in a Catholic church is what people mean by having a Catholic identity then it is a very fragile and inadequate form of identity for the world in which we find ourselves today.

Church authorities might spark more exciting and challenging discourses. They could include journalists in a communications project and warmly accept criticism and even harsh judgements. It seems to me that the idea of an Irish Catholic identity is idolatrous if it becomes a barrier to open hearts and open minds. But the chances of such a dialogue happening, from where I stand as an observer of the Irish communications scene, are next to nil.

I could have chosen, in this chapter, to devote my time to a consideration of many interesting questions that arise in the context of a study of identity and religion. Works such as *Mediating Religion: Conversations in Media, Religion and Culture*, edited by Joloyon Mitchell and Sophia Marriage,[7] or *Rethinking Media, Religion and Culture*, by Stewart Hoover and Knut Lundby[8] are among a growing number of titles that provide food for thought and debate. But they are so far removed from the everyday life of the Irish Catholic that I have preferred instead to speak frankly of what I believe to be the communic-

---

7. London and New York: T & T Clark, 2003.
8. London: Sage, 1997.

ations barrier between the authorities of the Irish Catholic Church and the Irish Catholic people, including journalists.

The almost non-existent structures of dialogue within the Irish Catholic Church, and the rudimentary level of theological debate and awareness that has been tolerated within it, the antagonistic and hostile forms of authority, the self-righteousness and contempt evident in judgemental phrases such as 'à la carte Catholic', the cosying up of authorities to bodies such as Opus Dei – these are just some of the ways in which growing numbers of Irish people have been alienated not merely from Catholicism but from religion and spirituality.

My personal 'Irish Catholic' nightmare is that a righteous and dominant rump of Irish Catholics will somehow coalesce informally with the reactionary forces of narrow nationalism, especially in the event of an economic recession or an outbreak of severe sectarian violence, and foster an idolatrous form of Catholic identity that will be every bit as narrow and suffocating as the version from which we thought we escaped in the twentieth century. This would reduce Irish Catholic identity to the level of a Balkan sect.

Finally, let me say (and I am not the first to say so), woe be to the scandal givers! For our mistakes and arrogance as journalists let us ask forgiveness and let us resolve to do better. But let those in power in the Irish Catholic Church look in the mirror and contemplate the image of what their Church became. If it is the image of Irish Catholicism that they think meets the needs of men and women in today's world then it is little wonder that the concept of Irish Catholic identity has been angrily shattered into a thousand pieces in the last few decades. If Jesus is a prisoner within the cage of Irish Catholic identity then let us destroy that cage.

Without a converted heart, no amount of media public relations or spin can generate new forms of worthwhile Irish Catholic identity for those who seek authentic spiritual experience and meaning in the twenty-first century. Hopefully, there will never again be a uniform 'Irish Catholic' but, instead, many Irish Catholics with personal identities based on open and authentic spiritual practice.

CHAPTER SIX

Representations of Catholicism in the Twentieth-Century Irish Novel

Eamon Maher

In spite of the fact that the earliest Irish novelists writing in English were Protestants (most notably Maria Edgeworth and Lady Morgan, alias Sydney Owenson), Catholicism became an extremely potent influence on the twentieth century Irish novel. This is not surprising when one considers that the majority religion in this country has historically been so closely bound up with our nationalism, politics and culture. Given the prominence of Catholicism in the evolution of Irish society, I think it would be enlightening to consider the reasons why there never emerged here a genre referred to as the 'Catholic novel', along the lines of what one comes across in France with writers like Georges Bernanos and François Mauriac, or in England with Graham Greene, G. K. Chesterton and Evelyn Waugh. In order to ascertain why we never had a Catholic novel in Ireland, we first of all need to establish what exactly Catholic literature is. In this respect, John Whitehouse's *Catholics on Literature*[1] is an invaluable reference. Whitehouse, in addition to two very insightful essays of his own, supplies extracts from a number of what are commonly considered the most important Catholic writers. In these essays, the authors try to tease out the ways in which their religious faith informed and influenced what they wrote. There is no accepted school of Catholic writers, in the same way as there is no specifically Catholic way of reading and critically assessing literature, which makes the task I have set myself quite perilous. Whitehouse quotes Jacques Maritain's *Art and Scholasticism*, in which the latter stated: 'A Christian work would have the artist, as artist, free.' (Whitehouse, p 14) This is a rule

---

1. John Whitehouse, *Catholics on Literature* (Dublin: Four Courts Press, 1997). Subsequent quotes from this book will be in brackets.

that all novelists, irrespective of their religious allegiance, would do well to follow. The work of art is not about edification or instruction; it is not implicitly didactic, even though one often finds a moral behind what is being expressed. Whitehouse draws a distinction between Catholic writing and Catholic literature. The former seeks to persuade and influence, even to convince, whereas the latter 'is fundamentally artistic, the fictional expression of idiosyncratic and subjective insights rather than general and analytical ratiocination' (Whitehouse, p 15). He concludes: 'In short, when we talk of Catholic literature in our own day, we are talking of a literature marked by faith, or the tensions of faith, and noticeable as such in the surrounding secularised world' (Whitehouse, p 17).

He goes on to speak of how the 'Catholic novelists' were explorers rather than expounders of their religious beliefs. They liked to delve into the dramas associated with faith. These dramas have a universal significance because they are at one and the same time human and metaphysical. Greene's whiskey priest in *The Power and the Glory* or the flawed police officer in *The Heart of the Matter*, are made up of flesh and blood like the rest of us and are thus prone to temptations and momentary weaknesses. What raises them above the ordinary is their unrelenting attention to Catholic dogma. Readers suspect that these men may well be saints in spite of their human faults. Many novels by Graham Greene have Catholicism as their central interest. This is also true of Bernanos's masterpieces, *The Diary of a Country Priest* and *Under Satan's Sun*, which have priests as their main protagonists. With Bernanos, the dramas of Catholicism are acted out in a spectacular fashion. Wrong decisions could well lead to eternal damnation: sin and grace, good and evil are omnipresent – God and Satan are vying for people's souls in a world that is tottering on the edge of an abyss. There is much theology in Bernanos's writing: reference is regularly made to the Communion of Saints and the substitution of souls, concepts about which you hear very little today! Satan assumes a human form and evil is palpable. With Mauriac, Catholicism is much

more subtly interwoven through the text. His main preoccupation is with the psychological probing of his characters, some of
whom, though fatally flawed, end up, as happens in Graham
Greene, as possible saints – there can be no doubting the fact that
Bernanos's country priest is a saint. The hero of Mauriac's *The
Nest of Vipers*, Louis, is a typical example of someone whose disdain for the hypocritical religious observance of his family
blinded him momentarily to the true value of Catholic teaching.
But before his death, this unwavering sceptic sees the light and
reconciles himself with God. What this novel and others like it
show us is that Catholicism has the right ingredients for producing powerful literature, provided, of course, that the writer remains at a certain remove from what he is portraying. Bernanos,
a man of trenchant views, especially when it came to
Catholicism, wrote:

> The first duty of a writer is to produce good books, in the
> light of his own ideas of his art and the resources at his dis-
> posal, without special consideration for anything or anyone,
> for every book bears witness and hence must above all be
> sincere ... Mediocre art is a scandal, and even more of a scan-
> dal when it claims to be edifying (Whitehouse, p 26).

These sentiments could have been uttered by the Irish novelist,
John McGahern, who has always maintained that the only responsibility of a writer is to 'get his words right'. When that styl-
istic element is properly rendered, then the writing will reflect
everything it is capable of reflecting. Bernanos is correct in his
assertion that art alone is what counts for serious writers. They
are keenly aware that a thick line must be drawn between literature and propaganda. This is probably why Mauriac, Bernanos
and Greene all rejected the tag 'Catholic novelist' and preferred
to refer to themselves as writers who also happened to be
Catholics.[2] The distinction is an important one: the quality of the

2. Both Mauriac and Bernanos were interviewed by Frédéric Lefèvre on
his radio programme *Une heure avec...* In 1923, in reply to Lefèvre's
somewhat provocative opening question, 'Monsieur François Mauriac,
Catholic novelist?', Mauriac replied: 'I am a novelist; I am a Catholic –

writing takes precedence over any theological or religious dimension in their works.

When you consider the flowering of the Catholic novel in
France and England, what is striking is the fact that it emerged
at a time when Catholicism was no longer the strong force it had
once been in both of these countries. Ever since the Enlightenment and the French Revolution, France had become a polarised
society and one in which Republicanism and secularism were
pitted in opposition to religion. There was an official separation
of Church and State in 1905 and in the novels of Bernanos, for
example, Catholicism had become obsolete for many people.
The curé d'Ambricourt felt that his parish was being eaten up by
a cancer and it is suggested that his own death from the same
disease is as a result of his assuming the evil he encounters at
every turn. Similarly, in Graham Greene's England, Catholicism
was a minority religion, which did not prevent him and other
novelists making it a central element of what is commonly regarded as their best work – Waugh's *Brideshead Revisited* is a remarkable illustration of this. In my opinion, what prevented the
emergence of a Catholic novel in Ireland is that up until the last
couple of decades Catholicism was too dominant a force (perhaps even too commonplace) for writers to engage with it in a

---

and there is the conflict ... I believe, in fact, that it is fortunate for a novelist to be a Catholic, but I am also quite sure that it is very dangerous
for a Catholic to be a novelist.' Mauriac appears to view the problem in
terms of a certain conflict between the role of novelist who must deal
with the miseries of the flesh and that of the Catholic who must not lead
his readers into moral danger. When it was suggested to him by the
same interviewer that the Catholic Novel does not exist, Bernanos concurred but then went on to explain that Catholicism is not an option,
not a particular optic on life which the writer can choose to adopt or
reject. All art which seeks to enlighten the inner life of Man is bound to
explore sin, and thus all literature which sets itself this aim is Catholic
literature: all novels are Catholic novels. From these comments it can be
seen just how difficult it can be to pin down the exact ingredients that
go in to making the Catholic Novel. To read the Lefèvre interviews in
full, see *Une Heure avec...* (Paris: Éditions de la Nouvelle Revue
Française, 1924).

sympathetic manner. There was little opportunity for critical appraisal of matters pertaining to faith here.

Whenever writers wandered from the status quo, by seeking
to engage with the daily human dramas, especially anything re-
motely connected to sexuality, they were promptly brought to
heel by the Censorship of Publications Board and had their
books banned. This even happened to those who, like Kate
O'Brien, displayed a great admiration and reverence for
Catholic practices in their work. Dermot Bolger makes the following remark about the changed climate in Ireland today compared to a few decades ago:

> Growing up in Ireland in the 1960s, it was like you had these
> huge puppets of oppression, or alleged repression, to whom
> you could take a baseball bat and smash them. There's a new
> generation for whom de Valera or John Charles McQuaid
> mean nothing – their shadows don't stretch that far – and
> that's great. But their targets are far less obvious than mine
> were.[3]

What Bolger is saying essentially is that the twin pillars of
Church and State were the normal targets of writers in the 1960s.
By the 1990s, this has changed dramatically and writers no
longer felt the same need to pillory structures that were exerting
less influence in a more progressive, global and secular Ireland.
In his play, *The Passion of Jerome*, Bolger decided to present what
he figured would be the most terrifying prospect for the average
Irish inhabitant of the Celtic Tiger period: a divine apparition.
That a secular-minded, middle-aged man who is having an affair with a woman in a flat in Ballymun should be visited by *stig-
mati* rendered many theatre-goers in this country extremely uncomfortable – the play was much more warmly received in
France. The wheel has come full circle to such an extent that
today countless Irish people are totally averse to even allowing
room for a reasoned discussion of Catholicism. This may explain

---

3. 'Being a Writer in Ireland in the 1970s and Today.' Interview between
Eamon Maher and Dermot Bolger, in *Doctrine and Life*, 55, 8, pp 28-38,
pp 37-8.

the wide variety of prisms through which the new generation of Irish novelists view Ireland and Irishness.

Seán Ó Faoláin had a continental perspective, which helped him to offer a good critique of Irish society in the numerous essays he wrote during the 1930s and 40s in reviews like the *Virginia Quarterly Review* and *The Bell*. Writing in the former, in 1935, he mused on the issue of Catholic writing and stated that the Catholic writer chooses to see man as midway between everything and nothing:

> I find in all of them [Catholic novelists] a painful self-consciousness, as if they could not forget they were Catholics, a timidity evident in their fear of the senses, a priggishness and a solemnity which has nothing to do with religion and for which there is no excuse, a lack of humour, and a tendency to underwrite about the emotions as if they feared to raise a storm they could not ride ... These tendencies, though ... highly laudable in the writer as a Catholic, are in the writer as a writer the signs of some basic weakness that is, apparently, fatal to his work.[4]

He expressed pity for the Catholic writer who suffers from the feeling that art poses some danger to religion – such a conviction deprives him of detachment. He continued: 'For, the whole human drama is surely the drama of the Seven Deadly Sins, and any novelist who attempts to avoid them is avoiding reality.'[5] Irish novelists did not, in fairness, neglect sin, as they knew that it possessed a fertile ground for exploration. But it was an area that troubled Mauriac quite a bit. If the source of the novel is ultimately humanity in its various guises, then there is a fair chance that it will involve portraying sinful behaviour. Sin is far more interesting from an artistic perspective than sanctity. Mauriac came up with the following solution to his dilemma: purify the source. By this he meant that he saw his responsibility as a novelist as being to write with a pure heart so that those

4. 'The Modern Novel: A Catholic Point of View', in *Virginia Quarterly Review*, Vol II (1935), pp 339-51, p 345.
5. Ó Faoláin, 'The Modern Novel', p 346.

who would subsequently read him would not be contaminated. Ó Faoláin did not recognise this as a legitimate approach. He felt it was not acceptable that the person of a religious disposition should distrust the flesh (as Mauriac most definitely did) and therefore do injustice to the natural impurity of life by glossing over what is unseemly. He maintained that Catholic novelists 'have falsified life by their refusal to handle manfully the drama of the Seven Deadly Sins. They have the strange delusion that they can present a brothel without mentioning the whore.'[6]

The position of the Catholic novelist in Ireland was often rendered uncomfortable on several fronts. Firstly, in a country that was coming to terms with its newly found Independence from British rule (in the 26 counties, that is) Catholicism was a bulwark of the ruling classes and was used as a means of distinguishing us from the English. The sort of Catholicism that developed here became strongly linked to republicanism, in spite of the fact that eighteenth-century nationalism was almost exclusively led by Protestants such as Robert Emmet, Wolfe Tone and Jonathan Swift. It should also be stated that the Catholic hierarchy was wary of nationalists and even went so far as to excommunicate members of the IRA during the War of Independence. It is ironic that the fruit of the armed struggle, which they opposed, opened the way for the most unchallenged period of clerical power ever experienced in Ireland. Once they became aware of the dangers posed by communism in the wake of the Second World War, the Irish Catholic Church began to reinvent a certain notion of Irishness being synonymous with Catholicism. Bishops like John Charles McQuaid in Dublin, who played a major role in the sacking of John McGahern from his position as a primary teacher after the banning of his second novel, *The Dark*, in 1965, felt secure enough to dictate to a largely submissive laity. Here is Louise Fuller's assessment of the bishops' approach:

The bishops repeatedly warned about the dangers of the

---

6. 'It no longer Matters or the Death of the English Novel', in *The Criterion*, Vol XV, No 58, October 1935, pp 49-56, pp 54-5.

modern world – dangers arising from dancing, 'evil literature', modern song, drinking and so-called 'company-keep-
ing'. In the minds of the bishops, these seemed to constitute
the concrete symptoms of the advancing tide of secularist attitudes which had already engulfed neighbouring countries,
and which they were determined to resist at all costs.[7]

It should come as no surprise that because the hierarchy pushed
such a repressive agenda, many of our novelists became es-
tranged from Catholicism in its institutional manifestation. That
did not prevent someone like John McGahern, a lapsed Catholic,
regretting the power and beauty of the religious symbolism and
rituals of his youth. Like many of his generation, his mother had
hoped and prayed that one day he would become a priest. In his
recent *Memoir*, we read:

> After the Ordination Mass I would place my freshly anointed
> hands in blessing on my mother's head. We'd live together in
> the priest's house and she'd attend each morning Mass and
> take communion from my hands. When she died, I'd include
> her in all the Masses that I'd say until we were united in the
> joy of heaven.[8]

The rift between most writers and their Catholic faith became
more pronounced as the power of the hierarchy began to grow.

---

7. Louise Fuller, *Irish Catholicism Since 1950: The Undoing of a Culture*
(Dublin: Gill and Macmillan, 2004), p 52.
8. John McGahern, *Memoir* (London: Faber and Faber, 2005), p 63. There
are close parallels between Patrick Kavanagh's and McGahern's love of
Catholic liturgy. This is how Antoinette Quinn describes Kavanagh's
memories of the church services of his youth: 'The liturgical aspects of
Catholicism appealed to the young Patrick's burgeoning aesthetic
sense: the altar dressed with flowers and candles, the gorgeous vest-
ments, the gleam of wine being poured into the gold chalice at Mass,
the pages of 'the Golden Book' reverentially turned.' (*Patrick Kavanagh:
A Biography* (Dublin: Gill & Macmillan, 2001), p 28) Compare this to the
following lines by McGahern: 'The church ceremonies always gave me
pleasure, and I miss them even now. In an impoverished time they
were my first introduction to an indoor beauty, of luxury and orna-
ment, ceremony and sacrament and mystery. I remember still the tex-

Many novelists felt that their Catholic faith was not really compatible with their artistic function. They therefore tended to treat of Catholicism in a negative fashion, emphasising how it led to twisted attitudes to sexuality. This is what McGahern has to say about the issue: 'Authority's writ ran from God the Father down and could not be questioned. Violence reigned as often as not in the homes as well. One of the compounds at its base was sexual sickness and frustration, as sex was seen, officially, as unclean and sinful, allowable only when it too was licensed.'[9] Other chapters in this book chart in far greater detail the complicated issue of Catholic identity in the last century and the first years of the present one. Catholicism does feature significantly in numerous Irish novels but never in a way that would lead one to attach the title Catholic literature to any of them. In this respect, I think the definition of the Catholic novel supplied by Albert Sonnenfeld is helpful:

> It is a novel written by a Catholic, using Catholicism as its informing mythopoeic structure or generative symbolic system, and where the principal and decisive issue is the salvation or damnation of the hero or heroine.[10]

There is no such tradition that I can detect in the Irish novel. There are Irish novels with Catholicism as their core element, without ever quite managing to be 'Catholic novels' and we will look briefly at two of those now: John Broderick's *The Pilgrimage* (1961) and Brian Moore's *Catholics* (1983). I have written elsewhere about Kate O'Brien and John McGahern's treatment of Catholicism and how both were keenly aware of the positive role the religion of their youth and early adulthood played in their lives. O'Brien's *The Ante-Room* is, in fact, the closest Ireland

---

ture of the plain, brown, flat cardboard boxes in which the red and white and yellow tulips for the altar came on the bus when there were no flowers anywhere. I think not of the great ceremonies of Christmas and Easter in that small church facing Henry's but of the Stations of the Cross in Lent and the feast of Corpus Christi (*Memoir*, p 201).
9. *Memoir*, p 18.
10. Albert Sonnenfeld, *Crossroads: Essays on the Catholic Novelists* (York (South Carolina): French Literature Publishing Company, 1980), p vii.

has come to producing a Catholic novel.[11] My choice of
Broderick and Moore is predicated on the fact that they are representative of a number of fictional representations of Catholic
preoccupations as represented in the Irish novel of the twentieth
century. Broderick (1924-1989) was born into the Athlone family
renowned for its bread. He lost his father at a young age and
was then very pained to see his mother remarry, especially as
her choice of husband was the debonair and flighty manager of
the family bakery, Paddy Flynn. In addition to his domestic
problems, Broderick also suffered from a common Irish failing,
alcoholism, a disease that was almost certainly exacerbated by
his inability to reconcile his homosexual leanings with his
deeply held spiritual convictions. Broderick was slightly paradoxical in terms of his Catholicism: he combined a serious aver-
sion to the 'progressive' tendencies of Vatican II – he fundamentally disagreed with the removal of Latin from the liturgy and
opened discussions on this topic with the line: 'Before the Mass
was abolished!' – with a desire to open up Ireland to more enlightened European influences. He was a friend of the French
American writer, Julien Green, and admitted several times that
Mauriac was the only literary influence of whom he was aware.
He read and spoke French well and it is certain that he was
aware of the impact of the 'Catholic novel' in France and elsewhere in the world. He does not appear, however, to have followed a similar course in his own writings. Nevertheless,
Catholicism is a permanent feature of his novels, some of which
were very daring for the time. For example, *An Apology for Roses*
(1973), describes among other things a priest's affair with a
female parishioner. *The Trial of Father Dillingham* (1982) deals
quite movingly with the love and care a homosexual couple lavish
on one another. Broderick shone a light into the dark recesses of
provincial Ireland at a time when most people were not quite
ready for such a stark delineation of the reality that was around

---

11. Kate O'Brien and John McGahern are deliberately omitted from the
present article as they form the basis of a book chapter the soon-to-be-
published 2004 IASIL proceedings.

them but that they failed to see. Broderick's commitment to his faith can be gauged from the fact that after his mother's death, in 1974, he went to discuss the possibility of becoming a priest with Fr Peter Connolly, then Professor of English in Maynooth College and someone who was most supportive of his literary efforts. In a robust interview with David Hanly shortly before his death, Broderick made the following comment:

> Anyone who is reared in a Catholic atmosphere first of all takes in that Catholic atmosphere more or less through their pores.

It reminds one of the heroine of Graham Greene's novel, *The End of the Affair*, who, baptised without her knowledge by her mother, imagines in later life that she caught 'belief like a disease'. Certainly, Broderick, in common with several other Irish writers, could do little to escape his Catholic upbringing. In fact, he often stated that any important religious decisions in his life were dictated by what he learned in primary school from Sister Margaret Mary's teaching of the Penny Catechism. But what of his first, and in my view, his best, novel and its treatment of Catholicism? Well, its plot is labyrinthine for such a short book. It recounts how Julia Glynn, the wife of a wealthy builder in a midlands town, engages in sexual adventures with various partners, most notably her husband's nephew, Jim, a doctor, and the manservant, Stephen, who is responsible for sending her anonymous and lurid letters describing her affair with Jim. Julia's husband, Michael, several years her senior, has been crippled with arthritis since shortly after their marriage, and is encouraged by the local priest, Fr Victor, to undertake a trip to Lourdes, where he may get a cure. Nobody really believes that the miracle will take place, but they indulge Michael by having Masses said for his special intention. Julia's main concern in the build-up to their departure is that Michael will discover her liaison with Jim, and so she is relieved when she learns that it is Stephen, mad with jealousy, who is responsible for the horrible letters. She ends up having an affair then with the manservant, which, because Jim's forthcoming marriage to the daughter of a wealthy and influential figure will deprive her of a regular sexual partner, suits her quite well. She is someone who appears to need lovers in the same way as others crave food or wealth. An easy conscience makes her adultery more pleasurable: 'She had never at any time suffered from a sense of sin.'[12]

While Julia is certainly no saint, she is not portrayed in a more negative light than those with whom she shares her life. During their honeymoon, her husband became besotted with a German man, with whom he subsequently carried on an intimate correspondence. His infrequent acts of intercourse with his wife were characterised by brutality. In fact, there is something prurient about the way the men in this novel regard sex. This is Julia's assessment of Stephen:

> She doubted if Stephen, who, she had no doubt, loved her in his own fashion, would ever be able to dissociate lovemaking from the furtive, the sordid, and the unclean. Few Irishmen, she knew, ever were. The puritanism which was bred in their bones, and encouraged in their youth by every possible outside pressure, was never entirely eradicated (p 171).

This is an excellent observation, not merely in relation to the Irish male psyche of a few decades ago, but also with regard to the difficulty presented to the Catholic novelist by sex. In the Ireland of the 1960s, much emphasis was laid on avoiding 'occasions of sin', 'bad thoughts' and these applied for the most part to any sexual practice or inclination outside of marriage. The challenge for the Catholic novelist is to reveal the workings of God within the world of humanity, without engaging in prurience or superficial piety. According to the famous French critic, Charles du Bos, those Catholic critics who place a blanket ban on 'impurity' in fiction are wrong because human life involves impurity. Broderick had a good grasp of theology. He recognised the frailties of the human state but also the possibilities of salvation afforded by prayer and faith. The last sentence of *The*

---

12. John Broderick, *The Pilgrimage* (Dublin: The Lilliput Press, 2004), p 24. All my references will be to this edition with page numbers in brackets.

Pilgrimage caused major controversy: 'In this way they set off on their pilgrimage, from which a week later Michael returned completely cured' (p 191). It may well have been this line, more than the daring descriptions of Julia's sexual escapades, that caused the book to be banned in Ireland. It was considered blasphemous that a sinner like Michael should be the recipient of grace. In his Introduction to the French version of the novel, which has been translated and included in last year's Lilliput edition, Julien Green stated his admiration for an 'extraordinarily gripping book', and asked why anyone should see blasphemy in the miraculous cure of an old, debauched man. 'Since when has healing been exclusively available to the just?' he asks (p 2). Green makes a valid point here: there are many examples in the gospels of God's understanding of, and love for, sinners. By introducing the notion of miracles and grace, John Broderick was dealing with material that had the potential to render many Irish people uncomfortable. It was one thing to suggest that an exemplary Christian should be the beneficiary of grace, quite another to have it bestowed on a sinner like Michael Glynn. But, as we have seen, from a theological standpoint Broderick was far from suggesting anything untoward in the cure of his protagonist. The core element of *The Pilgrimage* does not, however, revolve around the salvation or damnation of its main character, Julia. Michael is the recipient of grace but at no stage do we come to a good knowledge of what type of relationship he has with God. So we cannot describe this as a 'Catholic novel'.

Brian Moore's *Catholics* is more a novella than a novel and it too deals with the issues of faith and salvation. The setting is Muck Abbey, a remote island monastery off the Kerry coast, where the monks have started saying the Latin Mass again, in contravention of the ecumenical thrust of Vatican IV. The clash between the traditional and the modern is finely drawn as James Kinsella, a progressive American priest, is sent to Ireland with the task of bringing the monks in line with Rome's new stance. The Abbot of Muck, Tomás O'Malley, who has lost his faith, is a man who cares for his community and worries about what the

imposition of the ban will do to them. Pilgrims had flocked to
Cahirciveen to attend the traditional Mass said at the foot of
Mount Coom:

> Most could see the Mass rock and the priest only from a dis-
> tance, but all heard the Latin, thundering from loudspeakers
> rigged up by townsfolk. Latin. The communion bell. Monks
> as altar-boys saying the Latin responses. Incense. The old
> way.[13]

This is the type of ceremony that is so nostalgically evoked by
Broderick: the use of Latin and incense, the priest with his back
to the congregation, bells ringing. Sadly for Broderick, as for the
monks of Muck Abbey, 'the old way' is not Rome's way and this
is the message James Kinsella carries with him to the remote island. When bad weather and the refusal of two locals to take
him across in their boat because they do not believe he is a
priest, prevent Kinsella from gaining access to the island, he arrives in a helicopter. He is greeted by the Abbot with the following remark: 'You've brought us the symbol of the century. Just
when I thought we'd be able to close the hundred years out, and
say we missed our time' (p 30). There is a definite sense in which
Kinsella is depicted as the modern global cleric for whom there
are few, if any, obstacles that cannot be overcome. He has all the
trump cards, the power invested in him by Rome, technology,
sophistication. The monks resent his arrival, as they know that it
signals change. One, Fr Manus, asks what can possibly be wrong
with saying Mass in Latin. Surely the reverence of the sacrifice,
the adoration of the sacrament, are positive things:

> And we did it that way for nearly two thousand years and, in
> all that time, the church was a place to be quiet in, and re-
> spectful, it was a hushed place because God was there, God
> on the altar, in the tabernacle in the form of a wafer of bread
> and a chalice of wine. It was God's house, where, every day,
> the daily miracle took place. God coming down among us. A

---

13. Brain Moore, *Catholics* (London: Triad/Panther Books, 1983), p 10.
All subsequent references will be to this edition, with the page number
in brackets.

mystery. Just as this new Mass isn't a mystery, it's a mockery, a singsong (p 43).

Fr Manus is the mouthpiece for many of the reservations expressed by some Irish people in the wake of Vatican II. They found it difficult to adapt to the liturgy in the vernacular and hankered back to the time when the ceremony was shrouded in mystery.[14] Moore wrote this novel at a time when the Catholic Church appeared to be headed in a more progressive direction. During the last decades of the pontificate of John Paul II, however, that trend seemed to be largely reversed as more emphasis was placed on orthodoxy and conformity. The following statement by Kinsella is pertinent: 'We are trying to create a uniform posture within the Church. If everyone decides to worship in his own way – well, it's obvious, it would create a disunity' (p 55). This is a position that hasn't changed. The central authority vested in the pope is designed in such a way as to ensure that the faithful all over the world worship in a similar fashion and adhere to the same fundamentals in terms of dogma. Rome was alerted to the situation of the monks when television crews filmed the rock Mass and relayed it across the globe. This could not be tolerated.

The question of the Abbot's loss of faith is a central element in the novel and it has a connection with John Broderick's *The Pilgrimage*. It occurred during a visit he made to Lourdes when he was shocked by the tawdry religious supermarkets, the certifications of 'miraculous' cures, the lines of stretchers and wheelchairs on which lay the desperate and the ill. It caused Tomás O'Malley to flee to his hotel room where he was unable to say

---

14. Louise Fuller notes: 'A central theme of the Vatican Council had been that new symbols, new ways of communicating Christ's message, would have to be found, which would make sense in a rapidly changing world. However, a recurring theme, echoed by commentators reflecting on the Irish situation in the post-Vatican era, was that, despite the updated liturgy, the correlation between life and liturgy, as envisaged by the Council, had not been achieved. Writing in *The Furrow* in 1979, Fr Eamonn Bredin ... observed that the new liturgy seemed to "have left the inner core of people's lives untouched."' (*Irish Catholicism Since 1950*, p 122)

his prayers. He had not been able to pray since that time. Afterwards he immersed himself in his work and even managed to rule his abbey without betraying his loss of faith. When he is faced with the disappointment and possible rebellion of the monks, to whom he must announce the decision that he has reached – that they will conform to Rome's dictate – he finds somewhere deep within him the key to spiritual fulfilment. It does not matter, he tells the monks, what means you employ to adore God. He is there in the tabernacle when you believe in the real presence: 'Prayer is the only miracle', he said. 'We pray. If our words become prayer, God will come' (p 91). While he mumbles the words of the 'Our Father', readers have the impression that he may have regained his faith.

Moore comes closer than Broderick to writing a Catholic novel but, once more, there is not sufficient emphasis on the Abbot's salvation or damnation for *Catholics* to be placed in the same category as *The Power and the Glory* or *The Diary of a Country Priest*. Moore often admitted that he was fascinated with those who had faith and many of his novels explore the sort of loss of faith he himself experienced at a young age. His writings borrow heavily on Catholic rituals and practices especially with characters like Judith Hearne who finds that her religion, scrupulously observed for years, deserts her in her hour of need:

> God! Miss Hearne said bitterly. What does *He* care? Is there a God at all, I've been asking myself, because if there is, why does he never answer our prayers? Why does He allow all these things to happen?[15]

There is clearly a lot more that could be said in relation to Moore's representation of Catholicism. What this short exposé seeks to do is to underline how Catholicism is used by writers like himself and Broderick as a means of reflecting an important ingredient of Irish society that was beginning to wane, even as early as a few decades ago. Perhaps the time is now ripe, in an Ireland that has become increasingly secular and where conse-

15. Brian Moore, *The Lonely Passion of Judith Hearne* (London: Flamingo, 1994), p 229.

quently many are beginning to recognise that Catholicism, for all that it is not a perfect system, still meets a need for mystery and the transcendent that is keenly felt by many, for a Catholic novel to emerge in this country. It could be a voice from the margins, quietly suggesting the possibility that another world may exist beyond the material one. Maybe Ireland will one day supply what Whitehouse said has not emerged as of yet:

In the Catholic novel, there was a movement away from a picture of human beings working out their own destiny towards a presentation of them in a dialectical and critical relationship to their formative culture, where the old lexis – 'faith', 'grace', 'sin', 'salvation', 'redemption', 'hope', 'charity' – is largely meaningless. To date, there is no clear sign of the emergence of what may come next, a totally post-Vatican II Catholic novelist (Whitehouse, p 20).

CHAPTER SEVEN

'Mulcahy taught us God': Catholicism and Survival in the Poetry of Brendan Kennelly

John McDonagh

In 1963, Brendan Kennelly published the first of his two novels. *The Crooked Cross* is set in a fictional north Kerry village called Deevna and recalls a severe summer drought sometime in the 1960s and the villagers' desperate attempts to locate a water supply. The torpid nature of village life is compounded by the unnaturally warm weather, and the life that is depicted is one that is ravaged by emigration and consumed with petty political rivalries, unfulfilled sexual longings and chronic economic deprivation. The village itself is clearly based on Kennelly's home town of Ballylongford, which is itself shaped liked a crooked cross, the disjointed crossroads around which the town was built providing an architectural exemplar of the somewhat skewed life that Kennelly depicts in many of his poems. Of course the reader will find, in the extensive body of Kennelly's work, a scattering of the usual pastoral eulogies that nearly every poet feels obliged to write at some time or other, but largely the crooked cross image predominates. It is a place of metaphorical crucifixion, an unmerciful cauldron in which difference is not tolerated and those who do not conform to the unwritten standards of communal behaviour face an often brutal fate. Kennelly debunks the perceived utopian village community, describing an environment in which personal fulfilment and growth occurs in spite of and often in direct opposition to the predominant social and cultural forces of the time. Kennelly was seven years old when Eamon De Valera delivered his famous St Patrick's Day address in 1943, but the Ireland that De Valera dreamt of, with its comely maidens and sturdy youths, is far removed from the ambivalent, dystopian childhood that gradually emerges in Kennelly's work.

However, it would not do justice to the broad range of Kennelly's work to suggest that his childhood experiences were overwhelmingly negative. Indeed, the village of Ballylongford and its residents emerge at various points in Kennelly's 44 books of poetry as an eclectic gathering of just what one would imagine a bustling rural Irish town has to offer. The village of Ballylongford is the largest town for a considerable area in north Kerry and as a result it has occupied an important economic, social and cultural role in the lives of the local people. The Kennellys' business interests in the town were and continue to be considerable and the fact that Brendan grew up in the family pub exposed him to a range of social, cultural and economic events and transactions. His responses, therefore, to the various events of his childhood are by definition complex and varied. Equally, it would be disingenuous to suggest that he emerged from his childhood with any more or less traumas than those he grew up with and there are many instances of wonderfully evocative poems, such as 'I See You Dancing, Father', in which the nurturing, caring and supportive aspect of his childhood emerges. However, Kennelly has never been a poet to shirk from the dark, complex psychological difficulties associated with growing up in rural Ireland in the 1940s and 1950s and it is precisely this often raw and bruising honesty that gives his poetry such clout.

It is principally in his collection *The Boats are Home*, published in 1980 by the Gallery Press, that Kennelly portrays the dominant images of his childhood and early education, and given the centrality of both in the development of Kennelly's work this collection plays a crucial and often overlooked role in his canon. In this compilation, containing new and some previously published poems, Kennelly dramatises seminal childhood events as tangible memories full of fear, despair, violence and black humour. There are few of the cosy pastoral scenes one might expect from a poet growing up in a rural part of Ireland in the 1940s; instead the poems deal with a harsher existence, a daily grind of labour punctuated by rare moments of light relief. The poems range over a broad spectrum of rural life, including education, religion, violence, farming, singing and rituals associated with death. To Kennelly memories become like 'old loyalties'[1] that are not buried in the psyche but exist as tenable, tangible and reconstructed realities in the present. One of the main functions of Kennelly's poetry is not necessarily to deconstruct these memories but to assimilate the often phantasmagorical images of childhood into contemporary perceptions of the world and to tentatively position these images in the haphazard formation of the self, and these metamporphoses of the past into the present are one of Kennelly's great strengths as a poet. Indeed, this poetic methodology is developed further in *The Man Made of Rain*, published in 1998 by Bloodaxe Books, when Kennelly is taken on a journey that leads to his desire 'to see the dream absorb and transfigure its own violation by the "real"',[2] thus presaging our recollection of memories over whatever is perceived to be real in the present. This extraordinary epic poem takes Kennelly to his personal shadowlands and his journey into self is one that throws up as many contradictions as there are unstable memories:

> In the land of no language
> I beg understanding of shadows
> I look, listen, wait to be born
> In a word on the tip of the tongue
> Where I wander forever,
> A guest at the feast of silence
> Soon to return to the room where I lie
> Conscious (they say) scarred and still,
> Pigignorant of the words I kill (*Man Made of Rain*, p 23).

This absorption, re-evaluation and re-appropriation of memories and images form the past into the present, rather than a mawkish self-obsessed nostalgia, is a constant feature of his ear-

---

1. Richard Pine (ed.), *Dark Fathers into Light – Brendan Kennelly* (Newcastle-upon-Tyne: Bloodaxe Books, 1994), p 22.
2. Brendan Kennelly, *The Man Made of Rain* (Newcastle-Upon-Tyne: Bloodaxe Books, 1998), pp 8-9.

lier collection, *The Boats Are Home*, and indeed this could be seen as a key driving force behind most of Kennelly's epic work. This collection presents Kennelly as an occasionally detached, yet sensitive and emotional observer, capable of standing back and recording the detail that forms the essence of the captured moment his poem describes. In language that echoes Heaney's 'Digging', Kennelly has described this complex inter-relationship between the memorised past and the perceived present:

It's not a case of digging them up. It's not a process of disinterring. They revisit you. In a sense it's not the past as all. It's just images out of the past that happen to become living presence in your own life.[3]

Far from portraying a romanticised view of a rural idyll, Kennelly describes the key motivations of his early childhood experiences:

It was not a society that had set out to understand things. I remember very little understanding of anything. They understood that they had to cope with life. They understood that they had to make money ... All I remember is talking, trying to get on, lots of games, lots of football, lots of running.[4]

This frenetic life is a strong feature of the collection but perhaps the dominant image of *The Boats are Home* is that of a violence, both subtle and brutal, that permeates all aspects of existence and consequently each stratum of society. This violence manifests itself in an obvious physical aggression and in the subtle, more sinister, guise of those people entrusted with authority or influence. In his book *Poetry and Violence*, Kennelly muses over his translation of Eileen O'Connell's eighteenth century ballad, *A Cry for Art O'Leary*, a poem he admires for its 'violence – sexual, religious, political, forms of violence that occur again and again

3. Ciaran Carty, interview with Brendan Kennelly, *Sunday Independent*, 8 February 1981, p 16.
4. Daniel Murphy, interview with Brendan Kennelly in *Education and the Arts – A Research Report*, published by the School of Education, Trinity College, 1981, p 48.

throughout Irish writing.'5 He admires and desires the honesty that he perceives lies at the heart of a poetry that is not afraid to confront and challenge all sorts of cultural beliefs and practices, and his perception of the devious ways in which violence trickles through Irish society is both shrewd and provocative. Indeed, Kennelly concludes this fascinating essay with a maxim that could well be applied to a sizeable body of his own work:

> Violent poetry, the poetry of uncompromising consciousness, the poetry of hard, raw reality, continues to do its work of dramatic demonstration, of ruthless bringing-to-mind, of accusation and warning (Persson, *Journey Into Joy*, pp 44-5).

Kennelly certainly does not shy away from portraying the various manifestations of violence in his society and the collection points to a more subtle but no less dangerous psychological and emotional violence inflicted on children by the very people chosen by society to protect and cherish its young. The impression created by the collection is of an entire generation growing up despite, and not thanks to, the very institutions created to enable their transition into adulthood and it is this pervading sense of the betrayal of trust on such a huge scale that led Kennelly to overtly explore the notion of betrayal a decade later in *The Book of Judas*. The dominant forces of Church and State allowed little or no tolerance for deviance from a strictly imposed moral code, one that was shown to be laced with hypocrisy by revelations in the 1990s of widespread clerical child sex abuse. Indeed, Kennelly's poetry certainly hints at the scandal of child abuse long before such revelations became relatively commonplace. He recalls the chief characteristics of this time as:

> The repression in the Church, the suicides of girls, the schools, the brutal teachers, the notion that a boy could get fifty slaps on the hand for stammering or for writing with his left hand, the total lack of any sexual education – these are all in retrospect comic in a way, but at the time you're going through it, it was very puzzling (Pine, *Dark Fathers*, p 21).

5. Ake Persson (ed.), *Brendan Kennelly – Journey into Joy – Selected Prose* (Newcastle-upon-Tyne: Bloodaxe Books, 1994), p 23.

The Boats are Home presents the primary school not as a place of engagement and learning, but of fear, repression and brutality. In the opening poem, entitled 'To Learn', Kennelly contrasts the impression made on a young boy by the nine fields that lay between his house and the school. Each field is filled by the boy's imagination which is triggered by the different quality of land in each or by an animal which occupies it. The poem celebrates the wonder of a young boy who recreates his expanding world with images of familiarity and whose imagination can inspire both happiness and fear by the mere act of peering through a hedge. The 'real' process of learning has been active throughout the journey to school but it is a process that is not recognised by the regime of the classroom. The inorganic school stands out against the lushness of the colour of the fields in which it is set, and 'the gravely rise' on which the school is built presents education as a hard and stony process that reflects the physical difficulty of getting to the school. Kennelly concludes the poem thus:

He thought of the nine fields in turn
As he beat the last ditch and came
In sight of the school on the gravely rise.
He buckled down to learn.[6]

The last line neatly draws the boundary between the mysterious world of the nine fields, created in the freedom of the boy's imagination, and the stifling nature of the world presented by people with no other desire than to control a roomful of children. The final line 'buckling down to learn' is carefully chosen to highlight the weight placed on young children by a violent and insensitive educational system. The dual meaning of the word 'buckle' is intended to portray the leather belt that was the most memorable educational symbol for thousands of young children as well as the buckling of the individual under the repression of the pedagogical regime. Many of those who entered teaching did not do so out of a genuine vocation or desire to teach but rather because they were seeking the economic security and social

6. Brendan Kennelly, *A Time For Voices* (Newcastle-Upon-Tyne: Bloodaxe Books, 1990), p 9.

respectability of a teaching position. Kennelly describes his first teacher in far from flattering terms:

> Instead of finding security, all they found was mental frustration and bewilderment. The teacher didn't want to know, didn't want to feel the uncertainties of the students at all and all I remember out of that class was fear, beatings, crying, sticks and shouting – violence. I think I derive a lot of my thought from him, the opposite (Murphy, *Education and the Arts*, p 49).

This is a damning indictment of a system by a man who has spent the best part of 40 years as a teacher in Trinity College, one of the most respected educational institutions in Ireland. His commitment to what can only be called the art of teaching is unwavering and it is clear that his early experiences of negativity have forged within him the realisation that teachers are crucially important and formative figures in the lives of children and as such bear a huge responsibility. In fact, his next collection, due in 2006, is going to focus entirely on poems about education and knowledge and will feature over 500 poems.

Again, however, it would not be fair to brand all of Kennelly's experiences of education as negative and he largely escaped the worst excesses of his teachers by virtue of his extraordinary memory, an invaluable asset in coping with the constant questions and answers that he portrays as a central pedagogical tool of his primary school days. Indeed, one of the most influential figures on his development, as both a poet and academic, was Jane Agnes Mc Kenna, who ran a secondary school in Tarbet, Co Kerry, which he attended between 1948 and 1953. For each story of brutality and repression there is, of course, the often less currently fashionable story of a helpful, inspirational and supportive teacher, and Gabriel Fitzmaurice describes her as 'the significant event on Kennelly's early education' (Pine, *Dark Fathers*, p 32). Her positive influence on him is clearly reflected in Kennelly's love of French, which he learned at St Ita's, an influence that extended to his admiration of the work of Rimbaud and Baudelaire, amongst others. Indeed, he dedicated his 1992 collection *Breathing Spaces* to McKenna and the poem 'Entering' points to the long-term and often intangible effects of her tutelage:

> I touch, trust the strangeness in that thought
> As I parry the shrivelling demons
> Dodge the begrudging word
> Sidestep the withering eye
> And do my failing best
> To rest
> Among the flowing, growing forms
> That might open to my will
> Give access to their mercy
> And share their skill[7]

Given the influence of the Catholic clergy in the shaping of the ethos of primary school education in Ireland, religious education, otherwise known as 'catechism', was therefore regarded as one of the most important subjects in the entire school curriculum. Brendan Behan recounts his experiences of the preparation for the sacrament of confirmation at the beginning of his famous short story, 'The Confirmation Suit', and his experience of the preparation of this right of passage was certainly not unusual:

> For weeks it was nothing but simony and sacrilege, and the sins crying to heaven for vengeance, the big green Catechism in our hands, walking home along the brewery wall, with a butt too, to help our wits, what is pure spirit, and don't kill that, Billser has to get a drag out of it yet, what do I mean by apostate, and hell and heaven and despair and presumption and hope.[8]

Despite Behan's humour, this passage unveils a more sinister power struggle operating over the role of the clergy and Catholicism in the Irish education system and it is a seminal con-

7. Brendan Kennelly, *Breathing Spaces* (Newcastle-Upon-Tyne: Bloodaxe Books, 1992), p 16.
8. Augustine Martin (ed.), *An Anthology of Short Stories* (Dublin: Gill and Macmillan, 1987), p 244.

flict explored by Kennelly in *The Boats are Home*. In *A Time for Voices*, Kennelly's selected poems of 1990, 'The Stick' is counter pointed with 'Catechism', a poem that points to the reduction of mystery and wonder to pedantic questions and answers. Coupled with the inevitable beatings it occasioned, it is little wonder that the theory of God would be associated with the pervading atmosphere of fear, intimidation and confusion that characterised the classroom:

> Religion class. Mulcahy taught us God
> While he heated his arse to a winter fire
> Testing with his fingers the supple sally rod.
> 'Explain the Immaculate Conception, Maguire,
> And tell us then about the Mystical Blood.'
> Maguire failed. Mulcahy covered the boy's head
> With his satchel, shoved him stumbling among
> The desks, lashed his bare legs until they bled.
>
> Who goes to hell, Dineen? Kane, what's a saint?
> Doolin, what constitutes a mortal sin?
> Flynn, what of man who calls his brother a fool?
> Years killed raving questions. Kane stomped Dublin
> In policeman's boots. Flynn was afraid of himself.
> Maguire did well out of whores in Liverpool
> (*A Time for Voices*, p 21).

Kennelly's recollection of the treatment handed out to Maguire in the classroom is an interesting reworking of the treatment meted out to Jesus on the Via Dolorosa, 'lashed' as he stumbled along with a cross on his back. Kennelly replaces the carried cross with the schoolbag, imbuing the bag with the iconic status traditionally associated with the cross, namely that of the ultimate sacrifice and the inherent savagery of humankind. This is a poem that treads the fine line between tragedy and comedy that typifies Kennelly's recollection of his youth and the balance between the past and the future is cleverly handled in this tightly constructed work. The choice of the name Maguire for one of the central characters is perhaps an echo of the protagonist of Patrick Kavanagh's 1942 epic 'The Great Hunger', a man who

suffers from an emotional and spiritual paralysis and whose existence equally straddles both tragedy and comedy. As a result
of his failure to explain the 'mystical Blood', Maguire must shed
his own blood in the inevitable beating. This intended irony
highlights the gulf between what is being taught and how it is
being taught and the variegated responses such treatment elic-
its. Kane allowed the questioning and punishment to materialise
in his choice of career as a policeman, a tacit internalisation of
the way in which religion was presented and an appreciation of
the powerful social position of the Church. Flynn, so terrified
and overwhelmed by the whole violent educational experience,
is reduced to an emotional shell, suffering a form of pedagogi-
cally induced post-traumatic stress disorder. Maguire, the most
obvious victim, also internalises the violence and to an extent
replicates the model of morality presented to him in the classroom by profiting from the exploitation of prostitutes, cleverly
juxtapositioning Kane in a responsive binary. Each 'raving'
question, from the frightening concept of the mystical blood to
the exploration of hell, sin and salvation, was answerable with a
preset formula, and the consequent effects on Kennelly clearly
point to the origins of his often-expressed distrust of intellectual
and emotional complacency:

> There was no discussion, only questions and answers. If a
> question is framed in such a way that it says to you 'I'm
> going to ask you about this most amazing mystery and here
> is the answer; you must learn off his answers and give it back
> to me', it's a formula for total intellectual slavery and I think
> it took me many years to shake off that need to give an an-
> swer (Murphy, *Education and the Arts*, 52).

The catechism was the predominant pedagogical tool used by
the Catholic Church in Ireland from the inauguration of the
national school system in Ireland in 1831 until after Vatican II in
the early 1960s and the rote learning associated with it would be
an integral part of the collective memory of generations of Irish
people. The word catechism comes from the Greek *katekhismos*,
which means to teach by word of mouth and it refers to a sum-

mary of Christian teaching and principles built around a strict
question and answer formula. The catechisms became particularly popular in the post-reformation period when the Catholic
Church was extremely concerned with the preservation of doctrinal and moral truth and the elimination of the contagion of
personal interpretation. From the nineteenth to the mid-twentieth centuries catechisms were designed for use in an Irish classroom context and they condensed official doctrine into shorter,
easily remembered phrases. As the focus of the catechism
moved from the pulpit to the classroom the material was simpli-
fied to suit the more general needs of the teacher and pupil and
the general catechism soon became one of the staple experiences
of the Irish primary school system.

There were two Irish traditions of catechisms which exercised an enormous influence on religious instruction in Irish
schools for over 250 years. The first catechism tradition came
from the catechisms of Andrew Donleavy (1680-1746) and
Michael O'Reilly (d. 1758). The second tradition stems from the
Butler Catechism, so called because it originated from the catechism written by the Archbishop of Cashel, Dr James Butler
(1774-1791). Butler's catechism, which was originally published
around 1775, was revised in 1802 and it soon became known as
Butler's General because the hierarchy adopted it as a catechism
for general use in Ireland. A further revision of Butler's General
in 1882 became known as the Maynooth Catechism and it is important to note the crucial influence these texts had on the religious formation of Irish clergy and laity for almost two hundred
years. James Joyce illustrated how the catechism had permeated
the intellectual and social fabric of everyday Irish life as he set
the scene for his short story, 'A Painful Case', published in
Dubliners in 1914. He describes the contents of James Duffy's
gloomy Chapelizod room and notes that on a wooden bookcase
'A complete Wordsworth stood at one end of the lowest shelf
and a copy of the Maynooth Catechism, sewn into the cloth
cover of a notebook, stood at one end of the top shelf'.[9] For a

9. James Joyce, *Dubliners*, Introduction and Notes, Terence Brown
(London: Penguin, 1992), p 103.

writer so fond of narrative framing, it is fascinating to see the bookshelf bound by the consciousness-awakening power of perhaps the greatest of the High English Romantic poets on the one hand and the moral certitude offered by the Maynooth Cathechism on the other. This inclusion in *Dubliners* is a literary testimony to the social and cultural prevalence of the catechism and its central role in the formation of the Irish Catholic psyche, a psyche that so many late twentieth and early twenty-first century Irish writers have struggled to deconstruct.

For the first half of the twentieth century (Kennelly attended Ballylongford National School from 1940 to 1948) the catechism became so identified with religious instruction in primary schools that the two almost became identical. The catechism is in many ways an extraordinary document in that it attempts to dilute the most complex philosophical and religious questions to the most basic of formulae, yet the fundamental pedagogical flaws in its construction become apparent on close examination, and it can only be imagined what effect it would have had upon the more sensitive and receptive pupils in the classroom. Clear concise questions are followed by short focused answers and in one sense catechisms functioned as part of a rote learning system that was very much in favour in the early decades of the Free State, ranking alongside what were known in Ireland as 'tables' (rote learning of numerical addition, subtraction, multiplication and division). However, the reduction of some of the most complex religious and philosophical questions to a series of pedantic questions and answers elided any sense of wonder and enquiry that the children might have experienced. Indeed, religious education, as delivered through the catechism, probably caused a great deal of confusion in the minds of children barely old enough to grasp even the most simple of its constructs. A typical illustration of this fissure comes from a woman who tells of her confusion as a seven year old child, in a 1920s catechism class, when she had to rote learn that there were 'seven deadly or capital sins, namely: Pride; Covetousness; Lust; Anger; Gluttony; Envy and Sloth.' She was puzzled by this as she counted eight sins, since she was under the impression that 'namely' was a deadly sin. To a child of seven none of these sins made any sense and so the catechism cultivated parrotism where 'namely' was as deadly as covetousness or sloth. The theologically laden content of the catechism was hugely inappropriate for children. Very bright children experienced considerable difficulties in memorising the doctrinal content which they failed to understand. One can only conjecture how torturous the catechism must have been for children who experienced difficulties in literacy, comprehension and memorisation. While children could recite the catechism off by heart many had little or no knowledge of what it meant. Furthermore, the dichotomy between the child's lived experience and the cerebral, legalistic language and concepts of the catechism was enormous, and it is clear from many of Kennelly's early poems, published in 1992 in a collection entitled *Breathing Spaces*, that he has spent a good deal of his life attempting to reconcile these oppositional world views. While other educators were profiling the psychological and intellectual development of the child and attempting to design child-centred, age-appropriate learning experiences, Irish catechists continued to ply the catechism and do untold harm to their ultimate spiritual goal. In a brilliant early poem, published in 1966, Kennelly hints at the dichotomy between preceived truth and personal perception:

> But vision is not simply seeing straight
> And things discoverable without exist within;
> My shells and birds are different, yet elate
> Me utterly. Images that spin
> Within these limits are my own,
> With colours, shapes and forms that I create,
> Discovered somewhere in the blood and bone –
> I only see whatever I can make.[10]

The nature of Kennelly's response to the negative aspects of his education appears to be a deeper understanding of the parasiti-

10. Brendan Kennelly, *Collection One: Getting Up Early* (Dublin: Allen Figgis and Co, 1966), pp 34-5.

cal nature of oppositional forces, such as good and evil, despair
and hope, right and wrong, and the attempted deconstruction of
these binaries is a recurring feature of his work. Kennelly's personal perception of the classroom world is teased out by its negativity and violence which then acts as a catalyst to the sensitivity
already present within him. It is only through this attempted
understanding of the nature of contrary beliefs that he can arrive
at an attempted appraisal of the nature of these uncertain, indef-
inite and paradoxical beliefs. Interestingly, in his essay on the
poetry of Joseph Mary Plunkett, Kennelly notes that Plunkett's
poem 'Heaven and Hell' is a 'dream-battle' in which the dominant impulse is to 'see, plainly and precisely, what exactly is evil
and what is good' (Persson, *Journey into Joy*, p 105) and this impulse is also clearly visible in *The Boats Are Home*. In the poem
'The Smell', Kennelly presents a more benign and organic perspective on the areas of religious faith, ritual and belief, portraying faith as something to be encountered on the level of personal
contact with an open-ended experiential philosophy concerning
the nature of life. Kneeling beside an old woman in a church, a
six-year-old child is entranced by the mesmeric effect of the
woman's whispering prayers and the lines of age on her face.
The kneeling woman is dressed in black because of a personal
bereavement, and is on her knees before the image of Christ on
the cross:

> The rent, dumb Christ, listener at the doors of the heart
> The pummelled Christ, the sea of human pain,
> The salted Christ, the drinker of horrors,
> The prisoner Christ, dungeoned on flesh and bone
> (*The Boats are Home*, p 14).

It is the smell of the woman that initially transfigures the boy
and allows him to transcend the inside of the church and the
'pallid Christ on the cross', facilitating the realisation that the silence of the church and the figure of Christ, a dumb, battered
and damaged icon, provides hope and a sense of security and
identity precisely as a result of its humanity, vulnerability and
weakness. The woman finally takes the young boy's hand and

they leave the church together, a peculiar union of the old and the young, the bereaved and the bewildered, and a typical Kennellian symbol of a patched, odd, yet quietly determined humanity. They leave the church and enter the now purged 'rain-cleaned air', the woman's mere presence having spoken to the boy 'beyond lips' whispers and heart's prayers', freeing him into one of his first, tentative, confusing yet exhilarating experiences of self-revelation. This formative mini-epiphany occurs against the backdrop of the security provided by the physical space of the church building and hints at the emergence of a spirituality that will, somehow, survive the ravages of the very processes designed to nurture it. It is precisely in this vignette of humanity's infinite struggle to understand the complex forces at play in the construction of self that Kennelly's poetry achieves its most effective critique.

CHAPTER EIGHT

Bad Cop, Good Cop: Dualistic Theology and Stephen's Neurotic Response to the Hellfire Sermons in Joyce's A Portrait of the Artist as a Young Man

Brian Cosgrove

The hellfire sermons in Joyce's *Portrait*, and Stephen's response to them, constitute a crucial (if, in a work which refuses closure(s), not quite climactic) moment in Stephen's development. The final sermon, on 'the spiritual torments of hell', including 'the pain of conscience', so affects Stephen that, guilt-stricken, he seeks out a chapel in Church Street, desperate to unburden himself of his sinfulness in confession, and desperate to be absolved of the psychologically intolerable burden of his guilt and shame.[1]

My initial concern here is with the images of God projected in this final sermon. The first image is of 'a just God' for whom 'even venial sin' cannot be allowed 'to pass unpunished'; because 'sin, be it in thought or deed, is a transgression of His law, and *God would not be God if He did not punish the transgressor*' (*PA*, p 144: italics added). It would, I feel, be a fair summary of the italicised words to say that God is, of necessity, or by his very nature, a punitive God. It is this God who (as the previous sermon has stated) prepares the fire of hell which, though it rages with 'incredible intensity', rages 'for ever' (*PA*, p 131); thus, 'the immortal soul [is] tortured in its very essence amid ... glowing fires kindled in the abyss by the offended majesty of the Omnipotent God and fanned into everlasting and ever increasing fury *by the breath of the anger of the Godhead*' (*PA*, p 131: italics added).

---

1. James Joyce, *A Portrait of the Artist as a Young Man*, ed. Seamus Deane (London: Penguin Group, 1992), pp 137, 138; 152. Hereafter referred to in the main text as *PA*.

Yet the final sermon ends with an image of God which is dia-
metrically opposed to this punitive God. This is the 'gentle and
compassionate Saviour' with a 'sacred and loving heart', and in
this version of the deity fire is associated not with intolerable
punishment but with abundant love; for this God is 'burning
with love for mankind'. God, the preacher concludes, is in spite
of everything 'still the merciful Lord Who wishes not the eternal
death of the sinner but rather that he be converted and live' (*PA*,
p 145).

Now there is an obvious and traditional way of responding
to the dualistic theology evident in these sermons, and it re-
quires little extrapolation from the sermons themselves to arrive
at it. God, we say, is a God of mercy as well as a God of justice.
Yet in invoking such a glib formula we may tend to overlook the
possible irreconcilability of the two concepts involved. Can anyone, even God, be both just *and* merciful? More pertinently, do
we not (correctly, in my view) tend to think of mercy as an over-
riding, a cancellation, of the claims of justice? Indeed (and here
we approach what is perhaps the heart of the matter) is there not
a central theological tradition in Christianity which interprets
the 'good news' delivered through the life and teachings (and
death) of Christ in precisely those terms? Christ inaugurates –
or, we might say, embodies – the 'new dispensation' which (we
need not shrink from the word) 'cancels' the old. Here, then, is a
clear opposition which, if pushed in a certain direction, yields an
increasingly radical dualism; and even if it appears suspiciously
simplistic, it has nonetheless an appealing or seductive symmetry.
Over against the old dispensation (the mosaic law of 'thou shalt
not') we set the liberating 'good news'; over against the Old
Testament, the New; and over against Jehovah, Jesus.

One of the most striking and extreme versions of such a theological dichotomy (Jesus versus Jehovah) will be found in the
poet William Blake, emerging as he does from a particular cultural formation in late eighteenth-century England. In Blake's
own mythmaking, Jehovah transmutes into Urizen, seen as an
abstract sky-god which, projected from our own distorted psyche,

represents a principle of repression and punishment. Such a figure derives from such negative feelings within ourselves as self-
denial (self-repression), envy (because we are aware of others
who act outside the strict law which we insist on enforcing
against ourselves) and fear (from one point of view Urizen is a
manifestation of the punitive superego identified by Freud). But
on the other hand, Jesus – in what amounts to an extremely radical humanism – embodies for Blake the fullest potential of humanity, once we have succeeded in liberating ourselves from self-
imposed negations. Jesus, in sum, is divinised humanity, not as
uniquely manifest in one particular human being, but as potentially realisable by all mankind.[2]

The importance of this aspect of Blake's thinking to the present argument is that he provides an extrapolation into clear and
explicit terms of a dichotomous tendency that is always potentially present in the Christian tradition. Given, however, that
Blake's dualistic theology here is, in the final analysis, so far removed from Christian orthodoxy as to lay itself open to the
charge of eccentricity, it might be more useful at this point to
highlight instead the radical Protestantism which, prevalent in
late eighteenth-century England, acted as influential matrix for
Blake's ideas (even if it does not fully account for his original
handling of them). In this focus upon late eighteenth-century
Protestantism we emphasise not the Jesus-Jehovah dichotomy,
but that other opposition mentioned earlier – New Testament
versus Old. As we shall see, the implications of that opposition
are indeed far-reaching.

We may begin by noting that for Blake Jesus is an example of
the type he terms 'the Outlaw': that is to say, Jesus, in acting out-

---

2. The heretical implications of this view are fully spelled out in a famous conversational exchange between Blake and Henry Crabb
Robinson: 'on my asking in what light he viewed the great question
concerning the Divinity of Jesus Christ, [Blake] said – *He is the only God*
– But then he added – "And so am I & so are you".' See Edith J. Morley,
(ed.), *Blake, Wordsworth, Coleridge. Lamb, Etc.: Being Selections from the
Remains of Henry Crabb Robinson* (New York: Ams Press, 1967), p 3.

side the law, is an antinomian figure.[3] Now Blake's own antinomianism clearly derives from the antinomian emphasis to be
found in the radical religious movements of the 1790s in
London; and among those who have situated Blake in that radical religious context are Marxist historian E. P. Thompson and
critic/literary historian Jon Mee.[4] In the words of Jon Mee, the
word antinomian indicates 'a heretical hostility to the authority
of the moral law' (*Dangerous Enthusiasm*, p 57). Following certain
passages in the epistles of St Paul,[5] antinomianism begins by declaring that the Law, or Ten Commandments, is not the source
of salvation; salvation, rather, is to be found only in a passionate
commitment to the teachings of Jesus who, in effect, replaces the
Ten Commandments with the liberating 'good news' of forgiveness and love.

Of crucial importance here is what is known as 'the doctrine
of imputed righteousness' (Mee, *Dangerous Enthusiasm*, p 57);
and according to this doctrine, all the work of our salvation has
already been accomplished for us through the self-sacrificing
life and death of Christ. Thus it was possible to believe, in the
words of Jon Mee, in 'a finished state of salvation in the here and
now' (*Dangerous Enthusiasm*, p 58). We have been saved; and the
Law has therefore no longer any hold over us. There arises in

---

3. In *The Marriage of Heaven and Hell*, plates 22-24, it is argued that 'no
virtue can exist' without breaking the Ten Commandments, and that
the virtuous Jesus repeatedly acted in that way (for example, turning
away the law from the woman taken in adultery): see *The Complete
Writings of William Blake, with Variant Readings*, (ed. Geoffrey Keynes
1957) (London: Oxford University Press, 1966), p 158.
4. E. P. Thompson, *Witness Against the Beast: William Blake and the Moral
Law* (Cambridge: Cambridge University Press, 1993); Jon Mee,
*Dangerous Enthusiasm: William Blake and the Culture of Radicalism in the
1790s* (Oxford: Clarendon Press, 1994).
5. For example, Galatians 2-3, especially 3:13: 'From this curse invoked
by the law Christ has ransomed us ...'; Romans 8:1-2: 'no judgement
stands against those who live in Christ Jesus ...' (quotations taken from
*The Holy Bible: A Translation from the Latin Vulgate in the Light of the
Hebrew and Greek Originals* (London: Burns and Oates/Macmillan and
Co., 1957), pp. 194, 154). See also Thompson, *Witness Against the Beast*,
pp 10ff.

consequence (again in Mee's summary) 'an active rejection of the authority of the law, sometimes to the point of rejoicing in sinfulness as an occasion for the outpouring of God's grace' (*Dangerous Enthusiasm*, p 58). Grace, then, is abounding; and, to use a metaphor not unfamiliar in theological accounts of the redemption, we who had once been debtors now have access to an infinite and inexhaustible source of wealth.

In one formula, then – and it is a formula that bears on the opposition between the Old Testament and the New – Christ has 'liberated humanity from the curse of sin under the mosaic law by offering himself as a "propitiatory sacrifice"' (*Dangerous Enthusiasm*, p 199: Mee is summarising a view found in a work of 1792 by W. B. Cadogan). It is, however, E. P. Thompson who is most quotably explicit with regard to the consequences of such antinomianism. The Ten Commandments, he states, and the gospel of Jesus are now seen to be 'directly opposed to each other: the first is a code of repression and prohibition [as embodied, we might add, in Blake's Urizen], the second a gospel of forgiveness and love'. And in an additional remark Thompson very clearly spells out the theological dualism to which such a situation gives rise. The two, he says – that is, the repressive code and the liberating gospel – 'might have flowed from the minds of *opposing gods*' (*Witness Against the Beast*, p 14: italics added).

It might be objected at this point that the radical views found in some strands of the Protestantism in London in the 1790s are too unorthodox to be representative; but, on the contrary – and this is absolutely central to my whole argument – I would hold that what such radical Protestantism does is simply elevate into high relief a faultline that is latent in the very core of the Christian tradition. The tension between a punitive and judgemental God, and a liberating and compassionate Jesus who is companionate with man – evident once again in the sermons in Joyce's *A Portrait*; or (to shift ground a little) a transcendent omnipotence (the God, say, who appears at the end of the Book of Job) and the God of Christianity memorably characterised by

Hans Küng as the God 'with a human face'[6] – that tension, always latent, may emerge recurrently as a troubling dualism in both the historical record of our culture and in our human psychology.

We may appear to have wandered rather far from the immediate topic of this paper, namely, the hellfire sermons in Joyce and Stephen's response to them; but the relevance of the preceding consideration of dualistic tendencies in Christian theology should be apparent. What in effect happens in the course of the hellfire sermons is that the preacher succeeds in exploiting the possibilities in the broad theological dualism we speak of, and does so, arguably, for his own adroitly judged rhetorical ends – his purpose being, ultimately, the psychological manipulation of his listeners. Stephen is, in terms of that rhetorical assault, bounced back and forth between the contrary images of the deity: and just as the suspect/witness eventually breaks down under the well-known 'bad cop, good cop' routine, so Stephen, bandied between the theological polarities of the final sermon, is reduced to a quivering neurotic mess.

His sins are the filthy sins of the flesh; sins which, the preacher has made clear in the second sermon, provoke disgust in the very devils themselves. For those devils, when they sinned, 'sinned by such a sin as alone was compatible with such angelical natures, a rebellion of the intellect; and they, even they, the foul devils must turn away, revolted and disgusted, from the contemplation of those unspeakable sins by which degraded man outrages and defiles the temple of the Holy Ghost, defiles and pollutes himself' (*PA*, p 133).[7] Stephen's sinfulness, he is convinced, merits the utmost punishment; he has deserved pain and suffering and humiliation of the most extreme kind.

Later, in *Ulysses*, Stephen will have to grapple with the

---

6. Hans Küng, *On Being a Christian*. Translated by Edward Quinn. (London: Collins, 1977), p 300.

7. As Joyce would surely have been aware, this suggestion that lust is a greater sin than pride (the 'rebellion of the intellect') is a clear contradiction of central Christion teaching; but the preacher, of course, intends to make maximum emotive use of his material.

psychologically incapacitating guilt over his refusal to declare his willingness to act as an orthodox Catholic in the face of his dying mother's appeal to him from her death-bed. And in both instances – his response to the hellfire sermons in *A Portrait* and this later guilt in *Ulysses* – we do well to recall Nietzsche's investigation into the nature of guilt, and his suggestion that it relates to a masochistic tendency to inflict upon the self that innate capacity for (destructive) power we more usually (in Nietzsche's view) inflict upon others.[8] In a section called 'The Genesis of Christianity out of Resentment', Jorg Salaquarda, in his essay on 'Nietzsche and the Judaeo-Christian Tradition', comments on how, in *Genealogy*, Nietzsche describes the rise of 'ascetic priests' in western culture and the way in which they (in Salaquarda's summary) 'offered to the slaves a new scapegoat on which to blame their sufferings; their own sinfulness'.[9] Salaquarda, however, offers in a footnote a description, 'in terms of depth psychology', of those who accept such a proposition: 'The adherent of a religion of resentment is a neurotic who has become comfortable with his neurosis and resists therapy' (*Cambridge Companion*, p 113).[10]

Stephen's psychological predicament with regard to the hellfire sermons (to return to that) arises from his vacillation from a masochistically self-imposed abjection, to a desperate clutching

8. For example, Nietzsche, treating guilt under the heading of what he calls 'bad conscience', argues that the phenomenon of bad conscience, seen as a case of 'secret self-violation', arises when the 'form-creating and violating nature' of the will to power vents itself on 'man himself, the whole of his old animal self – and not ... the other man, other men' (*On the Genealogy of Morals*. Translated by Douglas Smith. (Oxford: Oxford University Press. 1996), pp 66-67).
9. See *The Cambridge Companion to Nietzsche*, Bernd Magnus and Kathleen M. Higgins, eds., (Cambridge: Cambridge University Press, 1996), p 106.
10. I am aware that my treatment of the idea of a religion of resentment (Nietzsche uses the French form *ressentiment*) is far too cursory; but the thinking behind Nietzsche's formulations would require a much lengthier consideration than is possible at this point. The reader might find it useful to consult Douglas Smith's 'Introduction' in the edition of *Genealogy* cited, especially pp xv-xx.

at a possible reinstatement through the merciful compassion of the alternative deity revealed in the preacher's cunning formulations. He is the filthiest and vilest of sinners; but lo! at the very nadir of his abjection and self-hatred, there approaches him that loving Saviour who will, out of his abundant love and mercy, raise and sustain and (above all) accept this wretched creature who has every right to fear the worst. It is hardly in a glib or superficial way that one may suggest the parallel with the bad cop/good cop routine as a means of understanding both the psychological pressures faced by Stephen, and his reaction to these. In any case, he undergoes, unsurprisingly, a temporary psychological collapse. He who had aspired to be free, mature and autonomous, ends up in the confessional, abjectly 'praying with all his trembling body, swaying his head to and fro like a lost creature, praying with whimpering lips. – Sorry! Sorry! O sorry!' (PA, p 155). The word 'whimpering' indicates that Stephen is not just less than mature here (whimpering like a child), but also that he has been reduced to something less than human (whimpering like an animal, or 'creature'); and whether or not one agrees with Nietzsche's precise way of expressing it, one can surely accept that guilt of this kind – induced, manipulatively, by the preacher – is a humanly debasing experience whereby the psyche masochistically punishes itself.[11]

*

The final questions I wish to pose here are really the same ques-

---

11. The specific question at stake here is whether or not guilt (or the even less rational experience of shame) is a pathological condition, or at least includes elements of the pathological; more generally, the question is whether or not there is a possible connection between religion and neurosis. Nietzsche's analysis in *Genealogy* is perhaps more persuasive than the notorious attempt by Freud to characterise religion as collective neurosis in such a work as the *Future of an Illusion*. Significantly, near the beginning of section V of *A Portrait*, Stephen, now more stable if not much more mature, on his way to university hears the voice of a representative holy celibate who is anything but mentally stable: 'a mad nun screeching in the nuns' madhouse beyond the wall'. Stephen, we read, 'shook the sound out of his ears by an angry toss of his head' (*PA*, p 189).

tion worded in two different ways. How are we to resolve the tension between the two (perhaps irreconcilable) images of God potentially operative within the broad Christian tradition? Or, do we really need to believe in a God who is severely punitive? The tension might be lessened (if not fully resolved) if we could translate the fearsome all-powerful God into alternative terms that would dilute our fears of God the punisher; which really entails the answer to the first question: do we really need a punitive God?

We might begin by recalling an established theological awareness of the inadequacy of all the (limited) human terms by which we undertake to describe the nature of God. Recently, the Anglican theologian Keith Ward has insisted on 'how deeply the idea of the ultimate unknowability of God is rooted in the major traditions of thinking about God'; and he points out that the 'absolute difference between God and anything else is basic for Jewish prophetic thought', which 'means that *none of the symbols and images of God in the Bible can be literally applied to God*'.[12] We can apply this general insight to the specific notion of God as 'wrathful' or 'punitive'; that is to say, such terms are the inadequate formulations of a limited human language, and may not be literally true of God. The terms, we might say, point to a divine reality which they cannot precisely describe.

One way of arriving at a somewhat different terminology whereby we register the notion of a fearsome God in a more acceptable form is indicated in Rudolf Otto's classic work on *The Idea of the Holy*. Speaking of the 'wrath of Jehovah', Otto relates such 'wrath' to the *mysterium tremendum*, to the awesome nature of the numinous as such. His gloss on the word 'wrath' is worth quoting at length. In using the phrase 'wrath of God', he says, 'we are not concerned with a genuine intellectual "concept", but only with a sort of illustrative substitute for a concept. "Wrath" here is the "ideogram" of a unique emotional moment in religious experience ...' He goes on to stress that this is not a 'natural'

---

12. Keith Ward, *God: A Guide for the Perplexed* (2002; Oxford: Oneworld Publications, 2003), pp 59; 46 (italics added).

wrath: 'rather it is an entirely non-[natural] or supernatural, that is, numinous quality', which arouses 'a terror no "natural" anger can arouse'.[13] He warns us later against the 'one-sided doctrine' whereby 'the mystical character of the "wrath"' is mistakenly taken 'as righteous anger or indignation' (*Idea of the Holy*, p 100). What the sense of God's anger points to 'is simply the non-rational element of "awefulness", the *tremendum*, for which "wrath", "fire", "fury", are excellent ideograms' (*Idea of the Holy*, p 107).

Those who are familiar with the rise of the idea of the sublime in aesthetic theory from the mid-eighteenth century onwards will readily discern a similarity between the 'awesome' or 'terrible' aspects of sublimity and the awesome nature of the numinous, of the *mysterium tremendum*. It would be a crass reduction to see the effects produced by the sublime as a vulgar kind of 'fear'; rather, the experience of the sublime can be expressed as a humbling of the mind before the immeasurable, accompanied by an expansive sense of the magnitude or even 'infinity' which the sublime experience mediates.[14] Equally, the 'fear' of the divine should be no vulgar fear, but a privileged insight into that which lies outside both human comprehension and human language – disorientating and disconcerting, of course, but not promoting the tight, self-regarding recoil which the word 'fear' may suggest. Fear of that kind would be generated only if – and this is the general point Otto wants to make – we allow ourselves to attribute to an awe-inspiring manifestation of the numinous such lower-order (human) characteristics as anger or vindictiveness.

With some of the discriminations made by Otto in mind, we

---

13. Rudolf Otto, *The Idea of the Holy: An Enquiry into the Non-Rational Factor in the Idea of the Divine and its Relation to the Rational*. Translated by John W. Harvey (1923; London: Oxford University Press, 2nd edn., reprinted 1969), p 19.

14. One of the most informative considerations of the sublime (although to some extent overtaken by subsequent studies), is Thomas Weiskel's *The Romantic Sublime: Studies in the Structure and Psychology of Transcendence* (Baltimore: Johns Hopkins University Press, 1976), which makes astute use of Kant's ideas on the sublime.

might now retrospectively argue that the angry God of the hell-fire sermons in *A Portrait* is a distorted or reductive version of that awesome deity who (as *mysterium tremendum*) rightly induces what we call 'fear' (though not fear of the kind induced in Stephen by the sermons). It suits the preacher, of course – who has certain pragmatic ends in view – to induce that kind of lower-order fear (as a prelude to what we call repentance); but, as we have seen, the psychological effects are destructive for Stephen.

Otto is helpful and illuminating in pointing a way forward beyond what has threatened to become an impasse; but even Otto cannot wholly move beyond the dualism which has been one of the main concerns in this essay. Thus, when he refers to the experience of the numinous as that 'unique emotional moment in religious experience', he feels obliged to add that it is a moment 'whose singularly *daunting* and awe-inspiring character must be gravely disturbing to those persons who will recognise nothing in the divine nature but goodness, gentleness, love, and a sort of confidential intimacy ...' (*Idea of the Holy*, p 19). And elsewhere he contrasts 'the bliss-giving character' of 'the God who "overbrims with pure goodness"' with 'the awe-inspiring character of the transcendent' as that is found in 'the God of sternness and punishment and justice' (*Idea of the Holy*, p 103).

Two final points. Even if we accept Otto's insistence on the difference between what we usually understand by 'wrath', and his own account of the numinous, we may still find ourselves treading a thin psychological line between the problematically similar notions of God as awesome and God as punitive/fear-inducing. Consequently the capacity for guilt and self-abasement before a punitive God remains a real possibility. But, on the other hand – and this is the second point – it might be asked whether we do not in fact need, not only to retain, but indeed to restore to our consciousness some sense of God as *mysterium tremendum*. In an increasingly secular world, we appear to be in danger of losing all sense of the category of the sacred. It seems, for example, a throwback to a pre-modern era to recall that

among the seven gifts of the Holy Ghost in the sacrament of confirmation (along with wisdom, understanding, counsel, forti-
tude and knowledge) was not only piety but fear of the Lord.

One difficulty will be to retain the high valuation we place on
the human and human freedom (part of the Enlightenment heritage), while at the same time trying to look to realities beyond
the human. A good test case or challenge might be found in the
conclusion of the Book of Job: and it may be appropriate to end
on a question. Anthropomorphically considered, the God who
at the end puts Job in his place comes across as Mr Big, himself
immune to the kind of suffering Job has undergone, and possessed of a power which allows him to call all the shots – a kind
of *capo di tutti capi*. But if we look beyond that human characterisation of the deity, might we not accept that what Job must rightly learn
(in an act of humility which is not a self-abjection) is that there
are indeed, as Job himself says, 'things far beyond my ken'?[15]

15. *The Book of Job*, 42:3; in *The Holy Bible* (as cited in footnote 5), p 478.

CHAPTER NINE

'I have looked on God and found him lacking': Catholicism and Homosexuality in the Plays of Frank McGuinness

Kenneth Nally

Today the Catholic Church is led by a man who has proclaimed homosexuality an 'evil',[1] a view which has informed the guidance offered to Catholic politicians and legislators in states preparing to offer legally to recognise gay marriages.[2] That the past decades have seen the main Irish political parties differ from the Catholic Church on a range of moral issues including contraception, the right to remarry and the decriminalisation of homosexuality, suggests Rome may perceive that Irish politicans could be in need of such direction. It was not always so, for of course Ireland has its own history of oppressing those who sought to challenge the moral authority of the Church and from its foundation, Ireland, infused with a Catholic ethos, was characterised by a generally conservative censorious climate. Through a consideration of the works of Donegal playwright Frank McGuinness this chapter looks at how Catholicism has shaped attitudes to homosexuality in modern Ireland and explores how McGuinness's work has challenged this outlook over the past twenty years. I also believe that an examination of McGuinness's work allows us to trace the demise of his religious

---

1. Congregation for the Doctrine of the Faith, *Letter to the Bishops of the Catholic Church on the Pastoral Care of Homosexual Persons*, 1 October 1986. Http://vatican.va/roman_curia/congregations/cffaith/documents/rc_con_faith_doc_19861001_homosexual-persons_en.html.
2. Congregation for the Doctrine of the Faith, 'Considerations regarding proposals to give legal recognition to unions between homosexual persons', Http://vatican.va/roman_curia/congregations/cffaith/documents/rc_con_faith_doc_2003073_homosexual-unions_en.html 28 March 2003.

belief, a process of secularisation that can be connected to disil-
lusionment with the Church's teachings, and that may be said to
be reflective of the increasing secularisation of modern Ireland.

The twentieth century was a century punctuated in Ireland
by the regular efforts of public bodies to resist and restrict the
liberalisation of sexual attitudes, efforts particularly prevalent in
Irish theatre. For Instance, Christopher Murray's *Twentieth-
Century Irish Drama* tells how 'when Behan's *The Quare Fellow*
was staged at the Abbey in 1956 Ernest Blythe was concerned
that the homosexual should not be performed as such'.[3] Nor
were such attitudes the preserve of de Valera's Ireland. In 1973
as the Gate Theatre Dublin prepared to present Mícheál
MacLiammóir's *Prelude on Kasbeck Street*, a play that explored
same-sex desire, director Hilton Edwards wrote: 'there is a tendency to fear the theme'.[4] Such fear was not without reason for
any theatre company seeking funding. In January 1977 Dublin
City Council refused to renew the annual grant to the Project
Theatre Dublin following the Project's staging of two plays that
dealt with homosexuality, while in 1990 Wet Paint Theatre
Company failed to receive financial support from the Dublin
County Council to tour the play *Tangles*, a play that used
Shakespeare's *Twelfth Night* as the framework for an exploration
of homosexual issues in 1990s Dublin.[5] Even such a cursory survey illustrates that Ireland was Catholic in more than Constitution. And even after the Irish State decriminalised homosexual
acts in 1993 its public representatives did not shy away from
voicing their homophobia. The 1994 Dáil Debate on Equality

---

3. Murray also points out that points out that Séamus De Búrca noted
that 'wisely the actor ignored the direction.' Séamus De Búrca, *Brendan
Behan: A Memoir* (Dublin: P. J. Bourke, 1993) p 29; quoted in Christopher
Murray, *Twentieth-Century Irish Drama: Mirror up to Nation* (Manchester:
Manchester University Press, 1997), p 173.
4. Christopher Fitzsimons, *The Boys* (Dublin: Gill and MacMillan, 1994),
p 295.
5. On Wet Paint's difficulties see Murray, *Twentieth-Century Irish Drama*,
p 175; On *Tangles* see David Grant, "'Tangles': Addressing an unusual
audience," *Sex, Nation and Dissent in Irish Writing*, ed. Eibhear Walshe
(Cork: Cork University Press, 1997), pp 235-251.

saw a TD protest that he was 'concerned about the possible effects on Irish society' and ask: 'will we now see exhibitions in
public by homosexuals holding hands, kissing, cuddling, etc?'[6]
Moreover, such homophobia remains in keeping with the most
recent of the Catholic Church's teachings, so much so that the
fact that homosexuality remains a taboo amongst broad sections
of Irish society is due in no small part to the teachings of the
Catholic Church. In light of this fact, gay men and women in
Ireland are no doubt thankful for the recent assertions of the
State's ability to determine its own morality independently of
the Catholic Church. While this development is laudable it is
also true that recent legislation gives a misleading impression of
Ireland as a liberal society at ease with diversity. The reality is
that if Ireland has belatedly liberalised in recent times, it is also
true that Irish society retains some of the repressive aspects of its
past, particularly in relation to homosexuality. The contradictions of Ireland today may be symbolised in the detail that a
State with a separated Taoiseach who feels comfortable attend-
ing State events with his female partner, with a Taoiseach who
has said he sees economic rather than moral obstacles to issues
such as same-sex marriages,[7] is also a State with a Taoiseach
who presides over a Dáil with only one inadvertently outed gay
TD. Southern Ireland has just seen the establishment of Garda
Liasion Officers for the Gay and Lesbian Community, a confidential service specifically aimed at those gay men and women
who feel unable to report homophobic hate-crimes for fear of
publicity while, in the North, Evangelical Christian groups are

---

6. Paul McGrath TD in a Dáil debate on equality legislation. Quoted in
Lance Pettit's 'Pigs and Provos, Prostitutes and Prejudice: Gay
Representation in Irish Film, 1984-1995', *Sex, Nation and Dissent in Irish
writing*, pp 252-84. p 252.
7. While Bertie Ahern remains reticent on the issue of same-sex mar-
riage he has acknowledged the rights of homosexual couples saying:
'These people are in relationships which are not illegal, they're not im-
moral, they're not improper.' Quoted in Kevin Rafter, 'Church and
State Agree on one Thing – Gay Marriage is Out', *Sunday Tribune*, 10
July 2005, p 10.

preparing to protest at Belfast's annual Gay Pride parade.[8] It is, then, an appropriate time to consider the relationship of gay men and women to religious and national identity.

As mentioned above, Pope Benedict XVI, in his earlier guise as Cardinal Ratzinger, outlined his interpretation of homosexuality in the starkest, most draconian terms. During his tenure as prefect of the Congregation for Doctrine of the Faith, Cardinal Ratzinger disciplined and silenced advocates of liberal theology with statements so forceful that the ICCL warned in 1995 that those who distributed his publications could be in violation of the 1989 Incitement to Hatred Act.[9] For instance, in October 1986 Cardinal Ratzinger published a document which is somewhat misleadingly entitled: *On the Pastoral Care of Homosexual Persons*, a letter which referred to homosexuality as an 'intrinsic moral evil',[10] while a more recent publication by the Congregation for the Doctrine of Faith, dated 28 March 2003, again describes homosexual activity as 'evil' and states 'those who would move towards tolerance to the legitimisation of specific rights for co-habitating homosexual couples need to be reminded that the approval or legitimisation of evil is far different from the toleration of evil'.[11] Such documents are 'intended to give direction to Catholic politicans by indicating the approaches to proposed legislation in this area' and are conceived in response to the 'troubling moral and social phenomenon' that is homosexuality in the eyes of the Catholic Church.[12]

It is clear from such publications that despite recent advancements in the Roman Catholic position on homosexuality, little

8. Protest group *Stop the Parade* claimed it was 'offensive' and stated that 'as evangelical Christians we believe what the Bible says regarding sodomy – that it is a sin – and for that reason we want to oppose a parade that we see is promoting a sinful life'. See BBC News (world edition), 28 June 2005. http://news.bbc.co.uk/hi/uk_news/northern_ireland/4629881.stm.

9. Liam Reid, 'Legal Warning to Church on Gay Stance', *The Irish Times*, 14 July 2005.

10. *On the Pastoral Care of Homosexual Persons*.

11. 'Considerations regarding proposals'.

12. 'Considerations regarding proposals'.

has really changed from the traditional doctrine of total rejection. Previously sexuality was exclusively viewed as a matter between males and females. This viewpoint was adapted during the twentieth century as behavioural research revealed that sexual orientation was not necessarily a matter of choice. Today the Catholic Church's position has become somewhat conflicted: homosexuality can be viewed as natural and even biological, but is still viewed at best as 'objectively disordered',[13] and at worst as 'an intrinsic moral evil'.[14] This leads to a critical distinction for the Catholic Church as theological teaching dictates that sin only occurs in matters where there is an element of personal choice. While it is possible to infer that if one's sexual orientation is not chosen, then it also cannot be sinful, homosexual behaviour and acts are still conceived of as sinful as they relate to personal choice. The Church argues that a person can choose to embrace celibacy and chastity so that by 'the virtues of self-mastery ... they can and should gradually approach Christian perfection'.[15] The Church's official position on homosexuality can be found in the Catechism, n 2358, which states that homosexuals 'do not choose their homosexual condition; for most of them it is a trial ... these persons are called to fulfil God's will in their lives and, if they are Christians, to unite to the Lord's Cross the difficulties they may encounter in their condition.' For the purpose of this chapter I want to look at how Frank McGuinness has challenged this notion that homosexuality is 'a trial'. Indeed McGuinness's works, as we will see, have often suggested that homosexuality is a trial because gay men and women are persecuted by religious bigots.

In 1986, McGuinness's work showed itself to be concerned with Catholicism on the most fundamental level. His play, *Innocence*, recreates the life of the late Renaissance Italian painter, Caravaggio. *Innocence* sees McGuinness's most in-depth exploration of the faultlines between gayness and Catholicism for it is

---

13. *Catechism of the Catholic Church*, n 2358.
 http://www.vatican.va/archive/catechism/cc_doc.htm.
14. *On the Pastoral Care of Homosexual Persons*.
15. *Catechism of the Catholic Church*, no] 2359.

a play which explores homosexuality in relation to Catholicism and Church leaders. Critical of the Catholic Church and its shaping of societal responses, the play set McGuinness on a collision course with the Church and its production drew protests from some people who deemed it sacriligious. Many may argue that late Renaissance Rome is hardly contemporary Ireland. But, despite its setting, the Gate production of *Innocence* was not designed as a purely historical work, something evident from the use of Irish accents, and the fact McGuinness 'used the city of Derry as … [the] model for the Rome' of Caravaggio's time.[16] In a similar vein, set designer Joe Vanek has noted that the play was distinguished 'by a refusal to be frozen in anachronism – *Innocence* did not belong to a specific period'.[17] Indeed what drew the ire of many of the protestors were the parallels that were to be drawn between Renaissance Italy and Ireland and the graphic representation of homosexuality in relation to 'Irish themes' such as Catholicism, land and the family.

The source for all of this was Caravaggio for his paintings provided visual and thematic inspiration for McGuinness. Using models and painting from life, Caravaggio had created an enfranchising religious vision and popular accounts tell that when he needed a Virgin, a local whore posed for him; and similarly how his saints and apostles were humble men illumined by their faith.[18] Somewhat unsurprisingly, the Roman priests and public both preferred conventional elegance and illusionism and works on Caravaggio tell of how his ideas were often so disturbing that his patrons often failed to understand or appreciate them.[19] For example, his *Calling of St Matthew* shows the

---

16. McGuinness, 'Introduction', *Frank McGuinness: Plays 1* (London: Faber and Faber, 1996), p xi.
17. Joe Vanek, in conversation with Derek West, *Theatre Ireland*, 29, (Autumn, 1992), p 26.
18. *The Death of the Virgin* [Louvre, Paris] is the last painting that Caravaggio painted in Rome. It was commissioned for S. Maria del Scala but the Carmelites turned it down because it lacked decorum.
19. For instance Howard Hibbard, *Caravaggio* (London: Thames and Hudson, 1983); Peter Robbs, *M: The Man who Became Caravaggio* (London: Bloomsbury, 2000).

future evangelist among a group at a public tavern. In this painting a significant darkness hangs over the table and its monetary
concerns. Despite the anti-materialist implications the work was
initially refused by the Church for which it was painted;
notwithstanding the fact that the story is told by Matthew himself, it was deemed to present the saint in a situation that was de-
cidedly too worldly. Caravaggio's paintings were also characterised by a determination to represent a physicality that could
not be cloaked. For example, in the best known version of
Caravaggio's *The Sacrifice of Isaac*, in contrast to previous austere
and academic representation, we witness Isaac's face twisted in
terror as Abraham's garnelled fingers press against the flesh of
his cheek. The terror and trauma evident emphasise the earthy
and uncomfortable aspects of the sacrifice. A somewhat similar
physicality and worldliness is evident in McGuinness's
Caravaggio in the scene where he recognises that he is both
'painter and pimp. Painter to Cardinal del Monte, pimp to the
Papal Curia, whore to the Catholic Church'[20] as much as it is
evident when he loudly proclaims that he has: 'been up the arses
of more priests'[21] than he cares to remember. And while
McGuinness clearly had a confrontational objective, for this
statement is designed to challenge the moral authority of a
hypocritical Church in Ireland, we should not ignore that this
was a reality of Caravaggio's time. McGuinness's Caravaggio
was a creation that had its origins in historical accounts, both of
Caravaggio and of Renaissance Italy, a society for which the existence of social networks involving male-male eroticism has
been particularly well-documented.[22] For example, the sculptor

20. McGuinness, *Innocence* in *Plays I*, pp 199-290. p 239.
21. McGuinness, *Plays 1*, p 247.
22. In his historical account of same sex categorisations, David F.
Greenberg points out that 'between 1432 and 1502, approximately 25
percent of the male population of Florence – by modern standards a remarkably high percentage – was arrested on Sodomy charges.' David F.
Greenberg, 'Transformations of Homosexuality-based Classifications,'
in *The Gender/Sexuality Reader: Culture, History, Political Economy*, Roger
N. Lancaster and Micaela di Leonardo, eds., (NY: Routledge, 1997),
pp 179-193. p 181.

Cellini, convicted twice of consensual sodomy, was handled quite typically. Despite having been both fined and placed under house arrest for convictions for activities the Church designated as sinful, he was commissioned by the Church and was buried with full honours when he died.

Perhaps as a consequence McGuinness does not pull any punches in *Innocence*. Caravaggio's inclusive vision rejected idealism in favour of realism and in writing *Innocence* McGuinness, inspired by the centrality of the marginalised in Caravaggio's paintings, sought to achieve a similar foregrounding of those whom the contemporary Catholic Church had marginalised, such as gay men and women. The result is that with a deliberate irreverence he subversively and defiantly queers Catholicism. Throughout the play, religion is continually presented in carnal terms that satirise the Church's condemnation of homosexuality: the whore compares Caravaggio and Lena to the Holy Family while Caravaggio quotes the Bible and the liturgy with an irreverence that is intentionally blasphemous. Sexuality and the Church are also connected through the actions of rentboys Lucio and Antonio whose mock ritual reconstructs the Catholic doctrine of transubstantiation into a process that offers a socio-economic rationale for their prostitution. In Lucio's and Antonio's adaptation they hope the sale of their bodies will enable them to have bread and wine. It will be, they proclaim, 'a reverse job. Flesh and blood into bread and wine.' They pray to God to give them 'a miracle', to give them 'a man'.[23] The reason for McGuinness's lack of reverence in these scenes lies in his belief that Catholicism was a negative and suppressive spirituality typified by the Catholic Church's choice of 'the crucified Christ as its central emblem'.[24] It is this view of Catholicism which McGuinness explores and highlights when depicting Caravaggio's life. In his view, the relationship between Catholicism and homosexuality was as crucial in understanding Caravaggio as it was in explor-

23. McGuinness, *Plays 1*, p 222.
24. McGuinness, 'The Out Interview,' interview with Gerald McNamara, *Out*, Nov/Dec 1986. p 20.

ing the situation of gay Catholics in 1980s Ireland, for in Caravaggio he identified a despair and a sense of rejection which he considered still relevant to Catholic gay men and women in Ireland. Thus in *Innocence*, where McGuinness explores the denunciation Caravaggio perceived to be emanating from the Church and Catholicism, a central theme is that it enforces Caravaggio's feeling of damnation, a sense of fate which is particularly due to his sexuality.

For McGuinness Caravaggio's sense of damnation was evident from many of his paintings and he drew on these paintings when reimagining Caravaggio's life. Many of the props for the play are found in Caravaggio's paintings while the play moves through a series of tableaux which visually recreate Caravaggio's paintings. For instance, the opening of Act Two shows Caravaggio with his head in Lena's lap in a recreation of *The Resurrection of Lazarus*. This painting also contains a red cloak, a common feature of many of Caravaggio's paintings. When writing the play McGuinness identified a red cloak as an intertextual emblem of both Caravaggio's sexuality and the forces that contributed to his sense of damnation due to his homosexuality. As a consequence *Innocence* is both framed and punctuated by this particular emblem and from the very start the red cloak signifies both Caravaggio's destructive sexuality and also its social and religious inhibitors. The stage directions at the opening of *Innocence* state: 'Detached from them, Caravaggio observes, fingering a skull. Lena caresses a red cloak, like a child. Antonio and Lucio caress each other. Whore rocks herself to and fro, weeping. Cardinal recites the Offertory from the Tridentine Mass, holding a host. Servant kneels at the Cardinal's feet, with Brother. Sister moves through the circle, repeating her prayer.'[25] As the Latin of the Mass transforms into animal sounds the red cloak begins to stretch and transfer wildly amongst the characters until its shape becomes that of a horse. Though what is being shown is but a dreamscape, it is one in which the Church has become a perverse debilitating force as indicated when the

---

25. McGuinness, *Plays 1*, p 205.

red horse cloak proceeds to wrap itself around Caravaggio, forcing him into darkness. This action seems to have been inspired
by Caravaggio's work *The Conversion of St Paul*, something also
suggested by the fact that in the play McGuinness's Caravaggio
has been blinded by a horse's hoof. McGuinness's interpretation
of the painting may be seen to be in keeping with Caravaggio's
artistic vision for this painting sees Caravaggio's characteristi-
cally free interpretation of religious themes. In it, Paul is not on
the road to Damascus but inside a half-darkened stable dominated by a large horse. Conversly McGuinness draws on such
realism to convey the transcendence of Caravaggio's vision. By
the play's end the cloak rests around the dead Antonio in a dia-
logic recreation of Caravaggio's paintings *St John the Baptist*, and
more playfully, *Death of the Virgin*. It is, however, in Caravaggio's
words that McGuinness allows us to find the play's religious
vision. In having Caravaggio say: 'I paint as I see in light and I
imagine in darkness, for in the light I see the flesh and blood and
bone but in the dark I imagine the soul of man, for the soul and
the soul alone is the sighting of God in man and it is I who reveal
God and it is God who reveals my paintings to the world',[26]
McGuinness signals that Caravaggio's painting is a spiritual act
of communion and praise. Ironically in a play that was de-
nounced as sacrilegious, it seems McGuinness sought not so
much to blaspheme as to pray. In this his vision truly connected
with that of the historical Caravaggio, for if McGuinness chose
to depict Caravaggio and the extremes of his sexuality within a
religious context, his method of depicting the socially marginalised within a religious context was Caravaggio's own. In the
play the cardinal explains that Caravaggio reminds 'us of important truths'[27] as McGuinness suggests that Caravaggio does
God's work in celebrating those who have been marginalised,
rejected, lost. The point is also made that gay men and women
are primary among those who have been rejected by the Church.

---

26. McGuinness, *Plays 1*, p 209.
27. McGuinness, *Plays 1*, p 243.

By the 1990s McGuinness seems less spiritually involved
with Catholicism. His later plays have demonstrated none of the
concern with damnation that characterised *Innocence*. Instead
the focus is on the suffering of gay men as a consequence of the
religious belief of others. What was a minor theme in *Innocence*,
namely religiously motivated familial rejection, now comes to
the fore in his work. *Innocence* had seen the inital development
of this theme of familial rejection as the institutions of Church
and family united through the figure of Caravaggio's brother
who is a priest. Through this figure we see that adjoined to
Caravaggio's religious guilt is his belief that he has failed in his
family obligations to marry and to have children. Touched upon
here is the idea that being queer is a way of rejecting the connections of family. Such intolerance, sourced in Catholicism, is for
instance a concern in *The Bird Sanctuary*, a play that again sees a
Catholic mother reject her son on discovering that he is gay. The
play reflects the fact that in the early 1990s Ireland still retained
Victorian constructions of morality and was deeply influenced
by the thinking of the Catholic Church. In *The Bird Sanctuary*,
Tina, the mother, associates birds with blood, misfortune, and
death through her tale of the robin 'which got its red breast from
the blood of Jesus on the cross'.[28] She then speaks as follows: 'I
never liked birds. They're unlucky. Big black birds. That's what
it is. AIDS. There was a film on the television over Christmas.
The birds started to attack human beings ... and what had started
the attacking? Maybe it was cruelty, human cruelty. I have been
a cruel woman.'[29] Her interpretation of Hitchcock's *The Birds*
(1963) rereads it in terms of the AIDS crisis of the nineteen-
nineties. Tina is traumatised not only by the fear that her son
may die of AIDS but also by the fact that her faith has contributed to her own inability to accept her gay son. In part it also
reworks the extremely homophobic quasi-religious viewpoint
that sees AIDS as a plague sent by God to gay men and women.

---

28. Frank McGuinness, *The Bird Sanctuary* (Unpublished ts. Dublin Gate
Theatre), p 50.
29. McGuinness, *The Bird Sanctuary*, p 51.

As a consequence, Tina's speech focuses on the havoc that an intolerance that is sourced in Church teaching can wreak and draws the allegory of familial rejection in the starkest terms.

McGuinness further explored the contribution Catholicism has made to the intolerance of same-sex desire in his play *Dolly West's Kitchen*. The play premiered at the Abbey Theatre on 1 October 1999, as part of the Dublin Theatre Festival. Set during World War Two, or 'The Emergency' as it was termed in Ireland, the play chronicles in three acts the developments in the personal and sexual relationships of the various inhabitants of the household in Buncrana, Co Donegal, with a particular focus on the difficulties of being a gay man in a Catholic family. In *Dolly West's Kitchen* McGuinness again highlighs the intolerance of Catholicism and explicitly blames the Church for the suffering and rejection that many gay people experience within society and within their own families. It sees Marco, a gay American GI, announce: 'All I want from the Catholic Church is an apology. A long apology. And I hope they will understand when I refuse to accept it'.[30] He proceeds to inform of how he has suffered the bigotry of his Catholic family, and in particular his mother whom he refers to as 'our lady of Second Avenue'.[31] Here we learn from Marco that his mother: 'once found some sketches I'd done of dresses when I was seven years old. She poured ketchup on every page, salt and lots of pepper. She made me eat them one by one until I vomited. I thought it was blood, the red coming up my throat.'[32] Unsurprisingly, Marco is haunted by nightmares in which the colour red is prominent. However, the play also presents a contrasting if implausible example of familial acceptance in the case of Justin West, a man who has repressed and ignored his latent sexual orientation. It is left to his mother, Rima West, to push Justin to embrace his true self. What is interesting is that McGuinness illustrates how Irish Catholicism and

---

30. Frank McGuinness, *Dolly West's Kitchen* (London: Faber and Faber 1999), p 60.
31. McGuinness, *Dolly West's Kitchen*, p 60.
32. McGuinness, *Dolly West's Kitchen*, p 61.

nationalism can serve as obscuring agents when it comes to recognising one's sexual identity.

As the play progresses, we discover that Justin sought to take refuge in the Church before joining the army. Fearful of admitting his sexual identity, Justin drifts from the ritual and doctrine of Catholicism to the regimentation of the army and the quasi-spiritualism he invests Irish nationalism with, but as the action develops we learn that Justin is a man struggling with the nature of his self and his sexuality. Here Catholicism and nationalism are presented as providing inadequate strategies for resolution. Where the border is used by McGuinness to separate home from otherness, Catholic nationalism offers the crutch of a ready-made identity. In setting the play in Donegal, McGuinness utilises national partition as a metaphor for personal divisions, as he has Justin find a mirror for personal and familial disintegration in the public/communal conflicts. As a result, the play emphasises the need for self-assessment as European war is appropriated for national, sectarian statements. Ultimately, Marco, the flamboyant American GI who wears rouge so that no Nazi will bitch about his bone structure, forces Justin to reassess his gender, sexual and political alignment. Within the first interaction of the flamboyantly camp Marco and the stiff repressed Justin, a conflictual innuendo allows sexual and gender delineations to be explicitly linked with political:

Justin: A right gathering of the allies.
Marco: Boys together – that's right.
Justin: You've crossed the border
Marco: Hasn't everybody.[33]

With this exchange we have a linking of geographical, political and sexual borders. Marco offers Justin the possibility of liberation, the chance to cross his self-imposed limits, demarcations explicitly connected with Ireland and its restrictive Catholic society.

In a Catholic context McGuinness's objective in the above

33. McGuinness, *Dolly West's Kitchen*, p 28.

mentioned plays may be seen to point to an aspect of the
Catechism which his work shows has often been ignored by
Irish Catholics, namely that which states in relation to gay men
and women: 'they must be accepted with respect, compassion
and sensitivity'.[34] His work has consistently presented homosexuality in a positive light while simultaneously highlighting societal and familial oppression of same-sex couples and in this we
see one of the fundamental contradictions between McGuinness's
work and the teaching of the Catholic Church. Deliberately presenting alternatives to the two-parent heterosexual unit which is
normative in Ireland to this day, McGuinness tends to show audiences alternative families such as an officer in the Irish army
and an American GI. In each case what we learn from
McGuinness's representation of the alternative family units is
that despite the contentions of the Catholic Church, and the Irish
State as expressed in the Irish Constitution, heterosexual marital
love is not the only possible basis for a family. This is one of the
primary concerns of his work and in this he has been largely successful. And if McGuinness has been critical of the Irish State he
has been equally scathing in relation to the Church which
shaped the State's ethos. In particular he notes that the teaching
of the cChurch has impacted negatively on Catholics and non-
Catholics alike. While his work does not suggest that all these
may have experienced the same sense of spiritual damnation he
perceived in Caravaggio's work, he does suggest that all have
suffered to some degree at the hands of Church members. As a
consequence, his work over the past two decades has continued
to challenge the Church and its exclusiveness. It is here that we
see the damning indictment of the Catholic Church as expressed
in Marco Devecarrio's request for an apology that he will then
reject. The implication is that the rejection and condemnation
that the Catholic Church has issued to its gay members has resulted in a fissure that can never be reconciled and is one that
serves neither it nor its members well. However, perhaps the
most damning statement of the relations between the Catholic

---

34. *Catechism of the Catholic Church*, n 2359.

Church, its gay members, and their God is found in *Innocence* in the blessing issued to Caravaggio by Cardinal del Monte: 'Blessed be the feet that walk the way of damnation. Blessed be the eyes that see the same damnation, for they have looked on truth and found it lacking. I have looked on God and found him lacking.'[35]

35. McGuinness, *Plays 1*, p 275.

CHAPTER TEN

'I'd like to be this family please':
Tom Murphy and the De/construction of the Irish Catholic Family Home

Sara Keating

Home: a house or household, where one lives or where one's roots are; an environment offering affection and security; the place of one's dwelling or nurturing; where important decisions are made.

Home: a place to which one properly belongs; where one finds refuge, rest, or satisfaction; where missions start and end.

To feel at home, to be at home, to come home to, to hit home, to be home-made.

To the fullest extent, to the heart, to a vital sensitive core.

Home: the place in which one is free from attack; the point which one tries to reach; the goal.[1]

Drawn from a variety of lexical sources, these meanings are all consistent in their relation to the personal or private spheres, offering home as a 'felicitous space', a physical, spatial, and environmental entity as well as a spiritual or mental frame of mind.[2] Home is associated with intimacy, comfort, the personal, the familiar. It is both origin, where one starts from in mind and body, and destination, the final resting place, where our greatest desires can be fulfilled.

Divorcing language from its ideological function, however, is impossible, and the assemblage of ideological associations in

---

1. Definitions from the *Compact Oxford English Dictionary* and *Webster's Complete English Dictionary*.
2. Gaston Bachelard, *The Poetics of Space,* (Boston: Beacon Press, 1969), p xxxi.

the definitions offered above delimits both the word itself and its field of connotations, establishing home as a *discourse* rather than a site of occupation,[3] a discourse whose shifting meanings can be impossible to pin down without ignoring recent, modern ideological change or essentialising historical difference.

This chapter will discuss the fundamental conflict between public discourses and private experiences of the Irish Catholic home, as represented through the recurring representational trope of the dysfunctional Irish Catholic family, and taking the plays of Tom Murphy as a representative example. Textual and dramaturgical analysis, however, will remain secondary to a larger argument about the general deconstructive tendencies of these dramatic domestic representations; for if this survey of dysfunctional families is to have any wider value than mere literary significance, it must be approached by way of the oppositional sociological and ideological discourses of home that provide the conflict through which the various family dramas are played out.

In order to begin discussing the implications of Murphy's deconstructive dramatic practices, then, it is necessary to historicise the instances through which the dysfunctional dramatic domestic experiences arise; firstly, by examining the development of a particular collective ideology of the Irish Catholic home, and secondly by suggesting how the plays of Tom Murphy offer an alternative narrative of domestic experience. For, while the individual families in the plays may be socially contained by the Irish Catholic ideologies that define them, the overall function of the plays is to explode these ideologies, which have shaped public expression of private life but have denied personal experience in the process.

Constructing an Irish Catholic Family Model
While Gaston Bachelard and Rosemary George have argued that the modern home was 'constantly re-imagining its reality',[4]

3. Chaudhuri, Una, *Staging Place: The Geography of Modern Drama*, (Ann Arbor: University of Michigan, 1997), p 6.
4. Bachelard, *The Poetics of Space*, p 17. Also see Rosemary George, *The Politics of Home: Postcolonial Relocations and Twentieth-century Fiction*. (Cambridge: Cambridge University Press, 1996).

in post-independence Ireland the idea of home was fixed within the ideological limits of a constitutional definition shaped by a particular domestic model of Irish Catholicism. Rather than sharing the surplus of meaning offered in the philological examples that began this chapter, this Irish Catholic domestic model functioned more as an ideological discourse deeply rooted in issues of cultural and political nationalism than as a site of either belonging or existence, locating it within a discourse of national fiction rather than historical objectivity (or actual experience).

It was Éamon de Valera who was largely responsible for the institutionalisation of an Irish Catholic family model. This institutionalisation, however, happened in tandem with the increasing dominance of Catholicism in social and ideological affairs, which had been steadily gaining institutional control since the late nineteenth century. The relationship between Church and State and Church and family is important for, as an ideological unit, the Irish Catholic family became defined almost entirely by the parameters of the dominant religious discourse through which the Catholic Church governed the various social networks of Irish life. Tom Inglis links the dominance of the Catholic Church to the parallel growth in institutionalisation and moral discipline that were a pre-requisite for the modernisation of Irish society in the first decades of the nineteenth century.[5] Inglis links Catholic control of the Irish modernisation process to the failure of the 'civilising processes' of colonialism; with the failure of the Penal Laws to take effect in Ireland, the British government gradually began to hand the moral education of rural Ireland to the Catholic Church in an official capacity – any control, even Catholic, was preferable to anarchy.

Inglis sees the widespread development of a stem-family system in Ireland following the devastated post-Famine period as the nexus point of Ireland's 'civilising processes'. This system changed structures of inheritance within the family unit to the Western European stem system, whereby one son inherits all the

5. See Tom Inglis, *Moral Monopoly: The Rise and Fall of the Catholic Church in Modern Ireland* (Dublin: Gill and Macmillan, 1987).

land, helping to reduce the strain on economic resources and improve impoverished standards of living for the family. The Church was crucial in encouraging this development, and by conforming to the Church's economic advice the family found that they could increase their social status and their financial position. This relationship of legitimation, however, was not one-sided: as the family relied on the Church for social legitimation, so the Church depended on the family for the consolidation of its own power, even, on the most basic level, for its recruitment processes.

It was through the force of moral education, however, that the Catholic Church extended its influence to ideological control of the family. The Church produced 'specific ways of being religious and ethical'[6] and they saw the home as the site in which these Catholic ways could be monitored in the private sphere. By situating the development of religious and ethical responsibility within the home, they co-opted the institution of the family to their own institutional ends, developing an ideological alliance with the home through which the behaviour and development of the individual was continually monitored through the lens of Catholic morality.

Supported and regulated by the Church, the Irish Catholic family worked along the same lines of authoritarianism and patriarchy that the religious order followed, advocating collective obedience and self-abnegation among its members. It also limited the field of independence for the individual, by emphasising passivity and conformity, and for the family unit within society, by ensuring its compliance with the Catholic-influenced nationalist familial discourse. Furthermore, the Catholic associations of this family model encouraged the use of 'outward shame and internalised guilt'[7] as the primary controlling mechanisms of individual behaviour and individual subjectivity, which, if nothing else, provided a coherent discourse within which the operations

---

6. Inglis, *Moral Monopoly*, p 11.
7. Kerby, A. Miller, *Emigrants and Exiles: Ireland and the Irish Exodus to North America* (Oxford: Oxford Univerity Press, 1985), p115.

of the family could be regulated and measured. The very structure of family relations within this model was, however, as
Miller argues, 'designed to include a sense of duty and emotional
dependence rather than individuality or self-reliance'.[8]

This ideological reinforcement of a Catholic orthodoxy within
the home established a coterminous, interchangeable relationship between the institution of the home as an economic unit
and the institution of the family as the moral centre of the Irish
state. Individuals within this Catholic-inflected social orthodoxy
were thus defined by related ideologies of spirituality, frugality
and celibacy, creating social subjects subjugated to greater religious ideals in private life (at home) and in public life (in society).

Such images of an ideal moral-based family culture were
absorbed into the fabric of the Irish State, but it was under de
Valera's tutelage that the glaring exclusions of these ideologies
came to light, as he enshrined these ideals in the Irish Constitution despite their glaring contradiction with the economic and
social reality of the struggling Irish State. De Valera believed
that a firm moral foundation was the key to upholding the integrity of the State, and the family, he maintained, played a piv-
otal role in developing the moral personality of the individual
and, therefore, in ensuring the preservation of the Irish nation.
While de Valera was committed on one level to proving
Ireland's viability as a modern nation, his refusal to modernise
the discourses under which Ireland gained her definition highlighted the disparity between his fictional national ideals and
the reality of Irish life. By placing the family and the home at the
very centre of his historical illusion and his vision of the future,
he conflated the social and personal functions of the family to
political ends.

The central place ascribed to the family was officially recognised in the 1937 Constitution, constructed under the guidance
of Father (and later Archbishop) John Charles McQuaid, which
declared 'the Family as the natural primary and fundamental
unit group of Society and as a moral institution possessing in-

8. Miller, *Emigrants and Exiles*, p 115.

alienable and imprescriptible rights antecedent and superior to all positive law'. It was 'indispensable to the welfare of the nation and the State', and the State guaranteed to 'protect the Family ... as the necessary basis of social order.'[9]

The privileged place that the Constitution thus granted to the family within the ideological framework of the State was a necessary element of a wider nationalist project. By insisting on the reality of national ideals on a personal, domestic level, de Valera hoped to secure its articulation on a public level. De Valera's politics, therefore, became defined by the morality of the home, while the home was defined for the individual in idealistic nationalist terms as the place where he/she believed he/she could and should be protected from the dangerous influences of burgeoning change.

It is interesting to place a contemporary anthropological text alongside the Irish Catholic domestic model communicated in ideological discourse, as the methodological problems that it throws up mark the beginnings of the process through which ideology was absorbed into the writing of national history. A study by anthropologists Arensberg and Kimball entitled *Family and Community in Ireland*, published in 1940, illustrates the problematic ideological functioning of the official model of the Irish Catholic home. Posing as a 'unified anthropological history', Arensberg and Kimball used the rural community of the town of Ennis in Co Clare as their unit of analysis, developing an experiential argument from which they developed a sociological model of kinship structures in Ireland. By extending their field of study in Clare to accommodate the community functions of Ireland as a homogenous cultural and social unit, however, regardless of such critical developments as Ireland's recent political independence and burgeoning urbanisation, Arensberg and Kimball inscribed the peasant Catholic family model that they observed in a classic portrait of stability that reinforced the nationalist ideologies of de Valera's post-independent Ireland. This is not, of course, to suggest that their entire study should be.

---

9. Article 41, *Bunreacht na hÉireann: Constitution of Ireland* (1937).

dismissed as ideological fabrication; *Family and Community in Ireland* remains one of the few contemporary sources describing familial function in mid-twentieth century Ireland. Along with secondary studies by revisionist historian J. J. Lee, economist Finola Kennedy and sociologist Tom Inglis,[10] their primary evidence is fundamental for contextualising the dysfunctional Irish Catholic dramatic families that began to appear in the late 1950s.

Suffice to identify in brief for the explication of the dramatic texts that will be discussed later in this chapter, the key trends that the structural mechanisms that the Arensberg and Kimball model identify complement the inflected Catholic conditions of the constitutional model, most specifically by identifying the attendant problematics of individual identity formation within the Irish Catholic family model. The promotion, or necessity, of prolonged cohabitation and the culturally specific phenomenon of late marriage, for example, meant the continuing subjection of children to adults even when adulthood/maturity had been passed. In fact the higher social position of the elderly within both the family and the wider social framework meant that 'sociological adulthood ha(d) little to do with physiological adulthood',[11] which in turn had significant implications for psychological adulthood, which we will see manifested theatrically in the experiences of the characters within the dramatic homes of the Murphy plays.

Meanwhile, Arensberg and Kimball also identify intra-familial relationships based on a system of interpersonal obligation that echoed the sacrificial discourses promoted by the discourses of Catholicism and nationalism that shaped the constitutional model that appeared just three years before their study was pub-

---

10. See Inglis, *Moral Monopoly*, Finola Kennedy, *From Cottage to Creche: Family Change in Ireland* (Dublin: Institute of Public Administration, 2001) and Lee, J. J., *The Modernisation of Irish Society, 1848-1918* (Dublin: Gill and Macmillan, 1973) and *Ireland 1912-1985: Politics and Society* (Cambridge: Cambridge University Press, 1990).

11. M. Arensberg and S. T. Kimball, *Family and Community in Ireland* (3rd ed with a new introduction by Anne Byrne, Ricca Edmondson and Tony Varley. Ennis: CLASP Press, 2001), p 147.

lished; within the domestic context this involved the sacrifice of personal preference for the well being of the people among whom one lived. In the same way that the family was valued primarily for its social and economic role, so the individual within the family was valued in relation to a familial role assigned by virtue of his position within the family hierarchy, and this role defined the configuration and expression of individual identity both within and outside of the home. For, while the private world of the home became the site in which identity was developed, it was ultimately – and paradoxically – the public social world, regulated by Catholic institutions as we have already seen, that held precedence over the *expression* of personal identity.

As developing economic and social frameworks throughout the 1950s and 1960s increased individual mobility within these domestic structures, there was no simultaneous development of a framework within the public social world that might compensate for moving outside of the closed secure familial structure. Thus by limiting identity development to the domestic sphere, even as its articulation was dependent on an arbitration process that lay *outside* of the home, the Irish Catholic domestic ideology, and the individual that it shaped, placed demands upon the family that it could not meet.

The conclusion of Una Chaudhuri's literary study *Staging Place: The Geography of Modern Drama* and C. C. Harris' social history *The Family and Industrial Society* complement this reading of the anthropological and sociological models, particularly when placed beside the Irish Catholic families of the Murphy plays as they demonstrate the failed realities of Ireland's domestic ideology. Where Chaudhuri suggests that the dramatic family of twentieth century drama becomes both the primary 'symptom of and obstacle to psychological coherence', Harris argues that suffocating modern family structures makes necessary 'escape into a public world' that the individual then finds 'impersonal and sterile'.[12] Physical independence from, and emotional de-

---

12. Christopher Charles Harris, *The Family and Industrial Society* (London: Allen and Unwin, 1983), p 165.

pendence on, the Irish Catholic home are, as our dramatic examples will reveal, false binaries in a world where ideology finds real experience secondary to its principled ideals.

Deconstructing the Irish Catholic Family in A Whistle in the Dark *and* The House

While the Irish Catholic domestic model, as we have established it so far, functioned as an ideological stronghold of Ireland's authentic origins, by the 1960s the pastoral, papist, puritanism of de Valera's vision was fading from the consciousness of the wider nation. It was in this period that Tom Murphy, whose career began as de Valera's tenure as Taoiseach came to a close, began to write for the theatre, and his socially astute dramas dealt with issues such as rural poverty and emigration. Finding its microcosmic expression in the home, however, his social critique was also focused inwards, offering a similar deconstruction of the Irish Catholic family model; as the public/private conflict between a wider society and the family home was represented as a public/private conflict within home itself, between the individual and the family unit, so it was also focused within the individual mind itself, split between the public spheres of performance and private manifestations of identity, between the 'I' of the public world and the 'I' of the individual ego that the split personality of Gar O'Donnell in Brian Friel's *Philadelphia Here I Come!* dramatised with such effectiveness.

The oppositional positions through which the fictional families of Murphy's plays experience their domestic environments problematises the accepted ideology through which the Irish Catholic home is imagined on an official level; Terry Eagleton has described it as 'the familiar discrepancy between rhetoric and reality'.[13] The fictional families in the Murphy plays expose an alternative history of the Irish Catholic home. By placing the constitutionally constructed ideology of the Irish Catholic family as the backdrop against which the disappointed, dysfunctional lives of the characters are lived out, Murphy highlights the es-

---

13. Terry Eagleton, *Heathcliff and the Great Hunger: Studies in Irish Culture* (London: Verso, 1995), p 6.

sential conflict between the family's private, individual function and its public, social function, and the difficulty, if not the impossibility, of reconciling the two. It is this tension, between the Irish Catholic family as a unit of personal experience (for the individual and the individual family) and the Irish Catholic home as a social construct, which pulls the ideological site of home in opposite directions. This contradictory obligation – between home as a site of political value and home as a site of domestic experience – results in the representational domestic dysfunctionality that we witness in the Murphy plays.

While the plays set themselves up within the paradigm of an accepted logic of the stable nuclear Catholic family home, they quickly renegotiate the operational terms of this paradigm by subverting inter-familial and inter-generational relationships, and by destabilising, through experience rather than rhetoric, the ideological foundation on which the Irish Catholic home is founded. The characterisation of domestic relationships within this dysfunctional pattern also destabilises the fundamental parameters of individual identity, by revealing the idealised structures of duty and dependency as the cause of the doubling, divided, and partial identities of the several characters in the plays. Furthermore, Murphy's manipulation of classic realist form lends the dysfunctional domestic representations a secondary deconstructive note by matching the characters' uncanny experiences in the home with the audiences' uncanny experience of the assumed realist drama.

It is also particularly interesting that the discussion of the two plays that follow place the Irish Catholic family within another social context denied by de Valera's constitutional vision, the social context of emigration; for, while fundamentally disrupting the stability of the Irish Catholic domestic ideal, emigration was actually fundamental to the economic stability of the domestic structure, to the extent that the family's dispersal pro-

14. Jim McLaughlin, 'The New Vanishing Irish: The Social Characteristics of New Wave Irish Emigration' in McLaughlin, (ed.), *Location and Dislocation in Contemporary Irish Society: Emigration and Irish Identity*, (Cork: Cork University Press, 1997), p 152.

vided 'the basis for the proper functioning of society'.[14] Emigration, or exile as it is thematised in the plays, is thus dually concerned with revealing the inherent problematics of the Irish Catholic home.

A Whistle in the Dark is set in what appears to be a fairly normal middle class living room and is couched within the framework of dramatic realism. 'The play opens on a confusion of noise and movement'[15] as Michael's well-dressed, well-mannered wife Betty, and his brothers Harry, Iggy and Hugo are busy preparing themselves for the arrival of their father. Our ease, however, is immediately disrupted as the domestic discord at the heart of the play reveals itself as a series of brutal and abusive marital, fraternal and paternal relationships. It is the tension between the ideal Irish Catholic home this could or should be and the destructive, disruptive home that it is which provides the backdrop against which the Carney's inter-familial and intra-psychic conflict is played out.

While the cacophony of the opening scene is a disruption of both the symbolic domestic space and the actual theatrical space, it also amounts to a psychic disruption for the audience. The apparent familiar structure of realism is violently exploded as the play moves steadily, without resolution, towards its inevitable tragic ending.

Despite the unity of the physical setting, the play really centres around two versions of home: home as place of origin (the Carney family home in Mayo) and home as self-created process (Michael's marital home in Coventry where the action of the play is set, which has become a second tribal enclave for the Carney family). The Irish Catholic family ideal permeates the discourses that surround both versions of home: from Dada's ideals of what a family should be, to Michael's romanticisation of Ireland as the homeland and Mayo as 'home'; from the brothers' selective recollections of their own childhood, to Michael and Betty's own aspirations for their marriage. While it is the

15. Tom Murphy, *A Whistle in the Dark and Other Plays* (London: Methuen Drama, 1989), p 3.

juxtaposition of these ideal familial constructions against the self-destructive reality of the Carneys' domestic experience that is crucial to the conflict and the deconstruction of the Irish Catholic family model, it is the aspirational commitment and unwavering faith that the characters instil in these ideals – despite the constant reminder of their impossible, illusory nature – that creates the play's tragedy. The importance of these Catholic inflected ideals, which emphasise family loyalty and responsibility, are evident in the encroachment of the family home upon Michael's marital home, the inevitable eradication of one version of home by the other and the ultimate destruction of both.

Michael is torn between the two ideas of home, between his responsibilities as brother and son and his responsibilities as husband; a conflicting conundrum that is reinforced by his dual responsibility to Ireland and his new host culture. Although Michael has left the family home of his childhood and founded his own home, through marriage, he is obliged to fulfil his familial duties when his brothers arrive in England. Paradoxically, however, while it is Michael's fulfilment of his familial duties that creates tension in his marriage to Betty in the first instance (he offers his brothers a place to stay despite her unhappiness), it is his refusal to fulfil those duties in another instance (that of the Mulryan fight) that destroys his marriage, both by heightening the pressure from his brothers in the house, and by highlighting for Betty the key issue at stake in Michael's crisis. By fulfilling his responsibilities to one family, he ends up betraying the other. Betty pleads with Michael to assert his independence and save their marriage and their home: 'It's us or them. Which is more important to you?'[16] she asks him.

Yet Michael's conflicted reality is only one instance in the destruction of this Irish Catholic family and the deconstruction of the Irish Catholic family model that *A Whistle in the Dark* bears witness to. The domestic authority of the mother, for example, is absent from the play, while her potential replacement, Michael's wife Betty, is banished from the stage. The emigrant Carney

---

16. Murphy, *A Whistle in the Dark,* p 19.

brothers may share tribal family affiliations but they are actually caught up in a cycle of dependency and loathing that manifests itself in their violent interactions and the inevitable tragedy. Dada, the father figure and hierarchical head of the family, meanwhile, is shown as the weakest of all the characters in the play. His refusal to concede seniority to Michael takes his patriarchal authority outside of its original domestic context. Patriarchal authority is the means through which he has masked his own haunting insecurities, and the fundamental dysfunction of the Irish Catholic family structures, where the individual, in real and identitarian terms, is subjugated always to the wider unit; when that unit collapses, as it does in *A Whistle in the Dark*, the individual resurfaces in a prolonged moment of crisis that the dramatic narrative of Murphy's play cannot resolve, thus Dada's final tragic moment: 'Boys … Ye're not blaming me … No control over it … Did my best. Ye don't know how hard it is. Life. Made men of ye … No man can do more than best. I tried. Must have some kind of pride. Wha? I tried, I did my best …'[17]

Similarly, *The House* dramatises a metaphorical quest for an idealised version of the Irish Catholic home, although it inverts the emigrant experience of *A Whistle in the Dark* by charting the return journey of its protagonist Christy Cavanagh. Murphy undermines the ideal that Christy creates around the de Burca family by exposing the fundamental dysfunction of his idealised version of home to the audience. While the audience, then, can see the disparity between Christy's perception of the de Burca home and its reality, Christy remains committed to his ideal even as he witnesses, and participates in, its destruction. The Irish Catholic home in *The House* is not a site of existence but a condition of existence, and Christy's quest is psychological, rather than material: 'I'd like to be this family please.'[18] He says, of the de Burca home, that 'this place will never change',[19] but it is his mis-guided insistence on its intransigence while the de

---

17. *A Whistle in the Dark,* p 97.
18. Murphy, *The House* (London: Methuen Drama, 2000), p 2.
19. Murphy, *The House,* p 6.

Burca family move on – echoing the perpetuation of the constitutional Irish Catholic domestic ideal despite the continuing modernisation of Irish society – that generates the conflict and tragedy of the play.

Christy sees the de Burca family through a lens of romance. For him they represent a familial ideal and he sees a place for himself within their family structure. From his various relationships (sexual and otherwise) with the de Burca daughters, to his decision to buy the de Burca home when he learns that it will be sold, Christy tries to possess a piece of what he sees as their ideal domestic existence. The de Burca home represents the values he believes in, and provides him with a sense of security and refuge through which he has forged his own sense of identity; an identity that has become inextricable with the de Burcas' fate. Christy hopes that by saving the de Burca home he can preserve the very values that he has imposed on them.

Christy believes that he can save the de Burcas from the decline that he refuses to acknowledge has already begun, yet this is a move of self-preservation on the symbolic level, as much as it is one of generosity on a material level. What he refuses to realise, however, is that not only do the family *want* to sell their house, and that the money he is prepared to give them will not necessarily solve all their problems, but that the de Burca family have problems of their own. They are not the ideal Irish Catholic family that Christy imagines as part of his socially inherited misguided idealism.

Mr de Burca's absence is merely the first indication of the breakdown in the de Burca family structure. His death symbolises a lacuna in the patriarchal system, which we have seen, in the failure of the patriarchal system in *A Whistle in the Dark*, as reflective of a fundamental reversal in the proper functioning of the Irish Catholic family model. The vacant fifth chair at the dinner table in Scene 6 is not merely, as Murphy notes in the stage directions, 'a mark of Mother's ongoing love for her late husband'[20] but also serves as a visual reminder for the audience of

---

20. Murphy, *The House*, p 46.

the important patriarchal absence in the family structure, which is only reinforced by the impotence of the other male characters in the play.

Meanwhile, Kerrigan the lawyer informs us that the de Burca family 'never fitted in here … They're – different.'[21] This difference could be traced to their Anglo-Norman Catholic heritage, yet the play ultimately documents the family's fall from a state of unity (albeit one imposed only through a physical site of belonging) to a fractured state of exile. Although our awareness that intra-family relations are less than perfect is continually awakened throughout the play, it is not until the actual auction of the house that the dissolution of the family, and the significance of this dissolution, is complete. The psychological implications of the family's demise, then, are worked into the symbolic and material texture of the play.

If the de Burca house functions on a symbolic level as an embodied representation of the Irish Catholic home, with its auction the metaphoric associations of home are also being sold off and the de Burca's 'difference' – that is, their idealised Irish Catholic conception – is normalised as they are physically established within the same discourse of domestic dysfunction that runs throughout and complements the important emigrant narrative. 'Now we know what it is like,' Mrs de Burca says, '… not to belong to a place anymore … We're being sent into exile.'[22] The de Burca home has become divested of its important symbolic qualities; its physical structure can no longer uphold its symbolic implications.

It is Christy, who defends and desires home above all else, who ultimately destroys the possibility of its realisation, either within or without of the framework of his ideals. The static theatrical picture created as he sits down with Marie, staring out at the land he now owns, provides a complementary tableau of impotence echoing that created at the end of *A Whistle in the Dark*. Marie's comforting reassurance that 'You belong here!' re-

21. Murphy, *The House*, p 25.
22. Murphy, *The House*, pp 77-79.

inforces the irony of Christy's fate and his irresolvable state of alienation. The house of the title is no longer a home, but Christy is now naturally at home there; he belongs in this world of failed ideals and disappointed realities, a world of disillusion and dysfunction that has failed him, but which he has also created himself.

Conclusion

Tolstoy's epic novel *Anna Karenina* opens with the declaration that 'all families are unhappy, but each is unhappy in its own way.'[23] While dysfunctional families are widespread throughout literature, teasing out the particularities of familial dysfunction on the twentieth century Irish stage through the plays of Tom Murphy is illuminating both of the plays themselves and of the wider sociological and historical reality out of which these representations arose. The failing structures of cultural myth and ideological fiction represented by the dramatisation of the failing structures of a particular Irish Catholic familial model reveal the reality of division, dispossession and oppression in twentieth century Ireland. As the Irish Catholic home is the primary site of this ideological deconstruction in the Murphy plays, it becomes an institution for deconstruction in and of itself; thus the conflict that drives the plays must be seen not just as a product of the conflict between parents and children in the dysfunctional Irish Catholic family homes but as a product of the disparity between nationalist ideals and actuality which shaped the constitutional ideal of the Irish Catholic family home.

---

23. Leo Tolstoy, *Anna Karenina* (Oxford: Oxford University Press, 1995), p 1.

CHAPTER ELEVEN

Trinities of Transition: Catholicism in the Novels and Plays of Dermot Bolger

Paula Murphy

Dermot Bolger is one of the most popular and prolific writers on the contemporary Irish literary scene, and his writing spans the genres of poetry, narrative and drama. This chapter examines Bolger's exploration of Catholicism in two of his novels, *Emily's Shoes* and *A Second Life* and one of his plays, *The Passion of Jerome*, arguing that through his juxtaposition of traditional religious values with modern secular ones, his writing is indicative of the transitive status of contemporary Irish culture. The last two decades in Ireland have witnessed tremendous changes in Irish Catholicism, with Mass attendance and vocations dropping, and clergy and laity being forced to deal with scandals surrounding clerical pedophilia, abuse of children in industrial schools and crimes committed in the Magdalen laundries. Bolger's novels and plays evaluate the role of Catholicism in Ireland and its in-fluence on identity by comparing institutional Church morality with the individual, secular, morality espoused by many of his characters. Through the opposition of the two, Bolger articulates how both can co-exist, if each is allowed to inform the other.

In *A Second Life*, the sea-change that has occurred in relation to Irish Catholicism is rendered succinctly in the anecdotes of two characters. An aunt of the protagonist, Sean, remembers what life was like in Ireland when she was a young woman: '[i]t doesn't seem that long ago, Sean, but looking back it could have been another planet. We weren't brought up to question. That doesn't mean we didn't, just that we felt guilty for even thinking of doing so.'[1] A man that Sean meets in the village where he comes from has similar memories of living in a repressive cult-

1. Dermot Bolger, *A Second Life* (London: Penguin, 1995), p 84.

ure and is quite amazed at how much things have changed. He tells Sean that in the early days of *The Late Late Show*, 'I remember all the shouting and fussing when the bishop condemned a woman for mentioning that she wore no nightie on her wedding night. Bedad, I was watching it last Friday night and they had a bishop's mistress on, talking about bringing up his bastard without a scrap of help from him.'[2] The two incidents that the man recollects are indeed indicative of the liberalism and critical debate that has replaced a more conservative culture. In the 1960s, a throwaway remark by a female member of the audience about her attire or lack of attire on her wedding night had the potential to cause a national debate about the demoralising influence of television. By the 1990s, Annie Murphy's appearance on the same show was received with less shock.

In *The Passion of Jerome*, Bolger depicts this transformation by comparing the rational materialism of modern Ireland with the inexplicable, illogical phenomenon of stigmata. The incongruity of a religious miracle in present-day urban Ireland makes manifest the transition from a religious to a secular culture, and suggests both what has been lost and what has been gained by the change. Bolger suggests that what has been lost is the ability to comprehend the spiritual. Speaking of his audience, he states, '[i]t's interesting to examine what makes them uncomfortable and the notion of the middle classes being one generation removed from the bog and also the possibility of the existence of the God their Grannies believed in intruding into their shiny secular world appealed to me.'[3] As Martine Pelletier notes, 'God is absent from Bolger's plays but the need for some transcendence cannot be avoided.'[4] This is precisely the situation that is unveiled in *The Passion of Jerome*. The play opens with Jerome

---

2. Bolger, *A Second Life*, p 138.

3. Emile Jean Dumay, 'Dramatic Terrae Incognitae: A French Perspective' in *Druids, Dudes and Beauty Queens: The Changing Face of Irish Theatre*, Dermot Bolger (ed.) (Dublin: New Island, 2001), p 206.

4. Pelletier, Martine, 'Dermot Bolger's Drama', in *Theatre Stuff: Critical Essays on Contemporary Irish Theatre*, Eamonn Jordan (ed.) (Dublin: Carysfort Press, 2000), p 254.

and Clara having sex in a flat in Ballymun. Jerome is using the flat to meet Clara, with whom he is having an affair. The care-taker relates to Jerome the story of the fourteen-year-old boy who committed suicide in the flat, and whose ghost has been causing havoc for tenants ever since. Jerome dismisses the idea out of hand and when asked what he does believe in, replies, '[m]y own eyes ... logic ... reason.'[5]

A lapsed Catholic, Jerome finds his stigmata inexplicable within the frame of reference of contemporary Ireland: '[m]obile phones are miracles, cloned sheep are miracles, Viagra is a mira-cle for those who need a bloody miracle. Logical miracles.'[6] The new secular, materialistic Irish society is contrasted with the old religious one. His only God, according to his wife Penny, is money. Yet Jerome's trendy, contemptuous demeanour is soon revealed to disguise a thinly-veiled inadequacy. The ghost of the boy who haunts him becomes a catalyst that forces him to con-front the ghosts from his own past. Drunk and raving in the flat, he shouts at the spirit: '[l]ook what you've reduced me to, my Daddy's son.'[7] It emerges that Jerome still harbours a sense of guilt about failing to prevent his father's drinking and abusive be-haviour when he was a boy. But in the society in which he lives, his guilt has no hope of being relieved. A priest tells him, 'When I was a child we'd whole legions of sins. Now that sin has evapo-rated we're stuck with guilt instead':[8] guilt without redemption. Bolger depicts a society that is, according to the priest, desperate to believe in something.[9] One need only consider the estimated three million people who visited the relics of St Thérèse, which toured Ireland in 2001, to verify that Catholicism may be disinteg-rating, but spiritual hunger is not.[10]

5. Dermot Bolger, *The Passion of Jerome*, (London: Methuen, 1999), p 29.

6. Bolger, *The Passion of Jerome*, p 30.

7. Bolger, *The Passion of Jerome*, p 41.

8. Bolger, *The Passion of Jerome*, p 67.

9. Bolger, *The Passion of Jerome*, p 69.

10. Tom Inglis, 'Catholic Church, Religious Capital and Symbolic Domination' in *Engaging Modernity: Readings of Irish Politics, Culture and Literature at the Turn of the Century*, Michel Böss and Eamon Maher (eds.) (Dublin: Veritas, 2003), p 51.

Bolger confirms this observation stating that in contemporary Ireland, 'there's still a huge desire to believe. As religion disappears … more and more bizarre notions populate the popular imagination and you have every kind of quack and mad belief wandering around.'[11] While it is of course unjust to dismiss all forms of modern spirituality as quackery, the popularity of alternatives to traditional religion cannot be denied. More and more Irish people are engaging in pursuits like yoga and pilates, which emphasise the mind-body relationship. Holistic medicine is even covered under some medical insurance policies now, and practices like acupuncture, reflexology, chakra realignment, crystal therapy and herbal remedies are attracting unprecedented interest. There is an apparently endless appetite for spiritual books like the international bestseller *Anam Chara* by John O'Donoghue. The overflow of emotion at the recent death of Pope John Paul II is an index of the desire for spiritual role models. Celtic meditative music like that of Enya and the enormous success of Fr Liam Lawton's CD of hymns, *Another World*, all substantiate the cultural longing for a spiritual dimension to replace or accompany traditional religious faith.

However, Bolger's writing is not content to merely lament the passing of more traditional forms of religion. Rather, it is fuelled by the hope that the vertiginous, painful restructuring of Irish society will bring about a more liberated, egalitarian one. At the end of the play, Jerome is honest with his wife for the first time in their marriage, admitting that part of his initial desire for her was what she represented to him. A Protestant, Penny represented exoticism but also an atonement that he could not find in his own materialistic life: he tells her, '[y]ou didn't just smell of soap and sex, you smelt of sins forgiven and redemption':[12] a suitable synopsis of the positive tenor of Bolger's writing. The transitory status of Irish culture is given voice in the thematic

---

11. 'Being a Writer in Ireland in the 1970s and Today.' Interview between Eamon Maher and Dermot Bolger, in *Doctrine and Life*, 55, 8, pp 28-38, p 36.

12. Bolger, *The Passion of Jerome*, p 71.

preoccupations of Bolger's work which focuses on liminal states between death and life, urbanity and rurality and tradition and modernity. Dramatising the dissolution of traditional signifiers of cultural identity, writers like Bolger not only catalogue but also accelerate cultural change. Presenting characters that struggle to coalesce the opposing forces of old and new in their own lives, he holds up a mirror to a nation which continues to experience the excitement but also the anxiety of rapid economic, social and cultural development, confronting the moral, sexual and spiritual dilemmas that these entail.

Bolger's writing is courageous in tackling difficult issues like racism, adoption, homosexuality, adultery and incest, and he is at the cutting edge of Irish writing from this perspective, examining topical and often controversial themes. *Emily's Shoes* is one such novel, which describes the life of a man called Michael McMahon, who has an uncontrollable fetish for women's shoes, the development of which is traced from Michael's first memories to his middle age. From early childhood, this obsession is revealed to be inextricably intertwined with two things: Catholicism and his relationship with his mother. Michael's first memory is of gazing up from a cot at three people looking down on him: 'three faces, feminine, familiar, bending forward into my line of vision'.[13] This image is repeated three times in the novel and its significance is threefold. Firstly, it symbolises the psychic operations of the fetish itself. The distinctive feature of the fetish is the distance between the fetishised object and the actual object of desire. Psychoanalyst Jacques Lacan argues that the fetish is a substitute for the symbolic phallus. It originates in the pre-oedipal triangle of mother-child-phallus and involves according to Evans 'both identification with the mother and the imaginary phallus'.[14]

The three faces that Michael sees over his cot may be said to symbolise the three elements of his fetishism. The faces may be of his mother and her two sisters. The first sister is either Aunt

13. Dermot Bolger, *Emily's Shoes* (London: Penguin, 1993), p 4.
14. Dylan Evans, *An Introductory Dictionary of Lacanian Psychoanalysis* (New York: Brunner Routledge, 1996), p 64.

Maire or Aunt Betty who dies soon after. The second is Aunt
Emily whom Michael goes to live with after his mother's death
when his fetish begins to manifest itself. His mother is the focus
of his horror during the castration complex and the cause of his
fetish through his identification with her and the maternal phallus.
Aunt Betty/Aunt Maire symbolises the link between the fetish
and the impossible fulfilment of desire in the real order of experience, from which the individual is cut off with the advent of
language. Emily represents the fetish itself, as it is with her shoes
that it begins. A second interpretation of the three female faces
who look down on Michael in his cot, links Catholicism to pagan
Ireland. In Celtic mythology, the Badbh is a triple goddess, com-
prised of the Maiden (Nemhain), the Mother (Macha) and the
Crone (Morrigan).[15] The three women who look down at Michael
could be said to fall into these three categories, with Aunt
Betty/Aunt Maire representing Morrigan, Michael's mother
representing Macha and Emily representing Nemhain.

These three elements symbolised by the three faces and reiterated three times also connect the fetish to an external influence
that is inseparable from Michael's fetish: Catholicism, which is
also based around a trinity of the Father, the Son and the Holy
Spirit. Although the same being, the Trinity has 'three distinct
divine persons'.[16] In relation to the three elements of fetishism,
the Father is its source, representing the symbolic castration that
must be endured to gain access into language by submitting to
the Name of the Father with resultant lost access to the real.
Jesus Christ is the fetishised object itself, an object onto which
desire is displaced, representing God. In Catholic ceremonies,
physical contact with the symbols of Christ, like kissing the
cross on Good Friday, adds weight to the fetishistic quality of
this relationship, a contact which takes on a specifically pedal
dimension in the washing of the feet ceremony or *Mandatum* on

15. Nancy Blair, *The Book of Godesses*, (London: Vega, 2002), pp 70-71.
16. Pope John Paul II, 'General Audience Given by Pope John Paul II, 4
December, 1985' in *God, Father and Creator: A Catechesis on the Creed*, Vol
1 (Boston: Pauline Books and Media, 1996), p 182.

Holy Thursday.[17] The Holy Spirit represents the link between the fetishised object (Jesus) and the *objet a* (God) through language, or in biblical terms, the Word of God. The link between the Father and the Son is through the Word, through language and through the symbolic order: the Gospel according to Saint John begins, 'In the beginning was the Word/And the Word was with God/And the Word was God.'[18] The Father, the Son and the Holy Spirit, corresponding to the source of desire, the fetishised object and the link between the two through language, also corresponds to another trinity: the real, the symbolic and the imaginary. The real is the fulfilment of desire, which through symbolic castration becomes impossible to access causing imaginary identification with the mother and the maternal phallus in fetishism.

Many of Michael's childhood memories, especially those of a sexual nature, are described in similies of Catholicism or by association with it. His childhood friend is a girl called Maggie who lives close by. During the month of May, Michael and Maggie steal birthday candles from the local shop and construct a makeshift grotto. Maggie kneels to pray in front of a plastic statue, with Michael, 'a few inches behind her, feeling guilty for staring at the scratched freckled thighs that vanished up beneath her short dress.'[19] Aroused by the sight of her bare legs, Michael tells her that he would like to play a new game: '[l]et's pretend that one of us is sick and has to be undressed by the other who is

---

17. This ceremony is derived from the biblical account of Jesus washing the disciples' feet before the last supper (John 12:3). In the Bible, there is a story about a woman washing Jesus's feet, drying them with her hair and anointing them with oil. Francois Mauriac describes the Holy Thursday ceremony as follows: 'the officiating priest divests himself of the cope, girds himself with a cloth, and begins the washing of twelve clerics or twelve poor men. He kneels in front of each one, washes, wipes, and kisses the foot held out to him, using the cloth that the deacon offers him' (Mauriac, *Holy Thursday: An Intimate Remembrance*. With a prefatory meditation by Mother Teresa of Calcutta (Manchester: Sophia Institute Press, 1991), p 43.

18. John 1:1.

19. Bolger, *Emily's Shoes*, p 11.

a doctor.'[20] Maggie is appalled by the suggestion and scolds him: '[y]ou dirty little boy … and us here praying to the Virgin Mary. The Holy Ghost is dwelling in my body and you want to touch it with your hands.'[21] Maggie eventually relents and agrees to play the game if she can be the doctor, so that Michael's first sexual experience is one of role-play (anticipating his desire to wear women's shoes during sex later in the novel) and is conducted in sight of the statue: '[t]he Blessed Virgin and I were both lying in the grass at the same angle',[22] setting out the associative relationship between Catholicism and sex. When Maggie's father is involved in a serious accident, she and her mother move to Canada, causing Michael to seek a replacement for what he perceives as the object of his desire. He finds this replacement in shoes, onto which his desire is projected.

Later on in the novel, the castration complex is enacted when Michael and Maggie dare each other to take off their underwear. According to Lacan, the castration complex is the most significant moment in the child's sexual development as it is at this point that identity is irredeemably divided and that desire is constituted as endlessly deferred. Michael tells Maggie, '[i]f you get to see my willie then I want to see yours too. I've never seen a girl's willie before.'[23] Taken aback by his naivety, Maggie replies, 'Michael, don't you know that I've no …'[24] It is likely, as Lacan suggests in his description of the castration complex, that the implication of Maggie's trailing sentence becomes clear to Michael only retrospectively. His confusion is made worse by the fact that Maggie leaves before he can speak to her about it. He has no other friends on the street apart from her, so when three boys ask him to come up the back field with them, he is immensely flattered. He tells them that he has to be back at half past two to say goodbye to her, but gets carried away with the fun of being part of a gang, until one of the boys pushes him

20. Bolger, *Emily's Shoes*, p 11.
21. Bolger, *Emily's Shoes*, p.11.
22. Bolger, *Emily's Shoes*, p 12.
23. Bolger, *Emily's Shoes*, p 94.
24. Bolger, *Emily's Shoes*, p 34.

onto the ground and demands to know, 'Did you see her cunt, did you? Did you ever stick your finger up it, what?'[25] When Michael escapes and runs home panic-stricken at the prospect of missing Maggie, she has already left, and he is left with a confused idea of the difference between the sexes and the impression that sexuality is shameful, violent and degrading.

Maggie's departure is the first of several traumatic events in Michael's life and the instability that he feels is compounded when his mother dies after an illness and he is sent to live with his Aunt Emily in England. His isolation is worsened because he is not informed about the severity of his mother's condition: '[n]obody ever tells me what it is that is wrong ... They have told me not to be frightened by the fact that she will be wearing a wig.'[26] While his mother is in hospital, Michael goes to live with his Aunt Maire. Here, the importance of Catholicism in Ireland is highlighted not only from a sexual point of view but also from a social one. Michael's attitude towards Maire is coloured by what he has been told by his mother: 'Maire had gone off to become a nun and not succeeded. When she returned home my grandmother told her that it would have been better for her to come back into the house inside a coffin than to be disgracing her family.'[27] Later, when Maire's husband dies, her mother attends the church but refuses to set foot inside her house. This contextualisation of Michael's relationship with religion is important, as Bolger makes it clear that his attitude towards sexuality and religion is a product of the culture of the time, or in Lacanian terms, is a product of the symbolic order, the realm of language, law and culture,[28] an order that he realises has

25. Bolger, *Emily's Shoes*, p 35.
26. Bolger, *Emily's Shoes*, p 48.
27. Bolger, *Emily's Shoes*, p 43.
28. The symbolic comes into existence with the advent of language in childhood. It is, according to Lacan, the determining order in subjectivity. Once the symbolic arrives, the pre-linguistic connection with the real is lost, because '[t]he symbolic order from the first takes on its universal character ... As soon as the symbol arrives, there is a universe of symbols.' Jacques Lacan, *The Seminar of Jacques Lacan Book Two: The Ego in Freud's Theory and in the Technique of Psychoanalysis 1954-1955*

changed at the end of the novel, a discovery that consequently changes him.

In Michael's childlike mind, Emily is a saviour who rescues him after his mother's death and his Aunt Maire is like 'an evil witch in a story',[29] linking her to the pagan crone. At his mother's funeral, Emily beckons Michael to follow her up the stairs, and the image of her shoes is burned on his memory:

> Her clothes were black, a sombre mourning coat, a short dark skirt and storm-cloud grey tights. But the only shoes that she could find in her haste, the ones that my eyes followed up each step, had the delicate stems of the slimmest high heels and were bright red as the most radiant lipstick.[30]

Although living with Emily in England is a more appealing prospect than staying with his Aunt Maire, the experience is a frightening one for a boy who has already had such upheaval in his life. Emily leaves immediately after the funeral, so Michael is forced to make the boat trip alone and meet her when he arrives. It is significant that the object which is situated at the border between his life in Ireland and England is a statue of Mary: 'a floodlit Virgin on a raised plinth high on the wall of the old train station, a harsh halo of electric light circling her head. I dread having to pass her, the guardian of a frontier between one world and the next.'[31] Religion is the only constant in the transition to his new life, but the disappearance of Catholicism's symbolic power is foregrounded by the Virgin's illumination in artificial light.

Michael finds his life in England terrifyingly lonely. Although Emily treats him kindly, he is left alone in her flat all day while she goes to work in a nearby factory. The local shopkeepers laugh at his accent and he becomes reluctant to leave the house for fear of being ridiculed. He feels threatened by Emily's anonymous boyfriend and has nightmares about him, but is too

(Cambridge: Cambridge University Press, 1988), p 29.

29. Bolger, *Emily's Shoes*, p 65.

30. Bolger, *Emily's Shoes*, p 65.

31. Bolger, *Emily's Shoes*, p 47.

afraid to tell her. He feels a proprietorial, sexual protectiveness for her and imagines her as his girlfriend or his wife, telling her, 'I wish you weren't my aunt and I was old enough to marry you.'[32] Although Emily is in her thirties, to Michael she is girlish and attractive, linking her to the Maiden of the Badbh trinity. Emily regards his comments as the sweet concern of a boy, but Michael's feelings are more than that. Her coyness about sexual matters means that Michael has no one to talk to about his confused emotions. One night when Emily returns from a night out with her face puffy and red from crying, she finds Michael asleep in her bed. For the first time, she seems to regard their relationship as potentially sexual and tells him that he can stay if he doesn't try anything. Michael is surprised, saying, '[t]he mistrust of her words startled me, turning me into a man.'[33] He goes to sleep dreaming of her and wakes up, 'after I came on the coverlet. I felt the sperm sticky and hot on my thigh ... had I hurt myself in some way, would my body ever be the same again?'[34]

One interpretation of these events is that Michael's sexual dysfunction is linked to his early indoctrination into Catholic shame surrounding sexuality and the lack of sex education at home or at school, but this needs to be balanced by a fair assessment of the role of Catholicism in Irish society and its contributions to wider social issues. Mary Kenny points out that it is unfair to blame the Church for 'instilling such a cult of chastity and continence into its flock that the Irish ... virtually turned away from sexual experience',[35] as the widespread adherence to what was perceived as Catholic regulation of sexuality in the 1950s and 1960s in fact influenced Protestants too. Both communities experienced a decline in marriages and in children in the 1950s, and Kenny suggests that this was not necessarily due to Catholic orthodoxy, but the result of a general post-Famine reluctance to marry without the necessary land and income to support a family

32. Bolger, *Emily's Shoes*, p 76.
33. Bolger, *Emily's Shoes*, p 78.
34. Bolger, *Emily's Shoes*, p 79.
35. Mary Kenny, *Goodbye to Catholic Ireland* (Dublin, New Island, 2nd edition, 2000), p 179.

comfortably. Kenny also points out that in the 1950s, America and most nations in Europe were characterised by conformity in the wake of the personal, political and social upheavals of World War Two. In Ireland, 'conformity and deference to authority took the form of strict adherence to the values of Catholicism',[36] but Ireland was by no means alone in its conservatism.

Rather than concluding that Bolger indicts the Church for its failings in the area of sexuality, it is evident from the novel, as has been suggested earlier, that Michael associates religion with his mother and that his dysfunction stems from a complex group of religious, social, familial and personal factors. What Lacan calls the Other, which is the way the individual experiences the symbolic order, is often represented by another person. Language is assimilated into the unconscious from the symbolic.[37] For Michael, his mother functions as the other who represents the Other even after her death, and his actions are carried out in the awareness of her presence and her judgement. This is evident in a scene that occurs after Michael has left England to return to live with his Aunt Maire. In his late teens, Maire becomes ill and spends a lengthy period in hospital, leaving Michael alone in a house again. This time however, he takes advantage of the independence it allows him, inviting his friends over and throwing parties. At one of these parties, Michael realises that his mother has never left him:

> Standing in Aunt Maire's kitchen, watching bottles being opened and someone being sick in the sink, there was a satisfaction in imagining her disapproval, her fossilised 1960s outrage. She was my prisoner, locked in time while I drifted towards each new experience. Yet it was she who set the boundaries, not of my behaviour but *how I perceived it*.[38]

---

36. Kenny, *Goodbye to Catholic Ireland*, p 182.
37. The radical alterity of the big Other allows Lacan to emphasise that language is beyond one's conscious control, it literally comes from an 'Other' place, which is why 'the unconscious of the subject is the discourse of the Other', Jacques Lacan, *Écrits: A Selection* (London: Routledge), 1989, p 61.
38. Bolger, *Emily's Shoes*, p 93.

His attempts at rebellion are rendered useless as they are all conducted in the pre-ordained knowledge that his acts are good or bad, according to his mother's judgement. Michael's struggles to deal with his sexuality and with the past in later life, are therefore as much about detaching himself from his mother, the cause of his fetish and the stumbling block to his progress, as they are about religion, which is just a factor, if an influential one, in the symbolic order represented by his mother to which he adheres.

In his twenties and thirties, Michael moves from place to place, metaphorically attempting to escape his past. In a desperate attempt to reconcile his sexuality with the religion that shaped it, Michael decides to go to confession in the hope of bringing his secret fetish out in the open. In the confession box though, his mother's voice taunts him: 'It's funny how the sound of it came back to me at that moment. I could hear her teasing me when I asked her how she knew something and she smiled and replied, *A little bird on a branch told me. A little bird on a branch.*'[39] The confession is aborted when Michael swears at the priest, who remains calm and sympathetic as Michael unleashes his anger at him. In *A Second Life* too, religious figures are depicted with humanity and humour. On a visit to the laundry where his mother was incarcerated before his birth, he meets a young woman in her twenties, who asks him if he is looking for St Martha's, which he is. They speak briefly and when she laughs, it is the laugh 'of a confident woman, aware of her good looks'.[40] She tells him that the institution has become the first interdenominational school run by the Catholic Church, indicative of the progressive outlook of her order:

> 'What do you mean your order?' 'Sister Anne is the name.'
> 'Sister …? … 'Well, fuck me.' She laughed at my surprise and tut-tutted in mock horror. 'I'm afraid our activities haven't quite broadened that far.'[41]

39. Bolger, *Emily's Shoes*, p 202.
40. Bolger, *Emily's Shoes*, p 252.
41. Bolger, *Emily's Shoes*, p 253.

This scene is typical of Bolger and his treatment of thorny social issues, bringing out the nuances of both sides in a manner that encourages dialogue and sympathy.

Just when Michael seems to have closed the door on religion altogether, he is forced to confront it again due to forces outside his control. His housekeeper, Mrs Brennan, tells him that she has seen the face of the Virgin Mary appearing in the knot of wood on the locked door of the spare bedroom. As in *The Passion of Jerome*, Bolger juxtaposes secular materialism with inexplicable religious experience. Although Michael terminates her employment, she returns that evening with a priest, Fr O'Rourke, and several women. Fr O'Rourke is a right-wing Catholic who has been defrocked for refusing to say Mass in the vernacular. Michael does not allow him to enter but permits one of the young women in his company, Clare, to stay and pray to the apparition. Clare is a vulnerable single mother who has already had to be rescued from the Hare Krishnas before being co-opted by Fr O'Rourke to help with his various schemes for purging society of its evils. Although Michael is a complete sceptic about the apparition, Clare's accusation lingers in his mind: '[m]aybe you're just too scared to look into it'.[42]

Like the protagonist of *The Passion of Jerome*, Michael feels angry at the unwanted intrusion of the otherworld into his modern home and modern lifestyle: 'I felt cheated. This was a new place, a clean sterile structure. There should be no room here for ghosts or spirits.'[43] Michael's troubles are only beginning, however, and the following evening, he returns home to find his housekeeper with six other women on their knees reciting the Rosary at his door, with a boy in a wheelchair looking on. The boy's mother pleads with Michael to allow her son inside: 'I beg you, Sir, the child is dying, we've been all over the country with him. To every grotto where she's appeared.'[44] Mrs Brennan and her friends are not the only ones who are desperately seeking

42. Bolger, *Emily's Shoes*, p 220.
43. Bolger, *Emily's Shoes*, p 223.
44. Bolger, *Emily's Shoes*, p 225.

spiritual guidance. Clare too reveals that she pretended to be able to see the vision in the door because she wants to believe that she has been chosen by God: '[D]o you know how many grottoes I've travelled to, how many people I've seen fall backwards, paralysed with joy? What have I done to make me different from everyone else who can see her face?'[45] At Clare's confession, Michael admits that he too is searching for something, although he has been unable to admit it, even to himself until that moment: '[T]here has to be more, or else we would all just lie down in that ditch there and never bother getting up.'[46]

In a final plea for divine intervention, Michael and Clare go to visit a field where visions of the Virgin Mary have been reported. The field is thronged with people chanting prayers, singing hymns and looking towards the night sky. The line of parked cars outside the vision field is a mile long, and others are travelling by bicycle and on foot. A reluctant visitor, Michael does not see the Virgin in the sky, but the atmosphere of joyful prayer does conjure up a vision of his mother:

> Memories were coming back to me, unwelcomed and unannounced. Lying in bed in the boxroom waiting for my mother to come home from the women's mission in church. The joy on her face as she described the visiting priest's sermon, the catch-phrase he had made them repeat over and over with their hands raised, *The family that prays together stays together.*[47]

Like Jerome, Michael's clash with religion is important not because of awesome miracles, but because it allows him to experience a miracle of his own: confronting the past that he was unable to access in the confession box and bringing his secret out in the open for the first time. At the end of the novel, when Michael defaces the ostensible vision of Mary in the knot of wood on his door, he does so not out of anger or spite, but out of a sense of triumph that he finally feels liberated enough to speak about his fetish and about the traumatic childhood that created it: 'I care-

45. Bolger, *Emily's Shoes*, p 238.
46. Bolger, *Emily's Shoes*, p 239.
47. Bolger, *Emily's Shoes*, p 223.

fully drew in two red high heel shoes underneath and then like a halo over her head I scrawled the letters EMILY.'[48]

Michael's act of vandalism reconciles the three trinities of the novel. He has made peace with his dead mother, the source of symbolic castration, he has rid himself of his shoe fetish which began with Emily and he has evaporated the distance between his fetish and his *objet a* (object of desire), realising that his desire may never be satiated, but that he may at least lead a contented life with Clare. He has resolved the tension between this trinity and the Holy Trinity of the Catholic Church, having, if not made peace with religion, then at least purged his hatred for it. 'No more shoes ... no medals, no miracles',[49] he declares. He has freed himself from the influence of the three feminine faces of pagan mythology, the Mother, the Maiden and the Crone and is finally free to live his own life by his own rules. *Emily's Shoes* illustrates the transitory status of the Irish symbolic order. It is between the old and the new, having neither abandoned the old order of Catholicism, piety and strict regulation of sexuality, nor completely embraced the new order of secularism, materialism and sexual liberalism. It also suggests though, that symbolic change is possible, as Michael eventually frees himself from the values and ethics of the old order and embraces the new order, more liberal and more accepting. Bolger does not provide a trite happy ending, however, and at the conclusion of *Emily's Shoes*, the reader is left with a sense of not only what has been gained, but also what has been lost. In some cases, old problems have merely been replaced by new ones. In *A Second Life*, Sean notes that, '[a]lmost one in every fifth baby in the State was born to a single parent now. But where every parish had once had a girl drummed out secretly at night, now they had a house, the corner of a field, a bridge, where an unexplained and unmentioned suicide had occurred in recent years.'[50]

Bolger's drama and fiction performs an imperative function

---

48. Bolger, *Emily's Shoes*, p 244.
49. Bolger, *Emily's Shoes*, p 266.
50. Dermot Bolger, *A Second Life* (London: Penguin), 1995, p 154.

in contemporary Irish society, re-imagining the roles and functions of Catholicism and the nuns and clergy who preach its message, refashioning both through his writing. For Bolger, the weakening power of the Church in Ireland can be considered positively: 'As the Church disintegrates more and more, it becomes in some ways morally more powerful because it moves to the margins to join the outcasts.'[51] In this way, Bolger cannot be regarded as either pro or anti-Catholic, because two such distinct camps cannot exist in an informed commentary. As he states, '[a]n artist's function is to stand outside these value systems and be sceptical, open to both sides of the argument',[52] an aspiration that he succeeds admirably in carrying out.

51. 'Being a Writer in Ireland in the 1970s and Today', p 35.
52. 'Being a Writer in Ireland in the 1970s and Today', p 36.

CHAPTER TWELVE

Cultural Chameleons: Religion in the Ryan of Inch Papers

Grace Neville

Inch House, north of Thurles in Co Tipperary, is described on its website as a country hotel with a cordon bleu restaurant that has been acclaimed by the prestigious *Bridgestone Irish Food Guide*. However, for the best part of two and a half centuries before it received its current five-star AA rating, it played a radically different role as home to a branch of a leading Catholic landlord family, the Ryans. The Ryans had bought their estate in the rich, rolling pasturelands of North Tipperary from the Fogarty family who had acquired it in the seventeenth century from a Cromwellian grantee, Edward Annesly. Their voluminous family papers, now held in the Boole Library, University College Cork, span almost three centuries of history, covering both public and private spheres, everything from land ownership and financial dealings to more personal matters (marriages made, babies born).[1] This present study explores the Ryan of Inch corpus in order to try to establish the Ryans' attitudes to religion, with a view to determining what part, if any, religion played in their identity. A word of warning, however, at the outset. As these papers track several generations of Ryans, along with Ryan relatives, neighbours, tenants, acquaintances and business associates over two centuries, the attitudes to religion evident here are inevitably multiple, varied and even contradictory: the people identified may share the same religion but they do not speak with *una voce*.

The Ryans' rarity as landowning Catholics in the early eighteenth century is evident from Roy Foster's assertion:

1. See *Ryan of Inch Papers. Descriptive List* (Cork: Boole Library Archives Service, University College Cork, 2001), with an introduction by Carol Quinn, Archivist, UCC.

By the early eighteenth century Catholics, though about 75 per cent of the population, owned only 3 per cent of Irish land.[2]

Not only were the Ryans fully integrated into the local landowning class, however, but they served in the British armed forces as late as the Second World War. They sent their children to be educated in England, their sons at public schools like Stoneyhurst and their daughters at schools like New Hall Convent, Chelmsford, described thus by Molly Ryan who was probably a pupil there in the late nineteenth and early twentieth century: 'Ladies of the noblest Catholic families have chosen it for their resting place in this life, and it is also under their care one of the favourite schools for the daughters of the Catholic gentry and nobility of England' (RI/627). The Ryans' nonchalantly cosmopolitan lifestyle, especially in the eighteenth century, is evident from their family papers relating to family members living in Brussels, Spa, Montpellier, Toulouse and Le Mans. In all, they are cultural chameleons, distinguishable only with difficulty from their Protestant Irish fellow landowners. It is precisely because they did not conform to the stereotype of the Irish Catholic which makes their case-history of particular interest in the context of the central theme of the conference – the exploration of Irish and Catholic identities.

At an immediate level, religion features here in salutations and other conventional loci. A typical example of this is found in a letter dated 1758 from John McCarthy, Thurles, on the death of his mother: 'God was pleased to deliver her from a great deal of pain and misery last Wednesday morning' (RI/866). Such formulaic utterances, however, hardly amount to evidence of religious fervour. Equally prominent throughout this archive are references to the rites of passage represented by the sacraments of the Catholic Church. The corpus contains, for instance, a significant number of baptismal certificates for family members born in France. The fact that such documents were carefully pre-

---

2. Roy Foster, *The Oxford Illustrated History of Ireland* (Oxford: Oxford University Press, 1987), p 165.

served by family members might be interpreted as an indication of the importance of religion (Catholicism) to them. However, I would argue that this is not necessarily so. Practical considerations may explain the preservation of these French baptismal certificates: it was known that they would be needed later, for instance when children came to make their First Communion or to get married. An Irish baptismal certificate may have been relatively easy to replace and would consequently not need such careful preservation. Delivered in France and in French, these documents may furthermore have exuded a soupçon of exoticism that contributed to their safe keeping. Given that they recorded the names of a godmother as Comtesse Bouiriaire de McCarthy (RI/536, dated 1790) and a father as George Ryan, Comte de Tipperary (RI/487, dated 1790), the decision to preserve them may owe more to (upper) class consciousness than to any particular fondness for Catholicism. After all, baptismal certificates must also have existed for generations of Tipperary-born Ryans. Of these, however, no trace remains. Death rituals are occasionally mentioned, though not necessarily in a religious context: the cost of a decent burial, for instance, is a matter of some importance: an account dated July 1778 refers to a family funeral costing 16 shillings and 6 pence for 'the best velvet Pall' and a further £2.14.6 for 'a sett [sic] of the best Ostridges Plumes for hearse and horses' (RI/372).

Deeper under surface-level formulae and milestones, however, a striking lack of any Christian sentiment marks some of these documents: witness a letter (RI/869) dated in the fateful year of Waterloo, 1815, from one T. Jackson in Brussels critical of his fellow Catholics, the anti-monarchist French (collectively dismissed as 'Johnny Frog') and urging the eviction back home in Tipperary of tenants unable to pay their rent. Christian charity thus counts for little when weighed against forces like money and monarchy. In two extended pieces of writing in this corpus, two travel diaries, one 117 pages long and dated 1775-6 (RI/371), and the other 56 pages long and dated 1820 (RI/672), there is little mention of religious affiliation or even of religion at all. In Saint Denis, north of Paris, in 1775, John Ryan saw 'nothing remarkable' apart from (by his own admission) ... a cathedral, a monastery, medieval stained glass windows, the tombs of the kings of France, the crown of Charlemagne, Holy Roman Emperor. The feeble highlights of Orleans, a historical city synonymous with France's fifteenth century saviour, Jeanne d'Arc, were – he tells us - a church under repair and a river (the Loire) full of sand. This Ryan wears his Catholicism lightly. Indeed, the word 'Catholic' features nowhere in his text. For him, Easter Sunday is memorable not for any religious ceremonies but for the opportunity it give to gaze on the King of France:

> During this last sejour in Paris, I made an excursion to Versailles on Easter Sunday the 7th April, it was principally to see the ceremony of the offerings made by the Royal family on that day, in which there is a great deal of respect and ceremony observ'd and at which I was not displeas'd, as I confess myself an advocate of these venerable ceremonies being kept up, with all their ancient splendour.

And then there is religion as a source of *mirabilia*: in Toulouse, Ryan visited a church in which

> there is a very remarkable cave or vault, which has the property of preserving whole bodies entire, by drying the flesh, without hurting in the least the outward skin; the bodies by the course of time turn quite black but it you touch them with your finger you will find the same resistance as if alive; I saw some in this vault which were four hundred years old, and which were almost entire.

This voyeurism hardly amounts to anything resembling religious belief.

In 1820, another Ryan relative on his way to France, refers, without further elucidation, to 'eight priests who were in the hold' of the ship he was travelling on (RI/672). This is the first and last we hear of them. His eight co-religionists lack any of the details that give reality and individuality to his other fellow passengers. They are afforded as little space in his narrative as they were on board ship. For the narrator, they appear to be underdeck, underground, underlings in every sense of the word. It could, of course, be argued that silence does not mean absence, and that their religious affiliation was so overwhelmingly obvious and omnipresent for the commentators in question that it needed no mention – no more than their gender or their taste in clothes. Nonetheless, travel accounts with landmarks like coffee houses and castles rather than cathedrals read suspiciously like the work of people for whom religion had limited importance.

That is not to suggest, however, that religion was some kind of empty shell for them. Adherence to Catholic belief is evident here from a reference (in a diary entry dated 1828) to money being earmarked for Masses to be said for the delivery of a soul from purgatory (RI/592). Furthermore, the corpus contains evidence of religious affiliation that involved not a little personal danger: more than mere rhetoric, in other words. A letter dated 26 December 1916, from Arthur Ryan, newly arrived in war-torn France, tells of miles of trenches, guns roaring all around and shells screaming overhead (RI/620). Ryan seemed positive in the face of such danger:

> I preached three sermons to the Irish soldiers and made a speech at one of their big dinners. All seemed much impressed. The General was at two of the sermons.
>
> Today I have spent in the trenches and under fire most of the day. It is strange to hear the scream of the shells over one. Two of my old friends of the R. Irish Regt., Col. Gregory and Major Farmer piloted me through miles of trenches. I found one of the O'Reilly boys in his dug out in a very hot spot.
>
> Then back to tea with the R. Irish, the guns roaring all round [...] I paid a visit today to the Blessed Sacrament, and there was an unexploded German shell under the altar. The Chaplain thinks it is best to leave it alone! [...] This is a strange Xmas, Molly, but I am surrounded by Irish soldiers and Irish priests, and good nuns are taking charge of me.

Religion as a security blanket should not be lightly dismissed.

It could be argued that, leaving aside – if that is possible – the appalling experience that involvement in the Great War must have been, at least those like Arthur Ryan believed themselves to be on the side of the angels, fighting for good against clear evil. Such black and white certainties are much less in evidence, however, in the three clusters of documents that I now wish to analyse and that form the heart of this study. These documents bring into focus the priorities of individual Ryan family members – and consequently their *mentalité* – through situations in which religion and family matters clashed, public and private spheres collided and painful choices had to be made.

The first concerns the tension between public advancement and private religious affiliation. Put bluntly, for much of the period covered by these archives, many senior public posts were seen as off limits for Catholics. Thus, in a letter from this corpus written to a certain Whyte (a Ryan family associate) in 1834, one More O'Farrell declares:

> I have long felt in common with many others that those who have most benefited by the repeal of the Penal Laws owe a debt of gratitude to you for the sacrifice you made of professional advancement (RI/861).

For him, Whyte's case highlighted the injustices done to Catholics, as it seemed clear that Whyte would never be offered the post of stipendiary magistrate that he wished for as no Catholic would ever be offered such a position. Whyte himself expressed his despair at ever being offered a post by the Admiralty. Here and elsewhere, one gets a sense of people quietly trying to navigate between rocks and hard places, loyal to their religion while all the time hoping and planning to move inexorably if slowly onwards and upwards. Roy Foster has commented:

> To be a Protestant or a Catholic in eighteenth-century Ireland indicated more than mere religious allegiance: it represented opposing political cultures, and conflicting views of history.[3]

However, throughout the entire period covered by these archives, it is striking to note the extent to which the Ryans go to smooth over or otherwise occult any perceived conflict resulting

3. Foster, p 163.

from their religion. A typical example of this is clear in a printed notice in these archives signed by the Ryans and a significant number of Tipperary Catholics in 1792, declaring their desire for peace, their abhorrence of violence, their loyalty to God and their King, their desire to take part in elections and their condemnation of anti-Catholic sentiment throughout the county (RI/665). The centuries-long narrative of the Ryan family, as traced in these papers, tells again and again how they minimised their 'Otherness' as Catholics in order to blend in to their preferred society. That their Catholicism could result in any perceived conflict or open opposition (*pace* Foster) thus appears, for them, to have been quite out of the question. That it did, and that they 'outed' themselves as Catholics on more than one occasion, as we shall now see, suggests that they found themselves quite simply with no alternative course of action.

In this context, the significance of the second and longest sequence of documents (twenty in all) that I now wish to analyse becomes clear, as they bring into sharp focus opposition, conflict and allied irreconcilables associated with religion. These concern a power struggle in which, it could be argued, there was no winner. In 1939, a bitter dispute arose between the Ryan family and the Catholic Church in the person of Archbishop John Harty of Cashel over the fact that the younger of the two Ryan sons, Arthur George, was a student at Trinity College Dublin. The rumbling disagreement escalated when the Archbishop threatened to remove the Blessed Sacrament from the family's private oratory at Inch House unless the young Ryan left Trinity College. The privilege in question had originally been granted by Rome in 1873, as is made clear in a letter to the then Mrs Ryan from a certain Rev Dr Leahy:

> I have obtained for you from the Holy Father the high privilege of having the Holy Sacrament constantly deposited in the tabernacle of your oratory. Holy Mass must be celebrated there *once a week* [...] a lamp must be kept lighted before the tabernacle day and night [...] the confessions of the whole family can in future be heard in the oratory (RI/302, dated 1873).

Permission to have the Blessed Sacrament exposed there was renewed through the subsequent generations, something that required not inconsiderable ongoing high-level negotiations between Rome, Cashel and Thurles, as is obvious here from the copious relevant correspondence in Latin and English on the subject. To lose this rare privilege would therefore be 'a calamity', writes Ryan senior who signs his letters to the Archbishop with formulae such as 'I have the honour to be your Grace's obedient servant.' In a series of succinct, powerfully argued submissions, Ryan advanced the arguments for allowing his son to stay in Trinity. These are summarised in his letter dated 22 July 1939 to Archbishop Harty which the latter had requested for submission to the Papal Nuncio. It is worth quoting at length:

In the first place I should state that [my son] has always been delicate and I had to withdraw him from school for this reason. He subsequently studied at Glenstal Priory for two years but I had again to take him home and revert to a private tutor for the same reason. In 1937 I obtained for him an opening with a very good firm Messrs Babcock and Wilcox, through acquaintance with one of the Directors. This opening was subject to his graduating at a University and taking a degree in Engineering. For health and other reasons his mother and I decided that he should study for a degree in Dublin, so as to be within easy reach. On pursuing the subject further we found that the entrance examination to the National University included an examination in Irish which my son had never studied and which subject it was impracticable for him to take up. His entrance to Trinity College appeared to be the easiest and in fact the only way of obtaining the necessary degree and we therefore entered him there, being unaware at the time of the very strict attitude adopted by the Church in Ireland on the subject. I need hardly say that we made careful enquiries as to the conditions under which he would study, the subjects he would take and the opportunities available for the practice of his religion, about which I consulted his prospective tutor in advance.

Having satisfied ourselves on these points we entered him at the University in October 1937, as an outside student, and he has continued his studies there until the present time.

He resides outside the University in rooms approved of by us and merely attends lectures in College on the professional subjects necessary for an Engineering degree. My son has now completed two years of his university education and I have searched without success every avenue by which he could continue it elsewhere (RI/302).

Elsewhere, his position is further elaborated:

I sent G. to Trinity in good faith and quite openly. No objections were then raised. Being young for his age it was undesirable to cut him off from his family – for instance by sending him to Oxford [...] My responsibility towards George, his education and future life is not a privilege but a duty which cannot be passed on to anyone else [...] His religion and morals are at present safeguarded particularly if he continues to live out and his subjects not including Scripture, Philosophy or even History do not in any way affect his religion or bring him under any undesirable non-Catholic influence (RI/302).

In fact, Ryan did seriously consider moving his son to University College Dublin. His request that he be integrated into the third year engineering programme there was rejected by the UCD Senate, however. As regards his son learning Irish *ab initio* which he would have had to do, in any case, in order to gain entrance into University College Dublin, he had this to say:

Already rather behindhand with his studies, due to reasons of health, I could not contemplate burdening him with a subject of no use to him in his future career (RI/302).

The suggestion that his son should move to Oxford or Cambridge (which did have reciprocal arrangements with TCD and which seemed less objectionable to the Catholic Church than TCD) was rejected by Ryan in a letter dated 16 July 1939:

The question of continuing my son's education in England

involves many difficulties, accentuated by the conditions existing at the present time in that country, where I am not anxious for him to become liable for military service and where a very considerable war risk has to be accepted (RI/302).

The conflict, in any case, was settled in a letter dated 19 July 1939 from Archbishop Harty, with an address at The Palace, Thurles. At a time when most of Europe was holding its breath, with matters of life and death on its mind, Harty stated:

In view of the general Church Law, the Maynooth statutes and the warning of the Holy See about Catholic boys in Trinity College, I cannot take it on myself to continue the privilege of the private Oratory. If you do not mind I shall put the matter before the Apostolic Nuncio who is always very helpful (RI/302).

Less than two weeks later, in a letter dated 31 July, the Archbishop conveyed the Nuncio's decision:

I put your case before the Apostolic Nuncio and sent him your letter explaining the circumstances. He failed to find any sufficient grounds to justify you in sending your son to Trinity College. Hence matters remain as they were, and I have no option but to withdraw the privilege of the private oratory if the boy continues to be a student of Trinity College (RI/302).

The Blessed Sacrament was removed by the parish priest on 5 August 1939 (a move which was relayed in a letter from the Archbishop dated 4 August).

A letter from a Bishop David Mathew (perhaps a Protestant or, in any case, someone who described himself as 'coming from a very different Church tradition') dated 3 August 1939 from 1 Woburn Square London, who had recently stayed with the Ryans may, one hopes, have provided some small consolation to them in difficult times:

with my feeling for antiquity I am so conscious of the great services which the Ryans of Inch have rendered to the

Church. But in this generation it is not the aid and sustenance which was given to the Church in the Penal days that are remembered. I have the greatest feeling for Inch and for your Chapel. I can only say that I am convinced that we all find that life is more unexpected and difficult for us in ways that we never foresaw that it ever seemed when we were beginning.

What we all need is a profound confidence in God and a certain detachment from transitory things of every kind (RI/302).

This was not the first time that religion had triggered off conflict and unhappiness for the same R. Ryan. As is clear from his 1937 diary (RI/648), his elder son's decision to marry a non-Catholic caused him and his wife much heartache. This time, however, there was no archbishop looking over his shoulder: both Ryan and his wife seemed genuinely distressed at their son's decision. In May 1937, they travelled to London to talk with the young couple who seemed to be resident there. Cryptic comments such as the following indicate that negotiations did not go well. 'M [his future daughter-in-law] would agree to conditions for RC wedding but wanted others as well'. Ryan was clearly well connected – in the Jesuit church at Farm Street in fashionable Mayfair, for instance:

20 May: to Farm St a.m. for advice re dispensation for Prot. Wedding. Little hope. Am to call again tomorrow.

21 May: to Farm St a.m. Apparently no hope for what I want. Advised to see Bishop Day […] rang up and went straight down to see him. V. nice v. sympathetic but unable to do anything towards dispensation. Not possible to get. V. depressed. Am advised to see Fr Beauchamp senior RAF chaplain at Halton […]

R. and Mary Taylor arrived lunch time. Took them to lunch at Harrods. Then had a long talk with each of them.
Went with R. to Halton to see Fr B. He said all well on the strength of something R. told him. No need for disp. All

much elated. but on way home rang up to find M.T. would not now agree to the conditions. Was very down and out about this.

23 May: wired K to come and gave him the bad news. Richie called a.m. and told me M.T. now declined to go to any church and would only be married in Reg. office. An advantage as far as scandal is concerned.

24 May: K [his wife] arrived …
Dr in law wouldnt meet k
We can do no more so returned home.
K v. done up (RI/648).

There is even, on 25 May, a reference to Ryan's wife partly collapsing. Then, in this very functional diary, amidst details of cattle and grass being tended to, an entry on 26 May reads: 'R. married in Reg. office' [presumably in London]. This news was added *post hoc* after a letter was received on 1 June: '1 June a letter from r. telling us the worst i.e. married last week in reg. office'. There is no further comment.

Belying the adage about lightning never striking twice in the same place, exactly twenty years later, in 1957, Ryan's younger son, George Arthur (the former TCD student) became engaged, like his brother, to a non-Catholic (RI/661). Ryan senior was at that stage nearing seventy. Again, negotiations were initiated:

21 June: Fr Lee here in the morning and had a talk with Elizabeth. Hope it may lead to something.

22 June: Fr Lee saw Elizabeth again

Then on 10 July, amidst news of calves being born and fruit being picked came the breakthrough:

'heard that E. is going to be a Catholic. Wonderful news.

Preparations were made for her admittance into the Catholic Church:

Fri. Aug 2: no less than 28 Pres. nuns turned up … to see gardens etc.! Chapel ready and finished for tomorrow.

The entry for the following day, 3 August 1957, is, unusually, written in red, a clear indication of Ryan's exultation that this time, at least, things had gone his way:

A red letter day.

Elizabeth was received into the Church in the Chapel. Conditional baptism and 1st Communion.

Fr Lee assisted by Fr Noonan. 2 masses in chapel ... cocktail party in evening (RI/661).

These mirror image events pose many intriguing questions regarding Ryan's attitudes to religion. In his dispute with Archbishop Harty, his priorities were clear, the choice was stark: what he saw as his son's welfare outweighed any religious privilege, however valued. In order to ensure the former, he was prepared to sacrifice the latter. At the same time, however, while he refused to bow to the Archbishop, his religion still mattered enough to him to cause him and his wife distress at the prospect of their sons marrying non-Catholics. Why was this? Richard Ryan was the youngest in a family of six and, as far as I know, the only one of them to have children (two boys). One could therefore surmise that he wished his family religion be continued through his two children; one senses his sense of responsibility as the sole link in a long chain that was in imminent danger of snapping. Particularly when his second son seemed ready to marry a non-Catholic (as his elder brother had already done), Ryan may have felt that this really was his last chance of continuing the family religion. He had to grasp it. This sense of urgency may have been heightened by evidence from his very own family archives of what his people had long been prepared to accept, that is, professional disadvantage, in their loyalty to their faith. And then there are the daughters-in-law themselves. Why did the said Elizabeth convert to Catholicism, unlike her sister-in-law twenty years earlier? How much did this have to do with religion? Was it, perhaps, an acknowledgement of all that Ryan senior had done on his younger son's behalf in 1939, a desire to spare the by now elderly man what he had been through with the out-marriage of his elder son? Or did the two young women simply have different attitudes to religion – per-

haps Mary Taylor's religion was too important to her to allow
her to leave it. Or was Elizabeth simply more accommodating? It
is perhaps significant that all negotiations with Mary Taylor
were carried out in London (did she ever visit Inch?) whereas
Elizabeth (though she later married Arthur George in London)
was a frequent guest in Inch. Were the relationships of the two
young women with their prospective parents-in-law very different? It is perhaps telling that one is referred to usually by her full
name (Mary Taylor) whereas the other is simply 'Elizabeth'. It
might take the nuanced spinnings of a Proust or a Joyce rather
than Ryan's functional agricultural diary to make all this clear.
In a wider context, it is regrettable that so little correspondence
exists from Archbishop Harty giving his side of the story. All we
have are two short handwritten notes simply saying no … and
no again, with no elaboration whatsoever on the reasons for this
decision, whereas the Ryan side of the argument is copiously
documented. I suspect that there was not much further docu-
mentation on Archbishop Harty's side however: indeed, the initial disapproval of TCD as the place of learning for Ryan *fils*
seems to have been conveyed verbally by the parish priest on a
visit to the Ryan household. It is tempting to see these two ways
of doing business as symptomatic of two different ways of being
in the world: one largely oral and informal, the other written
and formal, one dogmatic, the other a believer in the individual's right to follow his conscience – dare one say a more typically
Protestant way of doing things.

In 1985, some two hundred and sixty five years after it was
built, Arthur George Ryan (by now in his mid sixties) sold his
family home of Inch House, disposed of all his properties in Co
Tipperary and emigrated to New Zealand. The Ryan of Inch
family papers were subsequently bequeathed to University
College Cork in 1997. At a macro level, like similar archives elsewhere, they provide unique first-hand evidence of world views
(*weltanschaung/mentalités*) – in this present study, concerning
their religion, for instance. I would argue, however, that it is at a
micro level that they are most valuable and indeed interesting:

for it is here that they convey to us – up close and personal – the tensions and decisions, the soul-searching and struggles, the hopes and compromises – often difficult and messy ones – along with diplomatic silences, contradictions and gaps, that have, from time immemorial, been part and parcel of the human condition.

All in all, the close meshing between religion and social status in these archives is inescapable. Nominally, the Ryans subscribed to the same religion as did their fellow Catholic tenants: the reality was very different. They did not go to the priest, for instance: he came to them, to say Mass or hear confessions in their home. So normal was this that Ryan's shock is clear, one Christmas Day, when, as he writes, 'no Mass in house for first time in my recollection – priest could not come as curate in Borrisoleigh is sick'; similarly, when one of the Ryans is unwell during a visit to Lourdes in September 1939, no lesser a personage than a cardinal comes to visit her (RI/629). Ryan's reaction, when it transpires on 4 April 1937 that 'There is trouble over G. being at Trinity' is significant: he does not attempt to seek an audience with the Archbishop or to curry favour with him, nor does he plead: instead, as he writes in his diary that very next morning: '5 April in Thurles a.m. and *interviewed* the archbishop' (RI/650, italics added): in the relationship between Ryan and the Archbishop, Ryan is not the lesser personage! His links with the Church in England are resolutely up-market: the Jesuit church in Farm Street, Mayfair, the senior RAF chaplain, and so forth. The list of examples is endless. (It must, therefore, *soit dit en passant*, have added insult to injury for him that, in September 1939, the Blessed Sacrament was removed from the family's private oratory by the parish priest and not the Archbishop himself.) So close, thus, are these ties throughout this corpus that one could conclude that religion is just one of the many elements that make up the Ryans' overall social identity: a small and often silent one, but by no means the main one.

CHAPTER THIRTEEN

Return to Doolin:
A Reflection on a Changing
Irish and Catholic Identity

Patrick Claffey

Running water never disappointed.
Crossing water always further something.
Stepping stones were stations of the soul.[1]

Introduction

These few lines by Heaney have become something of a personal
mantra since I first read them in what is probably my favourite
Heaney collection, *Seeing Things* (1991). They speak of movement and hope. 'Running water, crossing water', these have a
certain excitement to them. The excitement of discovery and
more specifically, perhaps, of self-discovery. I am also very attracted to his idea of the 'stepping stones' as 'stations of the
soul', since at fifty-four and having moved about quite a bit in
my life, I do indeed see it as a series of stepping-stones that have
led me, not without the occasional splash, but not without grati-
tude, to where I now am.

I do not think it is difficult to see how these reflections can be
related to the question of identity and, in the terms of psychology,
the discovery of a personal identity, the sense of self, that is part
of the maturation process. I have no doubt that my own sense of
identity, both in terms of my Irishness, but also in terms of my
Catholicism, have indeed been formed by my various geographical displacements, mainly outside of Ireland. I do not hesitate in
describing myself as European by education, by cultural affinity
and by personal preference. It is within this framework that I

---

1. Seamus Heaney, *Seeing Things*, *xxxii* (London: Faber and Faber, 1991).

now look at both my Irish and my Catholic identities – albeit not always comfortably.

Let me fill in a little personal data. I was born in 1951, into what an American friend once described as a 'lace curtain Irish' family. This was the putative *petite bourgeoisie* of so many small Irish towns, and included the big farmers, who were the fathers of the big traders, solicitors, doctors and, of course, the parish priests who, it was expected, would become the elite of Home Rule Ireland. Although I never met him, and know nothing of his politics, I suspect that, for my grandfather and his nascent burgher circle, the violent birth of the Free State in 1922 came as something of a shock. Ten years after he had made a substantial investment in a large country business, the world suddenly changed. How were they to adapt to the new dispensation?

Several years ago I noticed a very interesting item in Clonalis House, Castlerea[2] which somehow illustrated this point. It was a parchment from the traders of the town of Castlerea, presented to the then O'Conor Don, Owen O'Conor, on the occasion of his wedding to his second wife, and second cousin, Gwedoline O'Conor in 1919. One of the first signatures on the document was that of my grandfather, Patrick Claffey, by that time apparently a burgher of this nascent, small but seemingly quite prosperous West of Ireland burgh. The thought that struck me when reading it was that these men must have been really bewildered by the maelstrom that had struck the country and the changes that would take place over the following years. For them, as for Yeats, life would indeed be 'transformed utterly' as the 'terrible beauty [was] born'.[3] Many were in fact wiped out financially in the years following independence and the subsequent economic war and worldwide depression of the 1930s. Our family business limped on for some time but it seems probable that by the

---

2. The Connacht sect included High Kings of Ireland, the last of whom, Rory, was born in Castlerea, Co Roscommon, in the twelfth century. He died in 1198 and is buried at Clonmacnoise. Clonalis House in Castlerea, is the ancestral seat of these O'Conors, whose ancestry included 11 High Kings of Ireland and 24 Kings of Connacht.
3. W. B. Yeats, 'Easter 1916'.

time of my grandfather's death in 1937 it was already in terminal decline.

By the time I was born, in 1951, our lace was indeed yellowing and somewhat tattered. A combination of my father's personal problems, the usual Irish demon drink, and a stagnant economy in the 1950s led to the final collapse of the family business. I can still remember my father and mother having their tea, alone at the dining room table, served from covered dishes. The nanny usually swept in after a last goodnight to put us to bed – before polishing my five year old's shoes for the morning. I also remember the departure of the nanny and the last of the domestic and shop staff, and I have little doubt that these years were indeed central to the development of my own identity and worldview. The fifties and sixties were not a cheerful period; in fact they were marked by a kind of hopelessness. It was a period of socio-economic limbo. Castlerea for me was never quite an *Angela's Ashes* scenario – though it did seem to rain a lot there too!

The bright spots in those years were fishing trips on Lough Corrib, Lough Mask and the River Moy, the part of my father's 'gentleman's existence' which he clung to until the end, and something for which I shall be forever grateful to him. It was in fact more than a gentleman's existence. He was, I think, more Yeats' 'freckled man', a 'wise and simple man', slightly out of his time, and certainly out of ours, who went 'at dawn to cast his flies'[4] because this, he thought, would never change. In those very impressionable years he gave me my sense of the Irish landscape that was to become and has remained the inner scape I now see as an essential part of my identity. As the sign on the bridge over the Shannon at Athlone says, the West for me has always been 'warm, wild and wonderful' – they don't mention the wet but even that has its charms as Hopkins rightly points out:[5]

4. W. B. Yeats, 'The Fisherman', *The Wild Swans at Coole*, 1919.
5. Gerard Manley Hopkins, 'Inversnaid', *Gerard Manley Hopkins: Selection* (London: Penguin, 1953).

What would the world be, once bereft
Of wet and of wildness? Let them be left,
O let them be left, wildness and wet...

Over the years of absence it has no doubt become romanticised for me but it is still very real. I sometimes think I only discovered Ireland when I left it. I suspect, however, that I was, and still am, more at home with the landscape than with the people of the country.

John Hewitt comes to mind:

I recognise the limits I can stretch,
Even a lifetime among you should leave me strange,
For I could not change enough, and you will not change;
There'd still be levels neither'd ever reach.[6]

Where did the strangeness come from? Did Ireland in some way let me down? I am not really sure but the personal, the social and the political concurred to colour my view and shape this narrative. A childhood fascination with travel books and exotic faraway places made flight seem like a good option. It was not an uncommon option for the time.

In terms of faith I am not sure I really came from a typical Irish Catholic family, although I can indeed share some of Heaney's sentiments in his wonderful little poem on Easter:

And rubrics for the blessing of the font.
As the hind longs for the streams, so my soul ...
Dippings. Towellings. The water breathed on.
The water mixed with chrism and oil.
Cruet tinkle. Formal incensation[7]

Nobody but a former altar boy could have written that, since nobody down the aisles ever actually heard the cruet's tinkle, the sound of pure crystal ringing on the cold air of a badly heated late nineteenth century town church. It was no doubt formative

---

6. John Hewitt, 'O country people', *The Selected John Hewitt* (Belfast: Blackstaff Press, 1981).
7. Seamus Heaney, 'Clearances, 6,' *New Selected Poems, 1966-87* (London: Faber, 1990).

and I have a lingering nostalgia for that kind of pre-Vatican II, 'smells and bells' Catholicism, with Mary Kenny's starched and well pressed altar linen. Benediction was more exciting than Mass precisely because it seemed to my childish sense to be all smells and bells, 'formal incensation' and mysterious incantation:

Tantum ergo Sacramentum
Veneremur cernui:
Et antiquum documentum
Novo cedat ritui:
Praestet fides supplementum
Sensuum defectui.

Down in adoration falling,
Lo! The Sacred Host we hail.
Lo! o'er ancient forms departing,
Newer rites of Grace prevail:
Faith for all defects supplying,
Where the feeble senses fail.

To The Everlasting Father
And The Son Who reigns on high,
With The Spirit blessed proceeding
Forth, from Each eternally,
Be salvation, honour, blessing,
Might and endless majesty. Amen.

We got glimpses of a rather distant, perhaps even smug, clergy who lived with a relatively simple faith in the secure knowledge that their flock was probably doing the same. My parish priest from the time I was born until I left home was the kindly Canon Patrick Duignan, so sympathetically evoked by John Waters.[8] Physical brutality in our schools was, however, not uncommon although it remained hidden from most of us for much of the time. I am aware from personal experience of two serious cases, although for some reason I escaped it myself and have nothing

8. John Waters, *Jiving at the Crossroads* (Dublin: Blackstaff 1991), pp 36-37.

but positive memories of all the teachers I encountered on my way through the education system, religious and lay. They struck me as kindly people, if not always inspiring teachers. I am aware of at least one case of serious sexual abuse which occurred long after I left the school and suspect that there were perhaps more instances. This was the shadow of the Irish country town school where there was always a teacher who believed that what was not bred into them could be beaten into them. I must note here that my own school, the small lay-run Mean Scoil Iosef Naofa, a semi-Irish language school now disappeared, was a notable exception. Here corporal punishment of any kind was banned and we were told this from the first day – though after a good tongue lashing from the formidable Mary O'Flanagan (another character in John Water's book) – one would almost have welcomed 'six of the best' just to get it over with. Hell held no fury, so to speak, but the heart was also there and her contribution has only recently been acknowledged.

I was not particularly close to the Church, nor was my family. We practised because everybody practised, but there no real emotional involvement with the Church. There were no sodalities, associations or other Church-run activities in which we became involved. I also have a very clear recollection of my father as someone who was not exactly anti-clerical, but certainly who looked at the Church with something of a wary eye and was suspicious of its intolerance and authoritarianism. He was aware of the foibles of some of the clergy and the brutalities of the school system, both of which I know he resisted. I still remember him telling the story of having to go to ask the permission of the then Bishop of Galway, Michael Brown, to hold what he said was the first Alcoholics Anonymous meeting in the West of Ireland, probably in about 1960. He reassured his Lordship that their reliance on a 'higher power' was doctrinally sound, and also that they would not be entering into competition with the Pioneer Total Abstinence Association, since, he explained, most of 'the lads' were well beyond anything the Pioneers might be able to do for them. His schooling in Clongowes in the 1930s left him with a particular coolness towards Jesuits and he occasionally told us stories of the ascetic Fr John Sullivan who he considered to be very strange, and the treatment of Jesuit students in the college which he came to consider as humiliating and even inhumane.

This independence, however, ran a little deeper. Having struggled successfully with alcoholism, I feel he developed a particular kind of spiritual autonomy which has certainly marked me. Another recovered alcoholic remarked to a friend of mine recently: 'Religion is for those who are afraid of hell, spirituality is for those who have been there.' I think there was something of this in his thinking. Having worked his way back from near destruction, he reached a point of certainty within himself which can only come from the deepest questioning of the self and certainly cannot be satisfied by pieties. I came to understand this in my very early twenties when, in the depths of quite a serious existential crisis, I read the following passage from James Baldwin which I now see as one of the defining texts of my life:

> I do not mean to be sentimental about suffering – enough is certainly as good as a feast – but people who cannot suffer can never grow up, can never discover who they are. That man who is forced each day to snatch his manhood, his identity, out of the fire of human cruelty that rages to destroy it knows, if he survives his effort, and even if he does not survive it, something about himself and human life that no school on earth – and, indeed, no Church – can teach. He achieves his own authority, and that is unshakeable.[9]

I think all of this speaks of a certain independence of mind that sat badly with the spirit of 1950s and 1960s Ireland. In reflecting on it, I have also come to understand that the middle class was certainly not as cowed by the clergy as some would have us believe. They were after all their own brothers whatever their clerical status. Ironically I have always found myself to be somewhat anti-clerical. I was born a Catholic, but I was not sure what

9. James Baldwin, *The Fire Next Time* (London : Penguin, 1963).

kind of Catholic. I had faith, but I was not sure what kind of faith and it certainly left room for many uncertainties, which happily still keep me thinking. An old French Cistercian friend, the late Dom Charles Foucher, once told me he could live without 80% of his certitudes and I felt and still feel the same: 'Do you thank God when you wake in the morning and when you go to bed at night? *Ça suffit!'* How he reconciled this with offices that started at 4.30 am and finished at 8.30 pm, I am not quite sure.

I am sure this narrative explains an uneasy relationship with both Ireland and Catholicism as I knew it. It ultimately explains my decision to join a missionary congregation and to leave Ireland. It was the combination of idealistic faith, curiosity about humanity, and malaise with Ireland that drove me to distant shores. Today, no doubt, I would have done something very different, but I have never regretted my choice. These were the 'running waters' that had to be crossed, the 'stepping stones' that would be the 'stations of my soul'.

I left Ireland in 1976 to study in France and from there to work in Togo and later in Benin (West Africa) from 1977 until 2002. Living in France, later mixing with French friends and colleagues and regular visits there over the past thirty years have certainly brought me to look at both my Irishness and my Catholicism again. By the 1970s France was the stereotypical secularised Catholic country. Being Irish there was, however, something refreshingly positive and certainly made a change from working in the Britain of the time where a quite nasty Paddy-bashing was still not uncommon. For French Catholics we remained the island of saints and scholars, *l'Irlande catholique et missionnaire qui nous a apporté la foi* (Catholic and missionary Ireland who brought us the faith). French *laïcs* seemed to forgive us our attachment to Catholicism because we were thought to have something of the *génie culturel* they find so attractive and, of course, we were not the despised Anglo-Saxons. In fact, as Wilde commented to a French customs official, we were *le contraire et mieux encore* the historical victims and avowed enemies of perfidious Albion – and this was long before the Common

Agricultural Policy, the rebate and the Olympic bid! I can still remember arriving in Charles de Gaulle airport from Africa very
early the morning after *Riverdance* made its first appearance at
the Eurovision song contest. On seeing my passport, the official
smiled benignly: *'Ah vous, les Irlandais, vous êtes formidables'*
('You Irish are just marvellous!'). I think he expected me to do a
few steps myself *parce que vous êtes tous comme ça là-bas* (because
you're all like that over there!). I almost believed it but remembered Yeats' remark to Synge that one line of *The Playboy of the
Western World* was worth more than all the clod-hopping lep-
rechauns in Ireland, and thought the better of it.[10] France was,
however, another perspective on Ireland and one I found very
positive even if a little romanticised. There were common roots
in Catholicism even if *les catholicismes* as it would now be fashionable to put it in France, were quite different.

In terms of the Catholicism I encountered in France, it was
certainly more diverse than anything I had encountered in
Ireland, ranging from ultramontane, reactionary royalists to
worker priests of the Guy Gilbert mode living in the HLM of the
major cities, perhaps, cynics would say, in a vain attempt to claw
back the losses suffered since the revolution, the Enlightenment,
modernisation and secularisation that had impacted on France.
The *idées de la France* (ideas about France) of these people were
often very different, coming from very divergent political positions, *réac, Catho ou laïc* (reactionary, Catholic or secular), but
they were reflected upon and argued about passionately. This
was the experience of a Catholicism of intellectual conviction
rather than social convention, which I found fascinating and
which certainly reinforced my own fundamental faith and gave
me a freedom I found I never had in Ireland. It was the
Catholicism of Charles Péguy, Gabriel Marcel, Jacques Maritain,
Emmanuel Mounier and Simone Weil, the latter believing in her
own tortured way but not fully belonging. It often contested *les
idées reçues de la modernité* (traditional ideas about modernity)

---

10. See Roy Foster, *W. B. Yeats A Life: The Apprentice Mage* (Oxford:
Oxford University Press, 1997).

but it also often contested a conservative and reactionary Church as in the case of Emmanuel Mounier (1905-1950), whose personalist philosophy was later to become so influential in both the development of liberation theology and the social teaching of the Church. In terms of the artistic expression, I became fascinated by the music of Louis Vierne, Charle-Marie Widor, Marcel Dupré, Jehain Alain and Olivier Messiaen, the whole school of French organ music I encountered for the first time as a member of the church music group attached to the Cathedral of Montpellier in the early 1970s. This was a *Catholicisme intellectuel, passionné, engagé et militant* (an intellectual, heartfelt, committed and militant form of Catholicism). It was a strange mix of social activism and mysticism, which bore little resemblance to what I had left behind in Ireland. It was often radical (both to the right and to the left), even troubled or *révolté*, as Weil and some of my own friends were for example, but it was always questioning. It was in a sense a counter-cultural Catholicism arguing its convictions and seeking its place in a modern France in a way we never had to in a monocultural Ireland.

At the same time it was interesting to encounter those French *laïcs sectaires qui bouffent du cure* (committed secular figures who 'eat priests') and have nothing but disdain for religion and all its trappings. These were the school teachers and other minor State functionaries who had become *le nouveau clergé républicain* so wonderfully captured in Yves Robert's film of Marcel Pagnol's autobiography, *La Gloire de Mon Père* (1990), and who in my opinion played an important part in the recent decisive *non* to the constitutional treaty.[11] They held robust opinions and expressed them with a sting that would leave many a DUP unionist seem lacking in real conviction.

This is, I believe, one of the things that is so lacking in the Irish Church, and indeed Irish society: lay intellectuals who are willing to argue their faith from a perspective of philosophical conviction rather than social convention. Dissenting voices were

---

11. See Jean Paul Willaime, *Europe et Religions: Les Enjeux du XXIe siècle* (Paris : Fayard, 2004), chapters 1 and 2.

always too few; we missed out on the Reformation and all that
followed. 1798 may indeed have been the biggest missed chance
in our history, as Roy Foster puts it, 'a moment when the Irish –
and possibly European – could have been decisively changed.'[12]
History did a dummy, however, and since then our would-be
dissenters have lived safely on the other side of the border and
have little interest in joining us. These were the people John
Hewitt described so well, living in

> the swathe left uncut, the blessed wheat
> wherein still free the gentle creatures go
> instinctively erratic, rash or slow,
> unregimented, never yet possessed.[13]

In the Republic things were much more regimented and there
was little debate leaving a situation that, I believe, has now
turned to often deep resentment. This was no doubt the fault of
an overweening clergy, although they were supported in many
cases by other elites. Unfortunately, there is still the tendency to
treat even mild dissent with great suspicion. The wagging finger
comes up when the faithful dare put their heads above the pews
and do anything other than 'pray, pay and obey'. And yet we re-
peat that that laity is the future of the Church

Like Friel's Fr Jack, I have come back – not without some
trepidation. Following my return from Africa, I spent five years
doing research in London, peering over at Ireland from the outside, making regular forays back and not quite sure how I felt
about it, before eventually taking the plunge and moving back
full-time. It has in many ways been a strange experience and yet
very interesting. I was never quite sure how I felt about the
Ireland I left and there is still quite an amount of ambivalence in
my feelings towards the country I have returned to. I was certainly very happy to have moved out and discovered myself in a
wider world – and part of me stays in the Africa I have not re-

---

12. Roy Foster, *The Irish Story* (London: Allen Lane, 2001), p 212.
13. John Hewitt (1943) 'The Swathe Uncut', *The Selected John Hewitt*
(Belfast: Blackstaff, 1981).

ferred to in this chapter. You will hardly be surprised, however, to learn that the Ireland I came back to in 2004 was a very different place from the one I left in 1977. Although I had the opportunity to visit over the years, it was only when I moved back here to live that I came to appreciate the breadth as well as the depth of the changes, and in some ways I am still trying to come to terms with that.

The pace of socio-economic change has been very rapid and seems to have broken all kinds of records. *The Guardian* last year reported that we were the 'happiest' nation in Europe. Another commentator notes that 'Ireland is ending the twentieth century on a high note ... national self-understanding is constantly evolving, nurturing and developing, but broadly the national project has been successful.'[14] Allowing for a certain amount of hubris on the part of a representative of the ruling party, Martin Manseragh, it is difficult not to agree with this without seeming to fall back into the stereotype (not unknown in Ireland, mind you) of the proverbial begrudger or party poop, as I think Charlie McCreevy notably described those who might burst the bubble of self-congratulation. I was quite surprised recently when my 18 year-old nephew told me that he was going to vote Fianna Fáil in the next election 'because we've never had it so good.' Both of his grandfathers would turn in their graves. When I was his age May 1968 had just happened in Paris and we spent the following summer with flowers in our hair.

But not everybody is so sanguine. Another observer of our socio-economic development is more critical, finding 'on the one hand a burgeoning underclass racked by drugs, gangsterism and poverty and on the other, spectacular wealth, vulgarity and indifference.'[15] The Central Statistics Office in a report entitled *Measuring Ireland's Progress 2004* depicts a country outperforming most other EU member States in economic terms but lagging behind on quality-of-life issues. Using national progress indic-

---

14. Cited in Diarmaid Ferriter, *The Transformation of Ireland 1900-2000* (London: Profile Books, 2004), p 27.
15. Ibid.

ators aimed at informing debate between the social partners, it notes that Irish people 'on average are better off, better educated and more productive than their European neighbours – but dirtier, more car-dependent and less sympathetic to the poor.'[16] This is certainly a sad reflection on our current state.

The sense of disillusion has no doubt been heightened in recent months by the apparent collapse of the peace process in Northern Ireland and a growing sense of pessimism in that area. Peace on the island would certainly have been the icing on the cake and left us facing into the twenty-first century with a lot of optimism. Hopefully, it can still happen but in the meantime there is a sense of uncertainty as we look at other processes and accords that have failed.

Humphries refers to 'spectacular wealth, vulgarity and indifference' and indeed it is at times striking. I live in Dublin 4, which at times can seem like the world centre of 'vulgarity and indifference'. Friday and Saturday nights on Baggot Street (though my posher side of the street is called Pembroke Road) can be noisy and binge drinking and the anti-social behaviour associated with it have become a genuine social and health concern. What is perhaps of even more concern on a deeper level is what lies behind it. I often listen to the voices of the young (and not so young) people shouting in the street and I try to hear what they are saying. A friend speaks to me of his son's constant need to socialise, which he now sees as almost obsessive, a constant running from Billy to Jack and talk of 'a brilliant atmosphere' where there is really only more noise. It seems to me that what lies behind it is a kind of emptiness, a purposelessness, an anomie that can only express itself in this way. We are *révoltés*, but by what? By ourselves? It is perhaps the illustration of the saying 'empty barrels make most noise' and these empty Baggot Street barrels make a lot of very silly noise. Listen to the mobile phone conversations in the bus they tell a lot when they are saying nothing.

16. Joe Humphries, 'Ireland's quality of life suffers as its wealth rises', *The Irish Times*, 1 April 2005.

I am reminded of this fragment of Eliot's 'Ash Wednesday' sequence:

Where shall the word be found, where will the word
Resound? Not here, there is not enough silence …

It was particularly striking on St Patrick's Day and the following few days, when apparently a record number of arrests were made. One newspaper reported 'Much of Ireland spent Friday suffering from a St Patrick's Day hangover: more than 700 people were arrested for alcohol-fuelled fights, vandalism and other abusive behaviour during the holiday.'[17] And this certainly raises questions. Where is the violence coming from if 'we never had it so good'?

I come from a rural area of Ireland and I was saddened on a visit there recently when one of the neighbours remarked that there had been four or five suicides in the area over the past two years, two in the previous six weeks. I know this statistic can be replicated in other parts of the country, particularly amongst young men in the 18-25 age-group. Surely there is a question here, a question as to the sense and meaning of life.

It appears to me that, whatever the prosperity, we also live in an age that is marked by dissonance, a shrill discourse where we seem to spend a lot of time talking past each other, even shouting at one another in a way I used to associate with New York taxi drivers. I believe that the problems in the North were primarily caused by dissonance, a failure to listen and from that a failure to communicate across the divide in any meaningful way. I think the situation of the Church in our society is quite similar. We seem to spend a lot of time shouting at each other in a kind of adolescent rage – we are no more thinking in our criticism than we were in our acceptance.

Catholicism in Ireland is at a particularly interesting crossroads – lying somewhere on the trajectory between, on the one hand, Poland, with its very traditional piety and belief in the inherent goodness of the institution, and France, on the other,

---

17. http://www.usatoday.com/news/world/2005-03-18-st-patrick's-mayhem_x.htm?csp=34

which feels it had to fight long and hard for its emancipation from the same institution. For the moment we seem to have taken the French route in that we are marked by an anger and resentment of the Church but without any of the other side of French Catholicism, its conviction that whatever the faults of the institution, a sincerely held and reflective Christian faith has something to say in the world. I suppose I still feel ill at ease with both my Irish and Catholic identities, to some extent I share Friel's Fr Jack's disillusion.

Let me conclude with a short story told to me by one of those very wonderful, parish-priest scholars one used to find scattered around the Church in Ireland, often in somewhat remote places perhaps because the bishop could not listen to these dissenting voices either.

Archdeacon Patrick Vaughan was administrator in Kilfenora, Co Clare when I met him in 1986. He was devoted to the Irish language and had an encyclopaedic knowledge of the Burren. He told me the story of what may have been the only missionary from Doolin.

The people of Doolin apparently had the name of being somewhat recalcitrant in their religious practice, more interested in pipering than in piety. There was something of Lughnasa about the place, an old paganism that refused to die.[18] There had never been 'a priest from the parish' (in fact, it was a half parish of Lisdoonvarna, so the clergy were at a safe distance). However, eventually one vocation did spring up and flourish like a rare flower on the Burren limestone. This was to a missionary congregation 'but sure wasn't it better than nothing!' The man was eventually ordained amidst much celebration. He was sent to Africa with the few pounds raised from dances and functions of all kinds, and Doolin had apparently done its part for the Kingdom of God and the spreading of the faith.

However, shortly after his departure came the news that Fr John would be coming back. This caused consternation in the parish house in Lisdoonvarna. What would they say to the peo-

18. Brian Friel, *Dancing at Lughnasa*, 1990.

ple? How would they explain the apparent failure of their first missionary? But the parish priest knew his flock. The weekend before Fr John was due back he went out and preached on the Sunday morning. 'You have no doubt heard that Fr John is coming back to us. And indeed you must be wondering why? Well it's like this. As Fr John's boat reached the port of Calabar it was met by native canoes. They came out from the coast, rowing and chanting, chanting and rowing, towards his ship. At first he couldn't hear the words, but as they drew closer it got clearer and eventually he heard them chanting: "Go back to Doolin, go back to Doolin." And so he is coming back to preach to his own.' If, of course, they will accept him!

I have come back to Doolin – or is it Lughnasa like Uncle Jack? – or at least to Dublin, and these were my observations.

CHAPTER FOURTEEN

Catholicism and Civic Identity in Ireland: Mapping Some Changes in Public Policy [1]

Kevin Williams

The school curriculum is used in most countries as an instrument of public policy through which national self-understanding is expressed and communicated to the young generation. This has been the tradition in Western Europe since the time of the Reformation when each ruler decided what was to be the religion of his region on the basis of *cuius regio, eius religio*. From the time of the Enlightenment, the conjunction of the civic and religious remits of schooling has been questioned and in France has been firmly rejected. Today the serious disagreement about the *invocatio Dei* in the proposed European Constitution and about the wearing of religious emblems in schools shows that the nature of the relationship between religion and civic life remains problematic in Europe.

This chapter aims to map the change in the profile of the religious dimension of citizenship education in the Irish context. From shortly after the foundation of the State in 1922 until 1971, education for citizenship was envisaged as having a strong religious dimension. In 1996, a new programme of civic education entitled Civic, Social and Political Education (CSPE) was introduced at junior cycle at second level and it contained no reference whatever to religion. The most recent revision (1999) of the primary curriculum shows an effort to produce a more balanced version of the relationship between civic and religious identity in educational policy.

But first I wish to note that it is mistaken to conceive of Ireland as polarised between Catholic and Protestant alone.

1. This article is based on research supported by the Irish Research Council for the Humanities and Social Sciences.

Diversity is a more pervasive and long-standing feature of Irish culture than is sometimes appreciated. Cultural diversity has been present among the inhabitants of the island long before the notion of diversity acquired its contemporary currency. To use some phrases from Louis McNeice's poem, 'Snow', the Irish ethnic/cultural/ moral landscape is 'incorrigibly plural' and consequently 'crazier and more of it than we think.'[2] The names to be found in Ireland today reflect wide and varied ethnic/cultural origins: Gaelic (the majority of Irish names); Norse (Harold, Sigerson, Sorensen); Norman (Norman itself, names with the prefix 'Fitz'); English (English itself, Green, Brown, Black); Scots (Scott); British (Britain); Jewish (Bloom, Wolfson, Goldberg); Huguenot (Blanche, Champ, D'Olier, Boucicault, Le Fanu, La Touche). Then there are names such as Fleming, Holland, French and Spain that also derive from continental Europe. As John Hewitt puts in his poem 'Ulsterman': 'Kelt, Briton, Roman, Saxon, Dane, and Scot,/time and this island tied a crazy knot'.[3]

Let us turn next to a brief survey of how Catholicism came to be associated with national identity.

Historical Context

One important reason for the failure of the Reformation to gain adherents in this country was the resistance by Gaelic Ireland to the attempts made by the English crown to promote the Protestant faith. This resistance led to an identification of Catholicism with freedom from foreign interference and this in turn prompted the development of a version of national consciousness that saw a fusing of religious, political and cultural elements. The closing years of the sixteenth century heralded the emergence of the tradition of Catholic nationhood and 'the elements of an ideology of Irish Catholic nationalism'[4] that has

---

2. K. Allott, *The Penguin Book of Contemporary Verse* (London: Penguin, 1968), pp 151-152.

3. The full poem can be found in P. Craig (ed.), *The Oxford Book of Ireland* (Oxford: Oxford University Press, 1999), p 14.

4. C. Lennon, *Sixteenth Century Ireland: The Incomplete Conquest* (Dublin: Gill and Macmillan, 1994), p 324.

endured to the present. Conversely, the later Plantation of Ulster was to lead to the emergence of a version of Irishness which was eventually (particularly in the nineteenth and twentieth centuries) to associate its political identity with Britain and with Protestantism. To this day many people associate their political and cultural sense of who they are with religion.

Awareness of the potential for social disharmony deriving from the 'crazy knot' of identities and the aspiration to separate religious from cultural and national identity formed part of the impulse behind the attempt to introduce a multi-denominational school system in the nineteenth century. The aim of the architects of the system of national education that was eventually established in Ireland in 1831 was therefore to promote a shared identity on the part of the inhabitants. The multi-denominational system that was introduced limited the remit of the State to secular learning and assigned responsibility for catechesis to the respective Churches. This attempt by Lord Stanley in 1831 to 'unite in one system children of different creeds'[5] was strenuously resisted by all the Churches with the result that education in practice assumed a denominational character.

Before the foundation of the State, a conception of a country that would be both culturally Irish and strongly Catholic was being articulated. This vision is communicated with considerable imaginative insight in *The Land of Spices* by Kate O'Brien set in the early years of the twentieth century. Even the version of Catholicism that was practised on Continental Europe came to be viewed with suspicion. A priest tells the English Reverend Mother of a convent of a French order that is was a 'shame' that Irish postulants were sent for their religious training to the 'barbarous' town of Bruges.[6] The local bishop whose views appeared to go beyond the 'untutored, unbridled nationalism' of the priest, nevertheless shared the spirit of the latter. 'Irish national life is bound up with its religion' he pointed out, and went on: 'it

---

5. Á. Hyland and K. Milne, (eds.), *Irish Educational Documents, Vol 1* (Dublin: The Church of Ireland College of Education, 1987) pp 100-101.
6. K. O'Brien, *The Land of Spices* (London: Virago, 2003), p 9.

may well be that educational work will become difficult ... for those Orders which adhere too closely to a foreign tradition.'[7] O'Brien attributes in an interior monologue the following wry comments to the Reverend Mother of this convent. 'How odd were these Irish, who believed themselves implacably at war in the spirit with England, yet hugged as their own her dreariest daily habits, and could only distrust the grace and good sense of Latin Catholic life.'[8] Later O'Brien allows the bishop, addressing a Protestant lady, to develop his points. Nationalism and Catholicism, he claims, are the only 'causes and platforms'[9] that the Irish willingly embrace.

'I believe it to be wrong that a nation fervently professing one Church should be subject to the rule of a nation professing an entirely other Church – so you see, for me, that platform is very closely allied to religion. And therefore I believe that, when such a state of things exists, education, for instance, should be very nationalistic indeed, even what is called narrowly so, until such a political anomaly is renounced, by the educational process.'[10]

He acknowledges that the tradition of the French teaching order is 'certainly very Catholic' but goes on to 'contend' that it is 'too European for present-day Irish requirements'. 'Its detachment of spirit', he concludes, 'seems to me to stand in the way of nationalism.'[11]

When the Irish State was founded in 1922, the government found itself free to pursue its aim of promoting cultural nationalism and reinforcing the denominational character of schooling. In the light of the salience of religion in Irish culture, this involved the continuation and strengthening through education of the connection between religion and national identity. As William Trevor tartly puts it: 'the emergent nation, seeking pil-

---

7. Ibid., pp 92 and 15.
8. Ibid., p 55.
9. Ibid., p 209.
10. Ibid., p 210
11. Ibid.

lars on which to build itself, ... plumped for holiness and the Irish language'.[12] In Ireland, the strong association between the Catholic Church and the struggle for independence has contributed to a close identification between loyalty to the nation and loyalty to the Church. The nationalist or republican tradition in Ireland is very different from that of France (or Portugal) where secularists perceive *l'église* together with *le château* as being in alliance against the republican institutions made up of *la mairie, l'école, et la poste*.[13]

Religion and Civic Identity 1966-1996

It was not until 1966 that the subject 'Civics' at second level was formally introduced into schools. This gave an opportunity to give focused attention to the relationship between religion and civic identity. Previously this had been affirmed in the course of comments on the general curriculum. The authors of the Department of Education's document in 1966 (aimed at junior cycle at second level) argued that religious education is primary and that moral education and, by extension, civic education, derive from religious principles. 'During his religious studies especially', they write:

> the pupil will have instilled into him the virtues of charity, honesty, self-sacrifice, purity and temperance and will acquire a complete moral code which will serve as the chief guide of his conduct and the mainspring of his actions and thinking.[14]

Although it is noted that civics is not:

> to be regarded as a substitute for religious and moral training

---

12. William Trevor, Extract from *Beyond the Pale*, in P. Craig (ed.), *The Oxford Book of Ireland* (Oxford: Oxford University Press, 1999), p 424.

13. G. Raffi, *Le nouveau combat des laïques, Le Monde de l'Éducation, de la Culture et de la Formation* (numéro 246, mars), pp 83-84, p 84.

14. Written in 1966, the relevant document was re-printed whenever the Department of Education's *Rules and Programme for Secondary Schools* was re-issued until it was superseded in 1996. The version used here is Department of Education's *Rules and Programme for Secondary Schools* (Dublin: The Stationery Office, 1986/87), p 165.

nor for that training in character formation and general behaviour which is an essential objective of all education, but
rather, again, as the complement to and extension of such
training. Its concern will be the imbuing of the pupil with the
social and civic principles which help in the formation of the
good citizen.[15]

The dependence of civic education upon religion is also evident
in the *Notes on the Teaching of Civics* published in the same year.

It is not difficult to see the importance of co-ordinating civics
with religious instruction ... It would not be very effective
for the civics teacher to discuss with his pupils the political
and social duties of the citizen unless the moral principles
underlying those duties had already been dealt with in the
religious instruction class.[16]

The following is a proposed sample treatment of a section of the
prescribed Civics syllabus dealing with 'Religion and the State:
the provisions of the Constitution regarding religion. The various denominations.'[17] This, it was pointed out, will involve
study of:

Religion and the individual's ultimate destiny; its importance to the family, to society in general, to the nation, to the
international community of nations; rights and duties; the
reasons for and the importance of religious toleration; respect for denominations other than one's own; a brief study
of denominations represented locally.

A brief study of the relevant sections of the Constitution
in the light of what has been discussed above.[18]

Civic identity in the 1971 curriculum for primary schools
The conceptual link between civic and religious identity is quite
not as pronounced in the 1971 curriculum for primary schools.

---

15. Ibid.
16. Department of Education, *Notes on the Teaching of Civics* (Dublin:
Department of Education, 1966.), p 3.
17. Ibid., p 4.
18. Ibid., p 5.

On the one hand, both areas are seen to 'share much common ground in the knowledge they seek to impart and the attitudes and virtues they aim to develop' and as a result 'there is obviously a very close affinity between Religious Education and Civics.'[19] But the authors go on to reject the 'narrow viewpoint that matters of morals and behaviour belong exclusively to the sphere of the Churches' and affirm the importance of encouraging pupils to 'embrace' moral values 'by personal choice' in the light of 'an upright conscience.'[20] Nonetheless, the religious dimension of civic education is articulated clearly. For instance, it is suggested that in the study of the family 'the love of Christ for His mother, His life as a member of the Holy Family and other aspects of the Divine example might be presented to the children as the ideal.'[21] The form of patriotism recommended must '[a]bove all ... prove itself in its consistency with duty to God and to the moral law.'[22]

The 1990s: Civic, Social, Political and Environmental Education
A great change occurs in the attitude to the religious dimension of civic formation in the 1990s. The notion of tolerance mentioned in 1966 emerges as a defining element in the document on Civic, Social and Political Education at second level published in 1996. This document endorses the secular values of liberal democracy and also places a very strong emphasis on communitarian values of social responsibility.[23] What is significant is the failure even to raise the possibility of a connection between religion and civic education. In a country where religion and culture have been so intimately related, this neglect is very surprising.

---

19. Department of Education. *Curraclam na Bunscoile: Lámhleabhar an Oide/Primary School Curriculum: Teacher's Handbook: Parts One and Two* (Dublin: The Stationery Office, 1971), Part Two, p 116.
20. Ibid.
21. Ibid., p 122
22. Ibid., p 124.
23. Department of Education (1996), *The Junior Certificate: Civic, Social and Political Education Syllabus* (Dublin: The Stationery Office, 1996), pp 10-12.

Whether this is a result of a considered change in policy or of an unselfconscious response to a new *Zeitgeist* is difficult to say, although I am inclined towards the latter explanation.

The salience of religion in Irish culture makes it a topic that should be included in any officially-sponsored programme of civic education. Apart from its role in the cultural self-understanding of both believers and non-believers, religion is a very significant feature in the political division of the island. There is also the role of the Church in raising awareness of disadvantage and exploitation. The missionary Church has animated much of the contribution of Ireland to the developing world and has highlighted the existence of poverty and exploitation in these areas of the world. Gene Kerrigan captures this aspect of the remit of Christianity by pointing out that it was inspiration from the Gospel that 'created the men and women, priests and nuns, volunteers, who went to the godforsaken spots of the globe to bear witness to finer values than accommodation to the local thug or dictator.'[24] Others, he writes, 'stayed home and stood by the oppressed or spoke out against the complacency of the comfortable classes.'[25] The ideals of human conduct enshrined in the Christian tradition (in the parable of the Good Samaritan or in the Sermon on the Mount, for example) form part of the moral capital of our civic culture. Indeed, a close connection exists between the values that are promoted in the CSPE programme (human dignity, interdependence and stewardship, for example) and Christian values in general. By contrast, the new syllabus in religious education has as one of its aims an exploration of the place of religion in civic life as well as a section on the topic.[26] So it is strange there is not a parallel treatment of the theme in the CSPE programme.

---

24. Gene Kerrigan, *Another Country: Growing up in '50s Ireland* (Dublin: Gill and Macmillan, 1998), p 118.
25. Ibid.
26. Department of Education and Science, *Junior Certificate: Religious Education Syllabus: Ordinary and Higher Level* (Dublin: The Stationery Office, 2000), pp 4, 43.

Diversity and the Christian Tradition:
The New (1999) Primary Curriculum

In the new Primary Curriculum published in 1999, however, the Judaeo-Christian story is acknowledged as an element in Ireland's cultural heritage. The spirit and tone of the aims as set out in the 1999 document are very different from those of its 1971 predecessor. In it we read that one of fourteen issues on which there was 'consensus' among those drafting the document was the place of 'pluralism, a respect for diversity and the importance of tolerance.'[27] The following are some affirmations of respect for diversity. Under the heading 'European and Global Dimensions', the authors state that:

> The curriculum acknowledges, too, the importance of a balanced and informed awareness of the diversity of peoples and environments in the world. Such an awareness helps children to understand the world and contributes to their personal and social development as citizens of a global community.[28]

This is consistent with the character of 'Social, Environmental and Scientific Education' which is described as follows:

> ... as children mature they encounter a widening range of people, events and periods. These are drawn from local, national, European and non-European contexts and from diverse social, cultural, ethnic and religious backgrounds, so that children acquire a balanced understanding of local, Irish and international history.[29]

One of the features of 'Social, Personal and Health Education' is that it will nurture '[c]oncepts of democracy, justice and inclusiveness ... through the learning experiences offered and through the attitudes and practices inherent in the organisational structures of the class and the school.'[30]

---

27. Department of Education and Science, *The Primary School Curriculum: Introduction* (Dublin: The Stationery Office, 1999), p 9.
28. Ibid., p 27.
29. Ibid., p 49.
30. Ibid., p 57.

The document endorses the importance of understanding and tolerating diversity and the value of pluralism within the context of an acknowledgment of the country's Christian heritage.

> The curriculum has a particular responsibility in promoting tolerance and respect for diversity in both the school and the community. Children come from a diversity of cultural, religious, social, environmental and ethnic backgrounds, and these engender their own beliefs, values, and aspirations. The curriculum acknowledges the centrality of the Christian heritage and tradition in the Irish experience and the Christian identity shared by the majority of Irish people. It equally recognises the diversity of beliefs, values and aspirations of all religious and cultural groups in society.[31]

Yet this was not the original text of the document. In the draft version of the document, as reported by Andy Pollack in *The Irish Times*, the Christian aspect of Irish culture was not mentioned:

> The curriculum acknowledges … pluralism in society and caters for a variety of differences while at the same time promoting tolerance and respect for diversity in both the school and the community.[32]

This begs the question as to whether the inclusion of the Christian aspect of Irish heritage is a confessional imposition. I do not believe that it is and in the concluding section, I shall try to explain why.

Religion as Belief and Religion as Culture

It seems to me that from a liberal perspective, it is not inappropriate to draw attention to this dimension of Irish identity in civic education. As the cultural identity of many Irish people has been associated with religion, does it then follow that the Irish

---

31. Ibid., p 28
32. Andy Pollack, 'New School Curriculum Leaves out God in Favour of Spiritual Dimension', *The Irish Times*, 22 August 1998, p 4.

must inescapably come to see their national identity in religious terms? Of course not. Although they live in a country where Christianity is deeply inculturated, Irish people do not have to be born or remain Christians. But whether in anger, like James Joyce, or in sorrow like John McGahern, the attitudes to life of its citizens are shaped by the religion which was a prominent feature of the culture in which they grew up.

Even Roddy Doyle, an atheist who dislikes the pope intensely, writes with bewilderment of his warm and positive reaction to seeing the pope meet the Irish soccer team before the World Cup quarter final in Italy in 1990. When the pope met the team, 'I couldn't fight down the lump in my throat as the lads in their tracksuits lined up to meet him. They were all Catholics, the reporter told us. Great, I thought; and I wasn't messing. It was strange.'[33] This response captures something of the resonance between the Catholic religion and national identity in the psyche of many Irish people.

There is an important distinction to be made between religion as culture and religion as belief. Like Leopold Bloom in Joyce's *Ulysses*, people can negotiate cultures without embracing their religious beliefs. This process is wryly captured in Polish-American author, Eva Hoffman's, recollection that her secular, Jewish mother when exasperated used to say 'Jesus, Joseph, and Saint Maria'.[34] The expression was part of the culture and its use reflected neither belief in Christianity nor belief in God. Hoffman's encounter with the Catholicism of Poland no more secured a transition to religious faith than did James Joyce's Jesuit education.[35] Novelist, Isabel Allende, makes a similar point about the role of Catholicism in the psyche of Chileans.

---

33. R. Doyle, 'Republic is a beautiful word' in N. Hornby (ed), *My Favourite Year: A Collection of New Football Writing* (London: H., F. and G. Witherby, 1993), p 20.
34. Eva Hoffman, *Lost In Translation: A Life in a New Language* (London: Vintage, 1998), p 30.
35. See K. Williams, 'The Religious Dimension of Cultural Initiation: has it a place in a Secular World?', *Ethical Perspectives*, vol 11, no 4 (December 2004), pp 228-237, p 232.

No one, she claims, refers to herself or himself as an atheist, preferring to use instead the term agnostic. Even convinced non-believers seek religious consolation on their deathbeds on the grounds that a last confession 'never hurt anyone'.[36] Significantly too she notes that the profile of the Church in Chile has been enhanced by admiration of its role in defending the poor and of the courage and self-sacrifice of the priests and nuns who opposed the régime of Pinochet. Allende herself rejected religion entirely at fifteen but has failed to shake off its cultural residue as is shown by her tendency to pray and to make the sign of the cross in times of need.[37]

Likewise, the embeddedness of religion in Irish culture means that an encounter with religion is not something that can normally be avoided. As a result, individuals have to choose what their attitude will be to religious belief which, rather than being relegated to the strictly private sphere, enjoys a profile in the nation's culture. Although religious belief can be accepted or rejected, religious sensibility is a salient feature of Irish culture. This is not a plea to return to the earlier version of civic identity with the pious over-emphasis on religion that the State sought to impose. Rather, it is to make the case for acknowledging the place of the Judaeo-Christian story in Ireland's cultural heritage.

---

36. Isabel Allende, *My Invented Country: A Memoir* (London: Harper Perennial, 2004), p 58.
37. Ibid., p 61-63.

CHAPTER FIFTEEN

Decoupling Catholic and National Identity: Secularisation Theories in the Irish Context

Timothy J. White

An earlier version of this chapter was presented as a lecture at the University of Missouri-St Louis on 15 September 2003, sponsored by the Jefferson Smurfit Corporation Professorship in Irish Studies and the Centre for International Studies at the University of Missouri-St Louis. I would like to thank Michele Dillon, Máire Nic Ghiolla Phádraig, Peter McDonough, Walker Gollar, Robert Snyder, Tom Inglis and two anonymous referees for their comments on earlier drafts. I would also like to thank Shannon Sweeney who served as my research assistant on this project and Nancy McDonald who provided editorial assistance.

Catholicism became a defining element of Irish national identity in the late nineteenth and early twentieth centuries. Once the Irish Free State was created, the Church's power was such that secular political leaders deferred to ecclesiastical leaders in making policies that related to public morality. In the last twenty to thirty years, the position of the Church has changed dramatically, both in terms of the direct influence of the hierarchy as well as the more diffuse influence of the Church in shaping public opinion. This chapter examines the influence of Catholicism as well as the nexus between Church and State by utilising theories of secularisation to explain the changing and diminished role Catholicism plays in defining Irish identity. While not agreeing with all aspects of traditional secularisation theory, this approach is much more useful in explaining the waning power of the Catholic Church in Ireland today than more recent theories of secularisation that emphasise the vitality of religion in a more pluralistic and competitive setting. I argue that secularisation in Ireland has meant that Catholicism as a source of national identity has diminished as religion has become more of a voluntary activity differentiated from other aspects of social and political life. This may not mean the end of religion, but it does mean the decline of the power of the institutional Church in Irish political life.

The Historical Fusion of Catholicism and Irish Nationalism
Several overlapping reasons account for the merger of religious and national identity in nineteenth century Ireland. The origins of Irish nationalism derived from a reaction against British imperialism and an attempt to reinvent a Gaelic culture. A dominant religion, Catholicism, played an important role in forging the unity that was necessary for nationalism to become an effective mass movement.[1] Religious elites do not need to lead political movements for religions to play a role in national politics. Politicians and nationalist revolutionaries can employ religion as a force for their own secular political cause. In the case of Irish nationalism, the Catholic Church became a powerful political actor because of its success from 1860 to 1870 in dealing with the British.[2] In addition, Catholicism was successfully conjoined with Irish nationalism by its identity as a persecuted Church, by the faithfulness of its followers, by the ability of the Church to organise and meet social demands, and by the need for nationalism to have some widely accepted source of identity.

As Gaelic Ireland increasingly lost its viability and receded to the western corners of the island, the Irish masses needed some common bond upon which they could maintain or create their national identity. Catholicism served this function perfectly because it united the Irish in their devotion to the same faith. Some

1. Steve Bruce, *Politics and Religion* (Cambridge: Polity, 2003), p 46, Brian Girvin, *From Union to Union: Nationalism, Democracy and Religion in Ireland – Active Union to EU* (Dublin: Gill and Macmillan, 2002), pp 3-14, Hans J. Kohn, *The Idea of Nationalism: A Study in Its Origin and Background* (New York: Macmillan, 1944), pp 14-15.
2. Emmet J. Larkin, *The Consolidation of the Roman Catholic Church in Ireland, 1860-1870* (Chapel Hill: University of North Carolina Press, 1987).

have argued that Irish Catholicism revived as Irish society began to industrialise and link itself with the outside world and felt threatened by modern liberal forces, but even in the rural Ireland of the early nineteenth century there was a unity between priests and the people in Ireland that provided much deference to ecclesiastical figures.[3] One of the commonalities upon which Irish nationalists could forge a nation was the widespread adherence and devotion to the Catholic faith, one that Larkin identifies in his work on the devotional revolution in Ireland.[4]

The faithfulness of the Irish to their religious heritage has historically provided the Church tremendous institutional power. In the past the Church has been able to utilise its power to transmit its message effectively from the pulpit and through its control of the schools and the administration of social services.[5] The result has been that Ireland is one of the most religious societies on earth. The Church has been able to influence the values and behaviour of the Irish people to conform to its doctrine and teachings. To the extent that Ireland's continued participation in the British Empire had ramifications relevant to fundamental Catholic doctrines, one would naturally expect the Church to play a role in directing the emerging Irish nationalist movement. The Church's remarkable development in the nineteenth century allowed it to emerge based on the needs and conditions of the Irish in that time period. Its control of education for Catholics gave it not only a formative power in shaping individual values,

3. For the argument that Irish Catholicism revived as society confronted industrialisation in the late 19th century see Tom Fahey, 'Catholicism and Industrial Society in Ireland', in J. H. Goldthorpe and C. T. Whelan (eds), *The Development of Industrial Society in Ireland* (Oxford: Oxford University Press, 1992), pp 246-248. Marcus Tanner in *Ireland's Holy Wars: the Struggle for a Nation's Soul, 1500-2000* (New Haven: Yale University Press, 2001), p 231 contends that deference to the Church had already been established in the early nineteenth century.
4. Emmet J. Larkin, 'Church, State, and Nation in Modern Ireland', *American Historical Review* 80:5, 1975.
5. David Miller, *Church, State and Nation in Ireland 1898-1921* (Pittsburgh: University of Pittsburgh Press, 1973) and John H. Whyte, *Church and State in Modern Ireland, 1923-1979* (Dublin: Gill and Macmillan, 1980).

but it also gained respect in society as the source and reservoir of intellectual thought. The Church also emphasised those values that were necessary in post-famine Ireland. Frugality and celibacy outside of marriage helped serve a social purpose of removing economic pressure from an impoverished economy. Thus, the Church played an important role in linking religious values and institutions with the everyday lives of the Irish.[6]

Although the Catholic bishops opposed violence as a means to pursue the Irish nationalist cause, the secular political need for a dynamic that could unify the Irish people nonetheless counteracted and overwhelmed the desires of the hierarchy. The rapidly growing support for Sinn Féin and elevated status of those executed as martyrs made the Church leaders overlook any theological argument against the practical political need to support the cause of Irish nationalism.[7] Nationalists utilised the common Catholic identity of the Irish to unite them for the cause of reinventing Gaelic Ireland. Nationalists were able to enlist Catholics for their cause since the vast majority of Catholics not only despised the English political domination of their island but also resented the historic British persecution of the Catholic Church. Thus, the need for a common bond overlapped with an anti-British antagonism concerning the right to freely practise one's faith. The Catholic religious identity served as a means of organising and mobilising the lower strata of society around the goal of defending the nation. By the late nineteenth century Catholicism was an integral part, if not the defining element, of Irish national identity.[8]

---

6. Thomas F. Inglis, *Moral Monopoly: The Rise and Fall of the Catholic Church in Modern Ireland* (Dublin: University College Dublin Press, 1998), pp 8-9.
7. Conor Cruise O'Brien, *Ancestral Voices: Religion and Nationalism in Ireland* (Chicago: University of Chicago Press, 1994), pp 118-120.
8. There are a number of sources who make this argument. See Kevin Collins, *Catholic Churchmen and the Celtic Revival in Ireland* (Dublin: Four Courts Press, 2002); Patrick J. Corish, *The Irish Catholic Experience* (Dublin: Gill and Macmillan, 1985); Girvin, *From Union to Union*, pp 15-16; David Hempton, *Religion and Political Culture in Britain and Ireland: From the Glorious Revolution to the Decline of Empire* (Cambridge:

Another important characteristic of Irish Catholicism that helped promote the successful integration of national and religious identity in Ireland was the traditional strand of authoritarianism in the Irish Church and Irish culture.[9] Because of its doctrine of infallibility and the fidelity of its followers, the Church was able to command an obedience and loyalty that made the Irish faithful willingly accept the directives of the Church. Eventually, as the Irish masses developed a devotion to the cause of nationalism, this movement could depend upon the fervent support of the Irish masses. This granted populist figures vast discretionary power to lead as they saw fit and expect as leaders an unquestioning acceptance of their decisions.

After the founding of the Irish Free State, the Church hierarchy played a more conspicuous role in Irish political life. This nexus was epitomised by the deference early Irish governments showed to the bishops of Ireland and the Holy See.[10] Nationalists who had effectively utilised references to the unique Catholic heritage of Ireland before independence continued to do so afterward. The passive role of the Church hierarchy during the Rising and its active opposition to the cause of violent revolution minimised its direct political influence in the years immediately after independence. Even though the heroes of the nationalist revolution did not heed the advice of Church leaders concerning the use of violence in the struggle for independence, the policies of the new State reflected their continued faith in the Church and in most if not all of its social teachings. These policies fulfilled the clergy's desire to maintain a viable rural community that linked national nostalgia with Catholic

---

Cambridge University Press, 1996), pp 72-86; Inglis, *Moral Monopoly*; James McEvoy, 'Catholic Hopes and Protestant Fears', *The Crane Bag* 7:2, 1983; Anthony D. Smith, *The Ethnic Origins of Nations* (New York: Blackwell, 1986), p 159.

9. See Ian McAllister, 'Religious Commitment and Social Attitudes in Ireland', *Review of Religious Research* 25:3, 1983 and David E. Schmidt, 'Catholicism and Democratic Political Development', *Éire-Ireland* 9:1, 1974.

10. Keogh, *Ireland and the Vatican*.

social principles. The Church endeavored to repel the threat it perceived from an urban lifestyle. For the Church this new lifestyle was antithetical to the traditional Irish national identity and threatened the ideal Catholic social order. As a result, the Church hierarchy quickly learned to co-operate with those whose previously violent methods they had condemned.[11] The Church's strength as a social institution meant that it could complacently oversee Irish politics without worrying that State policy might deviate from its teachings. Unfortunately, the tightening merger of Catholic and Gaelic identities after independence contributed to the institutionalisation of the religious divide that separates North from South in Ireland.[12]

By the time De Valera wrote and Ireland enacted a new constitution in 1937, the Catholic religion was guaranteed a special role in society and the entire document adapted principles of corporatism that were popular in Church thinking at that time.[13] Even though some claim that the bureaucratic tendency of the State to expand its sphere of control in society collided with the Church's desire to retain its sphere of influence,[14] the historic symbiosis of Catholic and Irish national identities permitted corporatism to be a successful means of organising politics in post-independence Ireland. De Valera's constitution provided an effective and formal merger between the Catholic Church and the Irish nationalist elites.[15] As long as the Irish masses continued to

---

11. For a more detailed analysis of Church-State relations in this time period see Dermot Keogh, *The Vatican, the Bishops and Irish Politics: Church and State in Ireland, 1919-1939* (Cambridge: Cambridge University Press, 1986) and Patrick Murray, *Oracles of God: The Roman Catholic Church and Irish Politics 1922-37* (Dublin: University College Dublin Press, 2000).

12. This argument is also made in John Fulton, *The Tragedy of Belief: Division, Politics, and Religion in Ireland* (Oxford: Clarendon Press, 1991) and O'Brien, *Ancestral Voices*.

13. Bill Kissane, 'The Illusion of State Neutrality in a Secularising Ireland', *West European Politics* 26:1, 2003.

14. For this general argument see John Cooney, *The Crozier and the Dáil: Church and Sate in Ireland 1922-1986* (Dublin: Mercier, 1986) and Whyte, *Church and State in Modern Ireland*.

15. Girvin, *From Union to Union*, pp 106-135.

equate their national and religious identities, there was no need to separate these two conceptually distinct aspects of Irish identity.

The Challenge of Secularisation

While some have been critical of efforts to apply theories of secularisation to the Irish case and critical of the traditional theory (ies) of secularisation, the decline in the status and power of the Church in Irish society justifies an effort to apply secularisation theory to determine how and if they apply to recent developments in Ireland. Despite the continuing power of the Church in terms of its control of primary and secondary education, as well as its ideological or ideational control exhibited by its parish priests and hierarchy, the Church no longer possesses its historic role both in defining Irish identity and establishing the cultural values of Irish society. By the late 1950s and early 1960s, the integration of Catholicism and national identity which had delayed or prevented the secularisation that had come to the rest of Europe finally yielded to those forces associated with the arrival of industrialisation and urbanisation.[16] Many scholars argued that the ascendance of science and reason in the western world meant the diminution of the mystical force of religion. Modernity tended to bring cultural and political pluralism. Ultimately, this liberalism was seen to be in conflict with traditional religious faith, including Christianity.[17] In the past thirty to forty years numerous efforts have been made to decipher the relationship between economic and social modernisation and the decline of religion. Theories of secularisation have proliferated and so have definitions and diverse meanings for this concept. Many assumed that a dichotomy existed between an ethnic,

16. Louise Fuller, *Irish Catholicism Since 1950: The Undoing of a Culture* (Dublin: Gill and Macmillan, 2002) and Hugh McLeod, *Religion and the People of Western Europe: 1789-1982* (Oxford: Oxford University Press, 1997), p 21.

17. Robert P. Kraynak, *Christian Faith and Modern Democracy: God and Politics in the Fallen World* (Notre Dame: University of Notre Dame Press, 2001); Thomas Luckman, *The Invisible Religion* (New York: Macmillan, 1967); and Bryan R. Wilson, *Contemporary Transformations of Religion* (Oxford: Oxford University Press, 1976).

rural society supportive of traditional religion and a conservative personal morality and an urban, cosmopolitan society more
liberal theologically and in terms of personal morality.
However, these static dichotomies could not detect the process
of change and interaction between different religious and socio-
psychological orientations of different national groups.

Many of the critics of the 'old' paradigm or traditional secularisation also contend that the empirical data does not support
the conclusion that modernisation yields a decline in religious
participation in institutional religions. Citing data that religious
participation in the United States has increased and held steady
in Europe despite rapid modernisation, a group of theorists
have developed a supply side theory of secularisation. Instead
of focusing on the transformation of the mass public and consumers of institutional religion, these scholars believe that the
lack of competition and organised State religions create stale environments for consumers of religion. Religious authorities have
little incentive to provide a comparative advantage to their consumers in religious services and thus their attendance and participation decline. Conversely, in regions and countries where religion has been separated from the State and more Churches
compete for followers, religious attendance and participation
rises. Thus, this new paradigm of secularisation emphasises the
failure of traditional monopolistic religions to provide a good
service to the people as the cause of decline in rates of participation.[18]

18. Roger Finke, 'Religious Deregulation: Origins and Consequences',
Journal of Church and State 32:3, 1990; Roger Finke, Avery M. Guest, and
Rodney Stark, 'Mobilizing Local Religious Markets: Religious
Pluralism in the Empire State, 1855-1865', *American Sociological Review*
61:2, 1996; Roger Finke and Lawrence B. Iannaccone, 'Supply-Side
Explanations for Religious Change', *Annals of the American Academy of
Political Science* 527, 1993; Roger Finke and Rodney Stark, 'The
Dynamics of Religious Economics' in Michele Dillon (ed.), *Handbook of
the Sociology of Religion* (Cambridge: Cambridge University Press, 2003),
pp 96-109; Lawrence R. Iannaccone, 'Religious Practice: A Human
Capital Approach', *Journal for the Scientific Study of Religion* 29:3, 1990;
Ted G. Jelen and Clyde Wilcox, 'Context and Conscience: The Catholic

While there are many defenders of this new paradigm of secularisation, there remain many critics of this new approach and
defenders of the traditional paradigm.[19] Most of the defenders
of the old paradigm insist that its critics do not apply traditional
secularisation correctly and that traditional secularisation theory
has not been disproven or falsified by the evidence cited in the
new secularisation literature. The core concepts of traditional
secularisation theory – differentiation, rationalisation, and
worldliness – have occurred in most States experiencing economic modernisation and industrialisation.[20] Examining data in
a large number of countries Chaves and Gorski found that increasing religious competition is not associated with increased
religious participation.[21] Thus, abundant evidence still supports
the basic conclusions of early secularisation theory that there is
increasing differentiation of religious institutions from other
social institutions in industrial societies and that religious institutions have a declining scope of authority over individuals,
organisations, and the society as a whole. This is because the
security provided by advanced societies allows individuals

Church as an Agent of Political Socialization in Western Europe',
Journal for the Scientific Study of Religion 37:1, 1998; Rodney Stark and
Lawrence Iannaccone, 'A Supply-Side Reinterpretation of the
"Secularization" of Europe', *Journal for the Scientific Study of Religion*
33:3, 1994; Rodney Stark and James C. McCann, 'Market Forces and
Catholic Commitment: Exploring the New Paradigm' *Journal for the
Scientific Study of Religion* 32:2, 1993; and R. Stephen Warner, 'Work in
Progress toward a New Paradigm for the Sociological Study of Religion
in the United States', *American Journal of Sociology* 98:5, 1993.

19. See Steve Bruce, *Religion in the Modern World: From Cathedral to Cults*
(Oxford: Oxford University Press, 1996); Jose Casanova, *Religion in the
Modern World* (Chicago, 1994); Mark Chaves, 'Secularization as
Declining Religious Authority', *Social Forces* 72:3, 1994; Frank Lechner,
'The Case Against Secularization: A Rebuttal', *Social Forces* 69:4, 1991;
and David Yamane, 'Secularization on Trial: In Defense of a Neo-
Secularization Paradigm', *Journal for the Scientific Study of Religion* 36:1,
1997.

20. Oliver Tschannen, 'The Secularization Paradigm: A Systemat-
ization', *Journal for the Scientific Study of Religion* 30:4, 1991.

21. Mark Chaves and Philip Gorski, 'Religious Pluralism and Religious
Participation', *Annual Review of Sociology* 27:1, 2001.

growing up in those societies to move beyond the religious values they inherit from previous generations raised in a less secure environment.[22]

Rather than debate abstract theories of secularisation, I would like to apply one specific theory that derives from the traditional secularisation literature in terms of the case of the Republic of Ireland. The model that works best in the Irish case is that of David Martin.[23] He believes that those who are late industrialisers, those experiencing the second phase of industrial revolution as he identifies it, have much more profound secular changes associated with the industrial revolution. Early developers had such a long transition to the modern industrial world that their religious institutions were more able to adapt to the slower changes that enveloped society. The later developers experience such a quick and massive transformation that the religious institutions of society do not have adequate time to adapt. As a result, large scale structures organised on the principle of bureaucratic rationality replace the human scale social structures of the small home, medium-sized school, the bounded town, and the family farm. Generalised empathy communicated through the new mass media replaces the traditional voluntary associations. Those experiencing the second industrial revolution tend to have their institutionalised religion and traditional structures of control or discipline give way to hedonistic consumerism. Thus, the societal level change associated with industrialisation transforms individual religious attitudes and behaviours.

Modernisation disturbs the pre-existing structures of meaning that religion traditionally provided. The cognitive level of secularisation results in a transition from a traditional institutional set of beliefs to the adoption of a personal orthodoxy. This means that individuals begin to question doctrines of religious

---

22. Pippa Norris and Ronald Inglehart, *Sacred and Secular: Religion and Politics Worldwide* (Cambridge: Cambridge University Press, 2004), pp 18-20.

23. The following theory is derived from David Martin's *A General Theory of Secularization* (Oxford: Blackwell, 1978).

belief and seek to develop their own private set of beliefs based on their own personal experiences and needs.[24] Individuals also alter their affective orientation to religion. As individuals become less inspired by the forces of religion, they become less committed to religion itself. They lose allegiance to a particular Church and become more committed to their own particular spiritual values. This changing commitment to one's own personal beliefs makes one less deferential to those religious institutions that had demanded so much allegiance in the past.[25] Finally, one can identify a behavioural transition from institutional religious devotion to private or personal behaviour or the use of other moral or ethical sources as determinants of behaviour. The sacred becomes a personal experience outside of the ecclesiastical teaching authority and bureaucratic control of a religious institution.[26]

Since secularisation typically threatens the political power of traditional elites in society, the clerics and their faithful followers will strive to maintain their power and the relevance of their religion in the modernising society. Hence, the onslaught of a new secular world typically results in a religious counterattack where religion tries to regain a public space.[27] This is especially the case in Catholic countries where the more encompassing holistic faith competes with secular progress instead of trying to coalesce with it as in Protestant societies.[28] Bellah identifies two different reactions to the threat posed by the forces of liberalism

24. This position is supported for Robert Bellah in 'Meaning and Modernization', *Religious Studies* 4:1, 1968 and Yamane, 'Secularization on Trial.'

25. Bryan R. Wilson, *Religion in Sociological Perspective* (Oxford: Oxford University Press, 1982) and Yamane, 'Secularization on Trial.'

26. William R. Garrett, 'The Micro-Macro Linkage in the Scientific Study of Religion: The Problems of Assessing the Influence of Religion on Individuals and Society' in William R. Garrett (ed.), *Social Consequences of Religious Belief* (New York: Paragon House, 1989) and Luckman, *The Invisible Religion.*

27. Casanova, *Public Religion in the Modern World.*

28. David Martin, 'Religion and Public Values: A Catholic Protestant Contrast', *Review of Religious Research* 26:4, 1985.

and secularisation. The first is that of Romantic Nationalism which stresses national solidarity based on primordial ties of language, ethnic origin, or religion. The other alternative is Radical Nationalism.[29] Clearly, the Irish of the late nineteenth and early twentieth century conformed to the pattern of Romantic Nationalism in terms of their attachment to the connection to their Celtic past. The conflict between a modern and more secular metropole and its less developed colony helped forge a Romantic Nationalism in Ireland. In the initial years after independence, the Irish continued to confront the threat of a secular materialistic culture emanating from the west by striving to maintain or promote their unique Catholic-Celtic identity.

Entering the twenty-first century, one would expect an even more strident Irish response to the inundation of secular western culture. Contemporary religious developments in Ireland, however, provide evidence that confrontation between the new secular society and the traditional religion need not result in indissoluble conflict. Religion may attempt to adapt to the changing context of the urban industrial era. The Catholic Church has attempted to make its peace with modernity and a more pluralistic, democratic society since Vatican II.[30] This Council attempted to forge an uneasy truce between the secular values of modern industrial societies and the Catholic tradition. Religion was to be demystified, to become more this-worldly. These changes, while most dramatic in some parts of the developing world where liberation theology seemingly removed the Church from supernatural concerns, have not been as evident in the Irish Church. A conservative hierarchy and the traditional fusion of Catholicism and historic Irish nationalism have made it difficult for both priest and prelate to bring about an *aggiornamento* of the Catholic religion in Ireland. Instead, Irish society has become more secular as the Catholic Church loses its 'moral monopoly' in society.[31]

29. Bellah, 'Meaning and Modernization.'
30. Peter L. Berger, 'Christianity and Democracy: The Global Picture', *Journal of Democracy* 15:2, 2004, pp 76-77.
31. This phrase is borrowed from the title of Tom Inglis' book, *Moral Monopoly*.

Corkery argues that Irish theology needs to change and take into account the cultural changes in society. The traditional desire for discipline and self-denial has not allowed Irish Catholicism to make an accommodation with liberalism or with valuing individual self-expression. The Church is thus put in a defensive position as it continues to interpret the materialism of affluence and indifference to spiritual values as its most immediate threats.[32]

Nevertheless, the Church in Ireland has begun to make changes in recent years that follow the spirit of Vatican II and that are changing the role of Catholicism in the social and political life of the nation. The Church has sponsored a growing ecumenical movement, emphasising the commonalities that all Christians share and thereby removing much of the parochialism that has historically been associated with Irish Catholicism. The Church has also allowed more freedom of discussion, and there is less clerical control as the laity has become increasingly involved in Church matters. Finally, the Church has loosened its tight control of the social sector making a pluralist Irish society more possible. Despite these modest changes, the Republic of Ireland remains an overwhelmingly Catholic State in terms of religious identification and the power of the Church remains remarkably strong in terms of its influence on many political matters.[33] This would seem to contradict the conventional wisdom that industrial high culture severs the historical link between faith and a dominant national Church. The evidence indicates that Ireland's comparatively high level of religiosity has begun to conform to other Catholic countries.[34] Weekly Mass attendance data since the mid-1990s indicate that religious particip-

32. James Corkery, 'Cultural Change and Theology in Ireland', *Studies* 88:352, 1999.

33. Kissane, 'The Illusion of State Neutrality in a Secularizing Ireland.'

34. This evidence can be found in Ronald Inglehart, Miguel Basanez, and Alejandro Moreno, *Human Values and Beliefs: A Cross Cultural Sourcebook* (Ann Arbor, 1998) and Máire Nic Ghiolla Phádraig, 'The Power of the Catholic Church in the Republic of Ireland' in Patrick Clancy, Sheelagh Drudy, Kathleen Lynch, and Liam O'Dowd (eds.), *Irish Society: Sociological Perspectives* (Dublin: Institute of Public Administration, 1995).

ation had indeed declined in Ireland and had fallen into the mid-sixties as a percent of population.[35]

While religious practices may not have declined as much as some have suggested, there has clearly been a decline in the Church's popularity and power as a social institution. The Irish public has lost confidence in the Church as an organisation, increasingly believing that the Church has too much power in society and increasingly disapproving of the Church trying to influence voting or the government. These attitudes diverge sharply from those found in the 1960s. Biever found that 82% of those surveyed then did not believe that the Church was too involved in politics.[36] Secularisation has meant that being a devout Catholic is no longer as important in achieving a position of power in Irish society, whether that position is in the world of politics, business, the media, sport, and most other ways of life.[37] If the Church has lost prestige in Irish society, it has also lost its ability to have the faithful conform to its teachings regarding sexual morality. There have been slight but statistically significant declines in Irish belief that sex should never occur outside of marriage and that abortion is always wrong.[38] Both the decline in fidelity to Church teaching and confidence in the Church have been declining since the 1980s. This decline as well as other survey evidence indicates that the Irish mass public is increasingly sceptical of the Church due to so many recent scandals.[39]

---

35. James S. Donnelly, 'A Church in Crisis: The Irish Catholic Church Today', *History Ireland* 8:3, 2000. Also see Norris and Inglehart, *Sacred and Secular*, p 74.

36. Bruce F. Biever, *Religion, Culture, and Values: A Cross Cultural Analysis of Motivational Factors in Native Irish and American Irish Catholicism* (New York: Arno Press, 1976), p. 307.

37. This point is made in Thomas F. Inglis, 'Catholic Church, Religious Capital and Symbolic Domination' in Michael Böss and Eamon Maher (eds.), *Engaging Modernity* (Dublin: Veritas, 2003).

38. Andrew M. Greeley and Conor Ward, 'How Secularised is the Ireland We Live In?' *Doctrine and Life* 50:10, 2000, p 601.

39. For a discussion of the scandals and their effect see James S. Donnelly Jr., 'The Troubled Contemporary Catholic Church' in Brendan Bradshaw and Dáire Keogh (eds.), *Christianity in Ireland: Revisiting the Story* (Blackrock: Columba Press, 2002), pp 277-284.

While the Irish have not abandoned the Church en masse, there clearly has been a failure in effectively transmitting aspects of the faith to the Irish youth – those most affected by the changes that have come to Irish society. Instead of a legalistic adherence to Catholic dogmas, the Irish youth were developing an individualistic faith. This increased alienation of the youth of Ireland from the Church has led Dobbeleare to conclude that we are witnessing the first generation of the unchurched and a growing secularisation as a result.[40] Survey evidence indicates that Catholic youth still identify with the Church and many core beliefs but exhibit lower levels of religious belief and participation than older generations in Ireland.[41] The abandonment of religious faith and practice among the Irish youth does not mean that they have disconnected the historical link between Catholicism and their national identity. Other behavioural indicators, such as rapidly increasing illegitimacy rates, demonstrate that even though the Irish remain identified with the Church they do not necessarily follow its moral precepts in terms of their own personal behaviour. The Irish are intellectually defecting from their Church's teachings while severing themselves from the social and emotional bonds they have with the Church to a lesser degree. The disaffection of the youth cited earlier may indicate a disintegration of the social bonds created by religion or may be the result of unsatisfying social experiences in addition to the intellectual defection more common in the general population. In any event, they indicate that secularisation is likely to continue in Ireland in the coming decades.

40. Karel Dobbeleare, 'Religion in Europe and North America' in Ruud de Moor (ed.), *Values in Western Societies* (Tilburg: Tilburg University Press, 1995), p 14. Noel Barber argues that while the Irish are increasingly becoming unchurched that does not mean that they are necessarily becoming secularised in 'Religion in Ireland: Its State and Prospects' in Brendan Bradshaw and Dáire Keogh (eds), *Christianity in Ireland: Revisiting the Story* (Blackrock: Columba Press, 2002) pp 294-295.
41. Greeley and Ward, 'How Secularised is the Ireland We Live In?'

Implications of Secularisation for Irish Nationalism

Although nationalism is typically depicted as a secular ideology, it often exists as in Ireland in a religious context. There are several reasons why Catholicism and the fusion of the Church and national identity have not followed the path of secularisation so common in the rest of the world. First, despite the secularising tendency of socioeconomic modernisation, social groups in general, and the Irish in particular, continue to desire a common fate. This common fate was forged a century ago when those advocating the independence of Ireland utilised the commonality of Catholicism on behalf of the cause of nationalism. This historical and institutional cohesion helped Ireland resist the secularising tendencies of western mass culture. Biever found that even in the early 1960s, the link between the Church and Irish patriotism remained very strong.[42]

However, the increased productive capacity of modern industrial societies makes religion no longer necessary for cultural integration. In the Irish case the arrival of cafeteria Catholicism, personally selecting those items on the menu of Catholic faith one wishes to believe, threatens to unravel the historical fusion of Catholic and national identity. The Irish continue to be dedicated to Catholicism as a badge of national identity, but a consumer orientation to the religious world undermines the Church's capacity to shape individual values. Instead of an unquestioning attitude and complete obedience to all Church directives, the Irish like many others are increasingly picking and choosing those moral precepts of the Church that they wish to believe and re-imagining transcendence outside of the context of the Church.[43] When many Irish abandon parts of their Catholic

42. Biever, *Religion, Culture, and Values*, p 314.
43. For this perspective see Ronald Inglehart, 'Postnationalist Values and the Erosion of Institutional Authority' in Joseph S. Nye Jr., Philip D. Zelikow, and David C. King, *Why People Don't Trust Government* (Cambridge: Harvard University Press, 1997), p. 225 and Catherine Maignant, 'Reimagining Transcendence in the Global Village' in Michael Böss and Eamon Maher (eds.), *Engaging Modernity* (Dublin: Veritas, 2003).

faith, they do so without feeling the loss of the fullness of the truth and the organic bond between their Catholic and Irish national identity. The traditional collectivist expression of identity Catholicism brought to the Irish is being undermined by the individual's ability to increasingly select and choose sources of social and national identity independent of one another. Secularisation has helped sever the connection between religious and national identity. The proponents of historic Irish nationalism supported the wholesale acceptance of the Catholic faith and a close relationship between the Church and State in Ireland. This is clearly no longer the case in the more pluralistic Ireland of the twenty-first century.

Even though the bishops had significant power and often close personal relationships with political leaders, they rarely became directly involved in the political debate of the nation.[44] In recent times, however, the Catholic hierarchy has made a more conscientious effort to remove themselves from even appearing to play a role in the political life of the nation. Perhaps this voluntary withdrawal from such an active watchdog role, in combination with the increased personal discretion individuals now have concerning their faith, explains why so many claim that Irish society is far less responsive to the teachings of the Catholic Church. The diminution of the authority and its voluntary retreat from partisan political involvement have begun to minimise the role of Catholicism in defining Irish national identity and in moulding public opinion in an increasingly secular society. This amounts to a move for the Irish State to play a more neutral role in regard to religion in society.[45]

To the extent secularisation has had an impact on Irish society it has threatened to undermine the faith of even those who maintain their religious beliefs. The difficulty in maintaining the veracity of faith and accepting another's as equal spawns a crisis

44. Garrett Fitzgerald, *Reflections on the Irish State* (Dublin: Irish Academic Press, 2003), pp 34-35.
45. This point is reiterated in Brian Girvin, 'Church State and the Irish Constitution: The Secularisation of Irish Politics?', *Parliamentary Affairs* 49:4, 1996.

of relativistic thinking. Those who make the compromise with a secular society simultaneously do so at the danger of losing their own capacity to sustain their religious beliefs. In Ireland this means that an increased tolerance for a pluralistic culture threatens the very religious and national identity of the Irish people. The historic separation of function if not of culture and ideology between the religious and partisan political worlds in Ireland has widened in the past few years. Whether the secularisation of individual attitudes or the voluntary retreat of the Church from attempting to influence partisan politics caused the widening of the gulf between Church and State, it is clear that the institutional power of the Church has been reduced in the political life of the nation even if the Irish State cannot yet be said to be neutral toward religion as in a classic liberal State.[46] Historically, personal friendships and relationships between politicians and the clergy guaranteed the influence in the partisan political debate.[47] Today, politicians pay less homage to prelates. An ecumenical Christian spirit dominates the Dáil rather than a divisive or parochial Catholic one. Thus, the Irish perceive religion to be less of an all-embracing ideology, but there remains a psychological pressure to maintain Catholicism as an element of national identity.

Although the Irish have become more secular, their religiosity may continue in the postmodern era. For example, it may appear that the youth of Ireland are abandoning the faith of their ancestors, but Inglehart and Baker argue that traditional religious values associated with the pre-industrial period may well survive into this postmaterial era of affluence.[48] Wuthnow believes religion can continue to be practised in this era of secularisation, but it is increasingly done so outside of the traditional in-

---

46. Ibid. and Kissane, 'The Illusion of State Neutrality in a Secularising Ireland.'
47. Keogh, *The Vatican, the Bishops and Irish Politics*.
48. Ronald Inglehart and Wayne Baker, 'Modernization, Cultural Change, and the Persistence of Traditional Values', *American Sociological Review* 65:1, 2000.

stitutional context.[49] Some even contend that religion may be even more necessary as individuals seek fuller self-realisation and expression.[50] Achilles finds evidence of this kind of post-modern religion in Irish dramatists who have increasingly turned to religion to search for redemptive factors in a world that increasingly seems to lack meaning.[51] Thus, religion may take a different form, but it is likely to persist and may even thrive under these new circumstances.

The changing role and character of Irish Catholicism may yet transform Irish nationalism into a more tolerant and accepting ideology, ready to accept the diversity of all who live in Ireland. Instead of religion serving as a signpost of distinct conceptions of national identity, a secular Ireland clearly erodes a principal source of parochial political identity in the Irish Republic and thereby minimises a source of political conflict within the larger Irish context. Perhaps the decoupling of Catholicism and Irish na-tional identity will allow a more secular and inclusive national identity to form that will be more able to compromise or at least co-exist in peace with the Unionist tradition, especially in Northern Ireland.[52] This may allow Irish identity to be recreated to be more inclusive of the growing plurality of religious practices and beliefs that is characterising the postmodern Ireland of the twenty-first century.[53] The growing plurality of religious beliefs, values, and behaviour may make the south of Ireland less of a homogenous Catholic State to be feared by Protestants in the north of Ireland, thus laying the foundation for improved relations between the two major religious and political traditions on the island.

---

49. Robert Wuthnow, *After Heaven: Spirituality in America Since the 1950s* (Berkeley: University of California Press, 1998).
50. See, for example, Luckman, *The Invisible Religion* and Wilson, *Religion in Sociological Perspective*.
51. Jachen Achilles, 'Religious Risk in Contemporary Irish Drama', *Éire-Ireland* 28:3, 1993.
52. John Coakley, 'Religion, National Identity and Political Change in Modern Ireland', *Irish Political Studies* 17:1, 2002.
53. Enda McDonagh, 'Church-State Relations in Independent Ireland' in James P. Mackey and Enda McDonagh (eds.), *Religion and Politics in Ireland at the Turn of the Millennium* (Dublin: The Columba Press, 2003).